INJUSTICE on the EASTERN SHORE

Race and the Hill Murder Trial

G. Kevin Hemstock

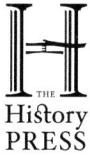

Published by The History Press
Charleston, SC 29403
www.historypress.net

Copyright © 2015 by G. Kevin Hemstock
All rights reserved

First published 2015

Manufactured in the United States

ISBN 978.1.62619.942.2

Library of Congress Control Number: 2014958798

Notice: The information in this book is true and complete to the best of our knowledge. It is offered without guarantee on the part of the author or The History Press. The author and The History Press disclaim all liability in connection with the use of this book.

All rights reserved. No part of this book may be reproduced or transmitted in any form whatsoever without prior written permission from the publisher except in the case of brief quotations embodied in critical articles and reviews.

To my lovely wife of so many moons. She puts up with my ways and is always there, with her puppies at the ready, to help me greet the sun.

CONTENTS

Acknowledgements	7
Introduction	9
Collecting a Debt	11
Millington in the 1890s	15
The African American Community	21
Hill Sets Up House in Millington	30
A House Call	39
Ford's Hill and Destiny	43
It Was No Accident	52
Lynching Prevented	64
African American Deliberations	73
Unpreventable Lynching	76
The Long Summer	83
Columbus Day	88
The Trial	102
The Merits of Hanging Eight	118
An Unexpected Visit	129
Another Surprise Visit	138
The Gallows Beckon	146
Foursome Finale	154
And Then There Were None	164
Was There a Miscarriage of Justice?	171

Contents

Executions Removed to Penitentiary	175
The Victims	180
Ripples to the Present	183
Jail Falls to the Wrecking Ball	185
Notes	189
Bibliography	201
Index	203
About the Author	208

ACKNOWLEDGEMENTS

When a project of this nature takes years to coalesce, those great and small who assisted come and go but are not forgotten. So many helped with this, whether it was to provide resource material or simply tap their memories, that it would be impossible to name them all.

There are some standouts, however. They include, in no particular order: Mark Mumford, clerk of the Circuit Court of Kent County, whose dedication to the preservation of county records is superlative and noteworthy; Nancy Jewell, Kent County register of wills, and her able and pleasant staff; Kent County Circuit Court judge Paul M. Bowman; Kent County sheriff John Price; former state's attorney Bob Strong; Craig O'Donnell, Trish McGee and Pete Heck, staffers at the *Kent County News*; the Reverend Larry Jameson; Karen Emerson, Steve Frohock and Joan Andersen of the Historical Society of Kent County; and Alex Rasin, able lawyer and inveterate local officeholder, who would have done more if he could.

But if there were space enough to mention only one, that one would have to be the late Ellen Lane, who not only assisted with her boundless mental genealogical database but also, however briefly, lived the story.

INTRODUCTION

One of the most sensational murders on Maryland's Eastern Shore, that of prominent Millington doctor James Heighe Hill, was a spontaneous outgrowth of racial tension in Maryland long abrew in the late nineteenth century.

It happened in an age when white America was still coming to grips with changes brought about by long-overdue freedoms incrementally extended to black Americans by the law but much more slowly by white society.

It was a time of racial mistrust that overshadows the present. Then, it was tangible and undeniable. Black communities were separate and unequal, as were opportunities in labor, property, education and at the polling places. The African American way of life mirrored that of whites, but it was a diffused and rippled reflection, running parallel to that which had dominated the continent since the early days of European settlement. Kent County, Maryland, was, and remains, a microcosm of race relations with all its warts and blemishes.

One area where racism failed in relevance and scope was in the mutual abhorrence of violent crime. Since the majority on each side of the racial divide were hardworking, family-oriented folks, mostly farmers seeking better lives for themselves and their children, they universally condemned acts that hyphenated social betterment. But what happens when the violence is racially motivated?

The homicidal coda in the life of an up-and-coming white doctor was an exclamation point in a sanguinary period of the county's history. It had

Introduction

its roots in another slaying that few noticed or cared about, but the final act in a tragic real-life drama would play out before a national audience, bring to bear more modernized police and investigative techniques and end with a gruesome display, multiplied times four, at the gallows, witnessed and recorded by numerous newspaper reporters and editors and, subsequently, shared with a national audience.

The case would demonstrate the intolerance of white American men, who dominated society, politics and local jurisprudence, for crimes—real or imagined—committed by blacks and the disparity in punishment of the races. It would also underscore the hypocrisy of a constitution and institutions that meant one thing for one race and something else for another.

It demonstrated, too, that intolerance was a two-way street and that citizens of all colors could reach the threshold where they were willing to set aside the rule of law.

The spectacle of death that resulted from the grisly outdoor execution would help feed the outcry against such public displays. It became painfully apparent that no sheriff, with the limited resources of a small jurisdiction, could know the extreme that some would go to in order to exercise their ghoulish urge to witness the machines of public death in action. It presaged opposition in Maryland to capital punishment. And four other perpetrators would become the grim bellwethers in the need for improvements in the state penitentiary during the era.

Ultimately, and more simplistically, it demonstrated that the crime of violence can strike anywhere, even in small, quiet villages or on the rural byways of the most pastoral, seemingly tranquil communities. It showed that the ripples it creates affect both the victims and the perpetrators. And that the scars it leaves last long beyond the lives of those directly involved.

COLLECTING A DEBT

It all started with a disagreement over a debt for carpentry work that flared up in a fracas on Christmas Eve 1891. The flashpoint was Thomas McWhorter's oyster saloon, on the northwest corner of Cypress and Sassafras Streets, in the busy little town of Millington, tucked away in the corn belt of Maryland's Eastern Shore.

It was the type of dispute that could be found in any Kent County justice of the peace docket of the day. In those times, a financial spat or an unpaid bill often resulted in small claims that could be handled by the local justice, whose office generally could be found within walking distance. That's how unpaid tabs at the local stores were often settled. That's where petty domestic squabbles were resolved. And that's where fines were levied for swearing on a Sunday.

The process allowed the injured parties to recover, in some cases, seemingly trivial amounts.

Getting the justice of the peace involved reduced the strain on the county's circuit court docket, which is where the cases ended up if they couldn't be resolved or were of a superlative nature, involved a serious crime or the justice felt they were beyond his scope or ability.

If Edward Jones had taken the simple step of filing a claim with the local justice of the peace, a fatal chain of events might have been avoided. But he opted to skip the middleman and collect the debt himself.

A white, forty-one-year-old house carpenter from the Queen Anne's County side of town, Jones had executed some improvements to a house in

Injustice on the Eastern Shore

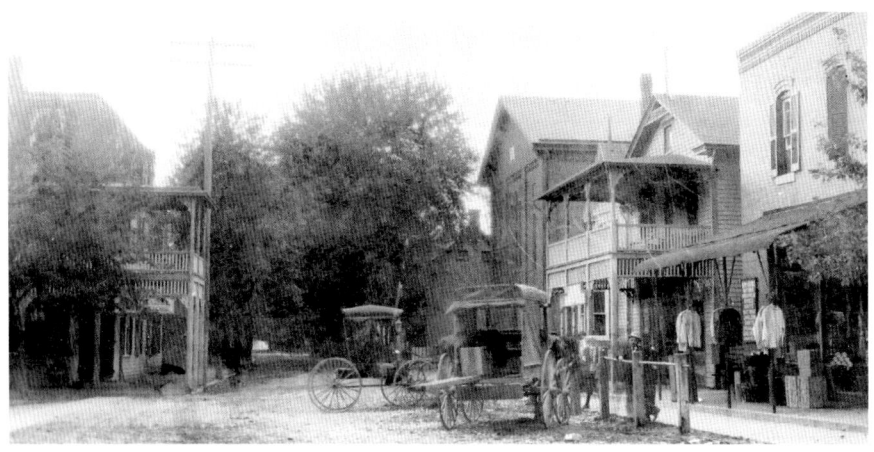

In this postcard image, the business district of Millington is seen about 1910. The structure at right replaced Thomas McWhorter's saloon after a fire in 1904. *Courtesy of Mark Newsome.*

Sandfield, the unincorporated, predominantly African American community dangling like a forgotten appendage from Millington's east side. The home's owners were black brothers John and Joseph Potts, sons of a family that had been in the area for many generations.[1]

Jones was a little liquored up when he went to collect. The brothers refused to pay, saying they had been promised that they could pay in installments.[2]

Jones threatened to file a lien. The fuse was lit, and it was not a slow burner.

On Christmas Eve, a Thursday, a group of white men, including Jones, was playing cards in the saloon.[3] The Potts brothers entered the establishment and engaged in verbal fencing. There was some pushing and shoving, but the men were separated. Joseph Potts "was worsted," receiving more than he gave. The black men would return looking for revenge.

About ten o'clock that night, John Potts, along with some friends, including a visitor named Thomas Campbell, promised to "do up the town."[4] After imbibing plenty of liquid courage, they marched up to McWhorter's place armed with little more than bad tempers. A similarly armed and alcohol-lubricated group of whites, arranged by McWhorter, was waiting. The door was locked or barricaded. Campbell, it is said, broke down the door, and a fray ensued.

McWhorter, forty-seven, the son of Jefferson McWhorter and originally from the area of Smyrna, Delaware, started in business in McDaniel's hotel on the old Osborn property about 1874, the same year he bought a house on Sassafras Street. He was Millington's first town commission president, comparable to being mayor, following the town's 1890 incorporation.[5]

Race and the Hill Murder Trial

One reason the town incorporated was over concerns about criminal activity and trouble with "rowdies." McWhorter had ample reason to be involved in crime prevention; his store had been robbed on at least one occasion.[6] By 1892, he had substantial commercial real estate holdings in town. Besides the oyster saloon in the old hotel, he had a two-story structure next door used as a dwelling and dry goods store and another building on Sassafras Street, on the site of the old Masonic Hall. In that building, he had a farm implement business on the first floor, and the second floor was rented out as a meeting hall for school functions, town meetings, civic groups and visiting performers. McWhorter was out of town government by then, but he still was not about to put up with any grudge match in his place of business.

Upon entering the smoky, lantern-lit eatery, Campbell, with his companions following behind, snatched up "a kettle from the stove [and] was in the act of dealing a deadly blow, when the white men sprang to their feet and dealt him a number of stunning blows over the head with bottles." One beer bottle was known to have hit him in the right side of the head. Bottles were made of thicker glass and were heavier in those days, and they likely made better bludgeons. Campbell fell to the floor. Knowing the tide had turned against them, the blacks left the business in a hurry. But Campbell was down, possibly unconscious. The oil lamps were turned down low, and the gang of assailants focused their rage on the inert form on the floor, kicking and stomping Campbell until he was motionless.[7]

When the lights turned back up, it was clear he was dead.

According to one account, when he fell, he hit his head on an iron stove and broke his neck, dying in minutes. But that's not what the autopsy report would say.

A jury of inquest was called the next day, Christmas.

In Kent County, these were official panels comprising primarily locals and peopled by white men only. It was a "badge of honor" to serve on such a jury. Not only was it a public acknowledgement of a person's integrity and stature in the neighborhood, but it was also a way to get firsthand information about a big case, such as a death resulting from something other than natural causes.

Dr. Alonzo R. Todd was first called on to examine Campbell's body during the inquest. Initially, the Jefferson Medical College graduate refused to do so unless his fee was paid up front. That's not how the county did business.

Dr. James Heighe Hill was then summoned and, after an examination of the body, reported that Campbell had died of heart disease,[8] for which the doctor had previously treated him. The implication of that determination was that Campbell had not been murdered.

Campbell's body was buried—probably at the John Wesley Cemetery—but it was later exhumed for another examination. Thomas Potts (it's uncertain what his relationship with the Potts brothers was) actually did the physical labor of digging up the body. He was paid $2.50. A second examination was again undertaken by Hill. He determined that "there were no evidences of the neck being broken as claimed," according to the *Kent News*. That report was also signed by Todd indicating that he assisted on the second autopsy, apparently no longer concerned about how quickly he would be paid. Hill received $10.00 for "post mort[em] examination," and Todd received $5.00 for "assisting in post mortem examination."[9]

No one was charged with a crime in Campbell's death, and the grand jury report for the April term of the circuit court, signed by its foreman, William B. Usilton, oddly had no mention of it at all. The truth is, there simply wasn't any interest in investigating the homicide of a black transient whose death had resulted from a liquor-fueled brawl in the far-flung First District of the county. According to the *New York Times*, "The best citizens of the county were opposed to any one being punished for the killing of the colored man, on account of the way the negroes had been acting."[10]

Hill's autopsy seemed an appropriate end to the probe into the Campbell affair. But in the African American community, there was no question that Campbell had been murdered. The rumor, though incorrect, was that Hill denied Campbell had a broken neck against Todd's analysis. The anger that manifested in some African American sectors would boil up the day after the jury of inquest made a final decision[11] in an act of violence that shocked the entire county and the state and rippled beyond the borders.

MILLINGTON IN THE 1890s

Internationally known travel writer and poet Bayard Taylor gave Millington scant notice when he toured the Eastern Shore in the summer of 1871. He was fascinated by the plight of former slaves, freed less than seven years prior to his visit by the state's revamped constitution of 1864, not by the Emancipation Proclamation of 1863. Lincoln freed the slaves only in the rebellious Southern states, not those in slave states like Maryland that had remained in the Union.

Many of Kent's affluent white residents, including its political strongmen, resented the emancipation effort and long held the belief that it was a Republican plot to supplant the Democratic majority.

The attitudes of the white "gentlemen" interviewed by Taylor no doubt lingered in the Kent County of 1892. And the South-like society of Kent was apparent in his description of Chestertown, the Kent County seat:

> The broad main street of Chestertown suggests the entrance to some ancient capital. Its venerable mansions, many of them in excellent preservation—its bank, court-house, hotel, and churches—would be disappointing if the corn fields succeeded them on the other side; but, instead, there is the broad expanse of Chester River, bordered by gardens and stately homes. Into one of these we were taken, nolens relens, and there, from a breeze portico in the rear, saw the twilight deepen over the charming water view until the hostess called us to crabs, fried chickens, and waffles, such as only the Eastern Shore can give. I could have believed myself in England, there was such an air of antique

Injustice on the Eastern Shore

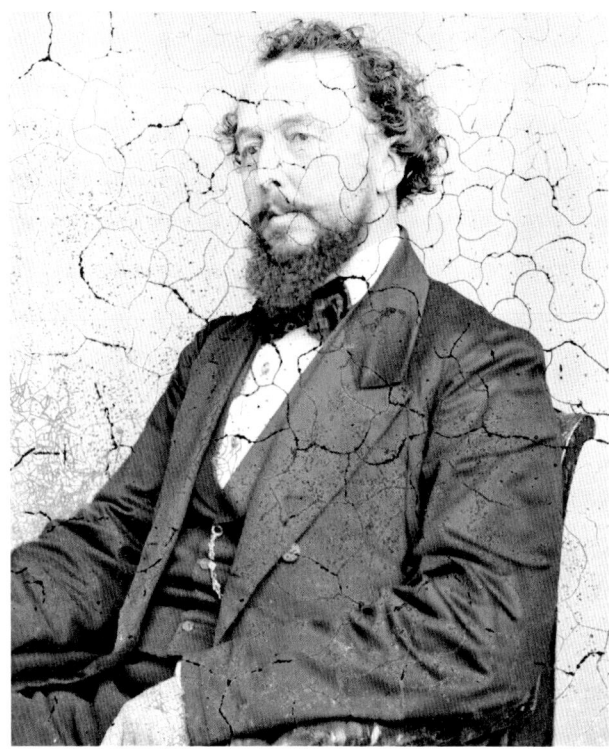

Left: Bayard Taylor. *Library of Congress.*

Below: The steam locomotive had become a common sight in Millington by 1870. *Courtesy of Mike Dixon.*

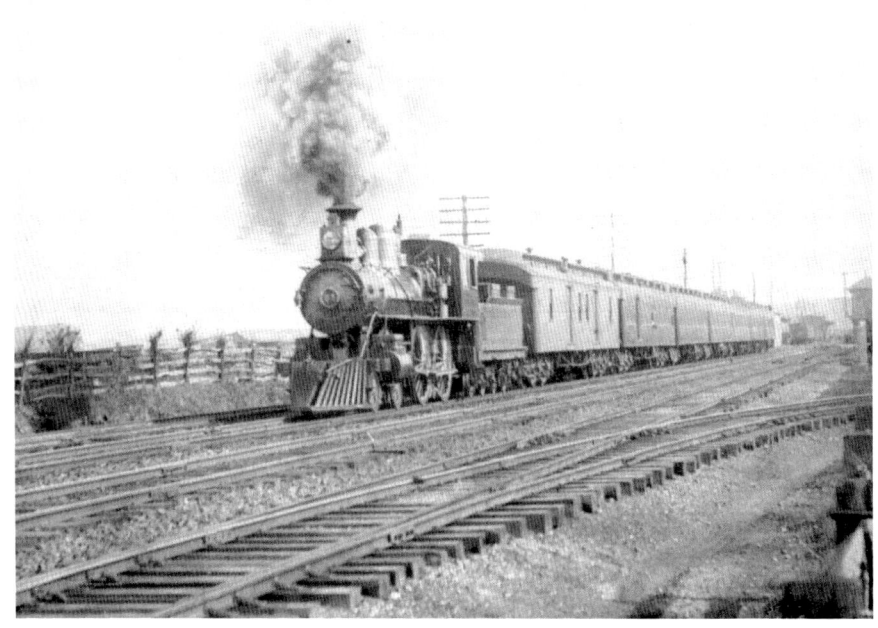

Race and the Hill Murder Trial

comfort and order about the place. It was only too attractive, for our plans commanded us to leave when the open-hearted hospitality of our host made us feel most at home.

On our return to the train, I heard the first indirect expression of opinion in regard to the change which came with the war. We met a company of negro laborers returning from their work in the dusk, singing as they went homeward. "A few years ago," said one of the gentlemen, "they always sang, but this, you will notice, is the first we have heard…"

"Are they, then, so unhappy since they are free?" I asked.

After a little hesitation he said, "They have cares now which they didn't know then."

"It is a good thing," I could not help marking: "If they begin to feel care for their future, they have already learned something."

This seemed to be a view of the matter which the gentleman had not considered. Similar opinions to his own were frequently suggested to us in a delicate way, but the tone was always regretful rather than bitter.[12]

Two rail lines met in Massey, four miles north of Millington; by 1872, travelers could take the train to that village, disembark and take another to Chestertown if they chose not to take a long walk, ride a horse or hitch up a carriage.

It was the Victorian age. Modern women wore their hair up, often curled with an iron heated on the wood or kerosene stove. Clothing was fancy, with pearls, fur, silk and lace aplenty trimmed with fine needlework. Hats had feathers, bows, lace and silk flowers. The wealthy shopped in Baltimore and Philadelphia, reached by train. Those of lesser stations made and mended their own clothes with a Singer. Every housewife had one. And they might take their fashion and social cues from *Godey's Lady's Book*, published monthly in Philadelphia. The February 1892 edition was dedicated to Valentine's Day and was appropriately filled with material of a romantic nature.

Fashionable men had handlebar mustaches and trimmed sideburns. They drank tea or coffee from "mustache cups," smoked cigars and ate farmloads of eggs, bacon, beefsteak, scrapple, fruit and fried potatoes for breakfast and steak, oysters, crabs, pork, venison, goose, duck and gobs of chicken for dinner. The male role was to provide for the family. For even the most casual public interaction, unless they dressed for a specific job, men wore ties and vests and shined shoes, repaired as needed at the local shoe repair shops. They wore hats—something wide-brimmed for the farm or a derby or top hat for important functions. Everyone went to church, and most gathered

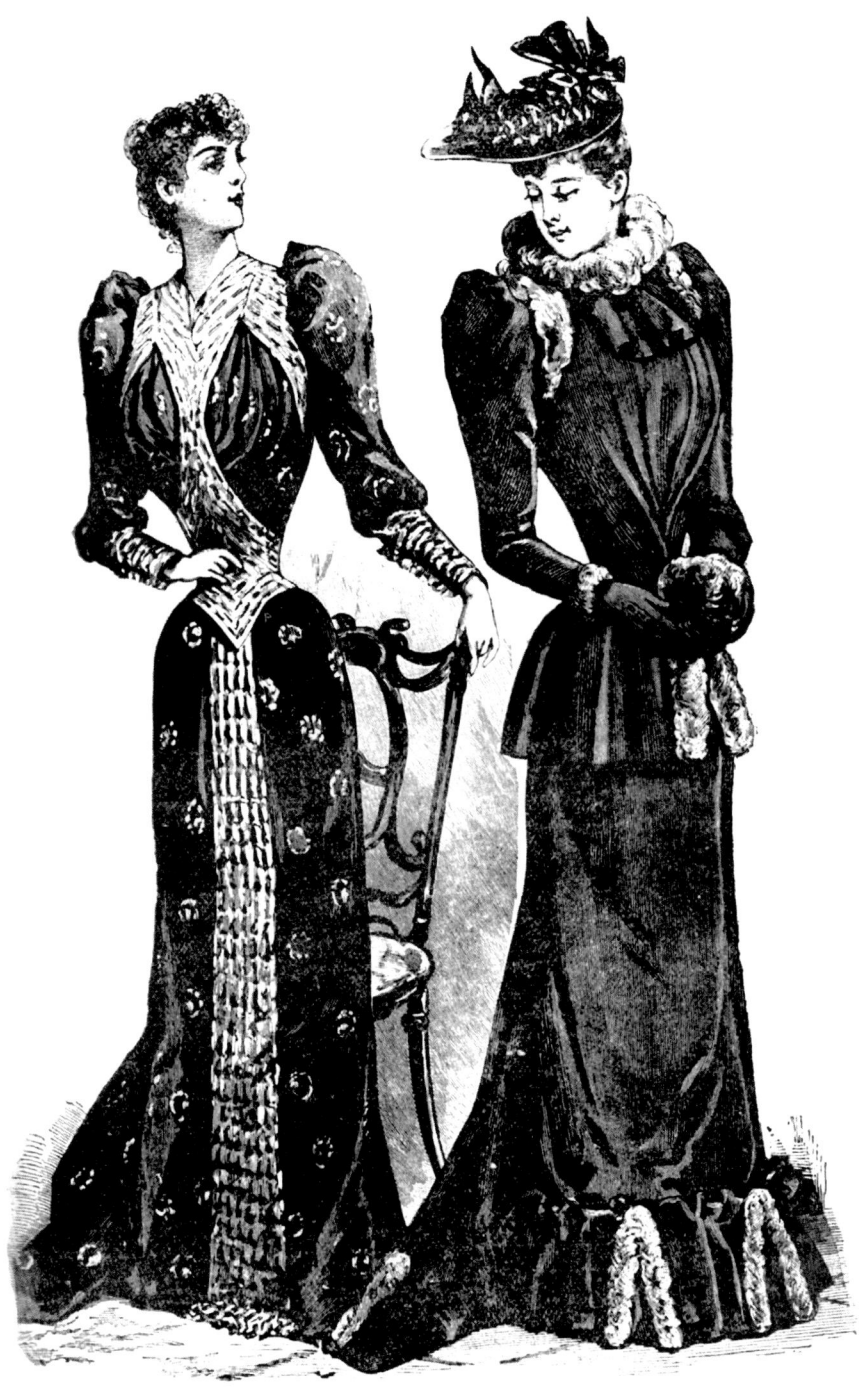

A fashion spread from *Godey's Lady's Book*, February 1892.

Race and the Hill Murder Trial

at the corner stores, blacksmith and barbershops for daily doses of gossip. There was plenty of that to go around, and most knew the real story before they read all the news that was fit to print and then some in the weekly *Kent News* and the *Chestertown Transcript*.

In the local "rags" people could find out the price of coal, ice, beans, corn and other commodities; how the kids were doing in school; whose house burned down; news on the newest commercial venture; courthouse news; who was elected; who was sick; and who had died.

And William Johnson, the justice of the peace, noted in an 1887 letter to the *Kent News* that the town had "four doctors and four drug stores." That, he quipped, was "pretty hard on the one undertaker."

And there were other improvements, noted "C.C.," the anonymous Millington correspondent to the *Chestertown Transcript*, in 1891:

> *Although some of our neighboring towns are a little in advance of us in the improvement line, still, we get there after a while. The long talked of street lamps have at last made their appearance. They were lighted for the first time on Saturday night last, and add a great deal to the looks of the town, besides being a very necessary convenience to those who find it necessary to be on the streets after dark. What we have lost in time in getting this long felt want supplied, we have made up in brilliancy of light. There are fifteen new lights, besides quite a number of private ones, which the town will now take care of, with the prospect of a dozen more new ones in the near future.*[13]

Lights or no lights, boomtowns, even small ones, can have their problems, not the least of which is a tendency for violence, often fueled by illicit hooch. Town residents could still remember a gunfight that occurred in 1884, when John Manning was shot by a Golts man after the two got into a fight one Friday night. It played out like a scene from the Wild West. The following night, Jack Darrell got into a fistfight with John Stewart, who then attempted to flee in a carriage. Darrell grabbed a shotgun out of a nearby store and got a blast off at Stewart with a full load, giving him a nasty leg wound.[14]

Fortunately, as Johnson had noted, the town always seemed to have plenty of doctors. In 1892, one of them was paid by the railroad to take care of its cases, most of which resulted from trauma. It was that job that brought young James Heighe Hill to the community. But a doctor was a doctor back then; there weren't many who specialized. They delivered babies, sewed up cuts, amputated limbs, knocked out or pulled rotten teeth and peddled pharmaceuticals by the box, bottle and pot. And when necessary, they were also freelance medical examiners, the unfortunate role that paved Hill's path to eternity.

THE AFRICAN AMERICAN COMMUNITY

Kent County's African American society in 1892 is best likened to a parallel universe or perhaps a different dimension than its white counterpart. The wounds of slavery and the Civil War still festered in Kent County. Many white farmers could recall the days when slave labor was the main farm engine in the fields and blacks could not vote. African American parents told their tales of slavery to their children. Blacks in and around Millington continued to blame racist whites for burning down their church and schoolhouse in 1865.[15] The flames of racial hatred were also fanned by local newspapers, which mongered fear among their white constituency that schools would one day be forced to integrate and the county would be run by blacks if the dominant Democratic majority was unseated.

While blacks continued to form the backbone of farm field labor for meager wages around Millington—most heads of households are listed as "laborers" in the 1880 and 1900 censuses—joblessness was high in the black community. Consequently, there was a movement to find work in the bigger cities.

The *Transcript* of March 12, 1891, reported:

> An exodus of colored people has set in from the vicinity of Millington, and the upper portion of Queen Anne's county. Fully twenty-six left Millington and as many more went from Pondtown and Sudlersville last week, all bound for New Jersey for higher wages.

Injustice on the Eastern Shore

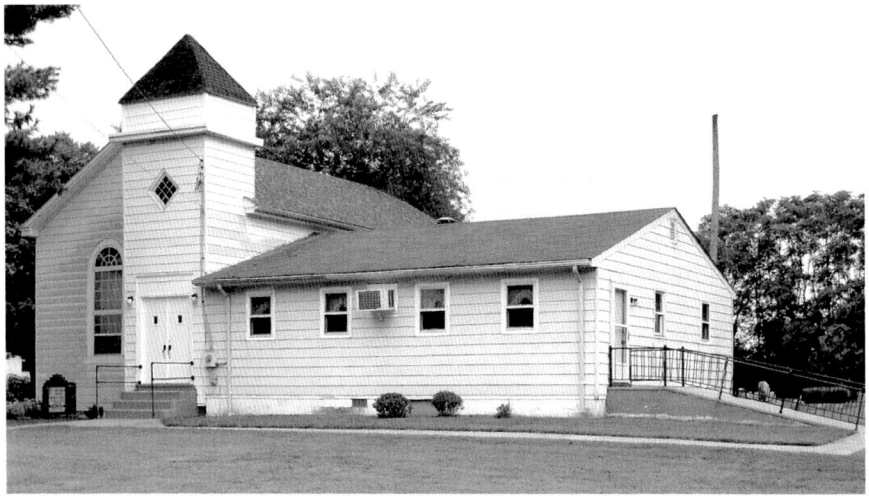

The John Wesley United Methodist Church has been a focal point of the black community in Millington since before the Civil War. *Photo by Kevin Hemstock.*

Nonetheless, black communities in Kent continued to grow,[16] seeded by increased property ownership (many blacks freed by emancipation twenty-five years earlier bought or were given property). Sandfield—not to be confused with Sand Town—was a good example. It had grown from a silk farm into a vibrant African American community.

The 1877 map shows sixteen properties, averaging one half to one acre, bordered by the millrace to the north, Cypress Branch to the east and Chester River to the south. The community, prone to flooding, was initially accessed by a road called Broadway east of the millrace. That road is no longer extant, but the southern part is now Race Street. There was also North Street (now Middle Street) and Charles and South Streets (now combined into West Street).

The population would grow substantially in the next two decades.

A county "colored" school, as it was called, augmenting the church school, was built there in 1893. By 1900, the population of Sandfield was about 150, almost all African American. At that time, the population of incorporated Millington (including the portion in Queen Anne's County called Sand Town) was 487, which included only 39 African Americans.[17]

The municipal boundaries, it seems, defined a population island of whites.

Sandfield was served by the John Wesley ME Church, now the John Wesley United Methodist Church, on the east end of Cypress Street. The church was a nexus of the African American community.

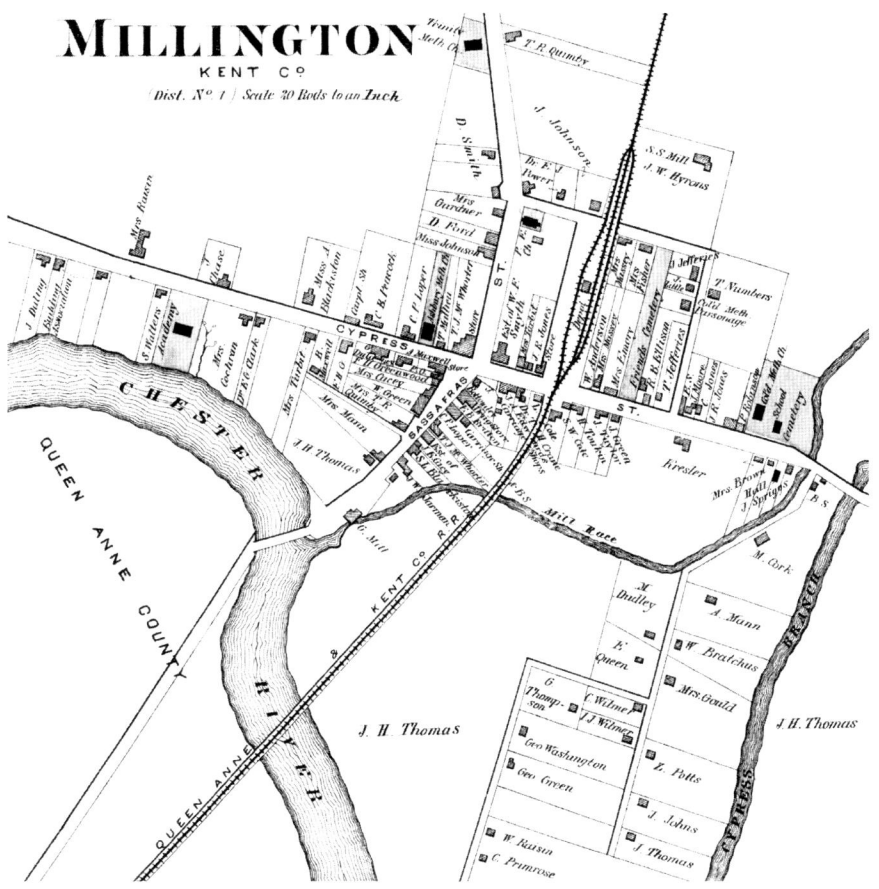

This 1877 map shows the town's configuration after the railroad was built. *From the* Lake Griffing & Stevenson Atlas of Kent and Queen Anne Counties.

In addition to Sandfield, there were small groups of blacks on family farms living along the edges of the former large white plantations, such as the Cacy, Jones, Davis, Johnson and Spear farms, between Millington and Sassafras, where their parents and grandparents had worked as slaves.

It was a period when Jim Crow ruled supreme. Racial prejudice was in its glory days. Whites thought African Americans should be inconspicuous and respectful and remain in their "areas." There were separate facilities, separate stores, separate churches, separate undertakers and separate cemeteries. Both races, however, understood the green color of money; a recently discovered account book for H.F. Jefferson millinery store in Chestertown, for the early part of the twentieth century, listed all the sales to white customers in the

INJUSTICE ON THE EASTERN SHORE

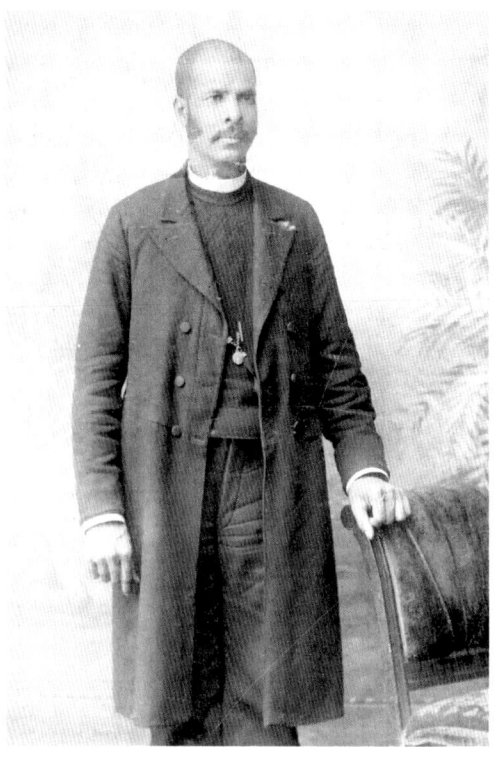

The Reverend Enoch E. Hughes was one of Kent County's first black newspaper editors and also served as the pastor of the Bethel AME Church in Chestertown. *Historical Society of Kent County.*

front of the book. But the store also catered to black clientele, whose purchases were listed in the back of the book.

Prejudice was clear in the county's two major white-owned newspapers. Blacks did not get obituaries or death notices unless there was some superlative, such as a crime involved or he or she was the servant of a wealthy white family. For example, Levi Murray's death was noted in the February 8, 1873 edition of the *Kent News* because he died of smallpox, an often-fatal, contagious disease the mere mention of which was guaranteed to cause a stir anytime there was an outbreak. In 1871, the *Kent News* reported the murder of twenty-one-year-old Robert Hackett at the hands of two drunken white men. Hackett, of Sassafras, had come to the defense of two women and was stabbed to death. The paper reported, "The deceased was formerly a servant of D.C. Blackiston, Esq., and is said to have been a very industrious and inoffensive boy."

As seen, African Americans were subtly or not so subtly diminished in the papers. Color-centric white editors used "boy" or "girl" to describe adults; first names were often used in discussions of blacks in the news and deformalized: Deborah would become Debby; James, Jimmy; and Robert, Robby, Bobby or Bob. Whites had their full names used and received titles: Mr., Mrs., Messr., Messrs. or Mesdames. Blacks seldom did. African Americans were sometimes quoted in vernacular; that is, the paper would try to transcribe "accents" for blacks but not whites. They also used what today are seen as derogatory names. For example, an African American man was asked by the *Kent News* reporter to describe his experience with the tornado that killed eleven people in and around Still Pond in 1888. The newspaper quoted him:

> *Uncle John H. Wilmer, an old darky, was working around the factory, when the cyclone picked him up and hurled him through the air at a lightning express rate for a hundred yards, and then put him on his props before he knew what had struck him. They tell it upon Uncle John that the storm discovered what it had, and would have nothing more to do with him. Uncle John says, "Deed I thought de judgment day had cum, right away, en I was gwine ter be en engel, becus I was flyin' through de air."*[18]

Sometimes this imbued prejudice led to outright violence if an African American "stepped out of line."

In one such case, a black man wanted to shop at a church sale at the Asbury ME Church in Millington in 1875. His effort ended in violence.

The *Kent News* correspondent "Traveler" reported what no doubt was a scandal among local whites:

> *The audience were a little surprised on Saturday evening by the appearance of a representative of the fifteenth amendment, who attempted to carry out one of the points of "Civil Rights," by deliberately stepping up to one of the ladies' flower tables to buy an orange, which he was refused; and being ordered out he went down stairs heels over head out into the street, where it is said he received several knock-downs, and retaliated with a pistol, shooting a young man by the name of Solloway, the ball taking effect in the fleshy part of his thigh. The wound was examined by Dr. Clark, who failed to extract the ball, it being buried so deep in the flesh it was impossible to remove it. The darky made his escape without much injury, and Solloway is said to be doing well.*[19]

It wasn't beyond the papers to use the most disgusting and demeaning of derogatory terms. In 1866, when the white population was at the height of its fear about how newly freed African Americans would affect society and politics, the *Kent News* had this political item, headlined "Union with the Nigger":

> *The Radicals have latterly been making a great ado about the "Union." The Jack Hamilton Convention, which met two weeks ago in Philadelphia, demonstrated that their "Union" means nothing more or less than Union with the negro, Fred. Douglas and other negroes being present, and*

participating in the proceedings. The prayers offered were prayers for the negro; the speeches made were only so many appeals for the negro; the proceedings looked to the enfranchisement of the negroes—Union with the negro *is the feast to which these worthies invite the laboring white men of the country. In supposing they can carry the country on such a negro platform, they reckon without their host.*[20]

Most of the African American community, while still oppressed by the white majority, was nonetheless aglow with the newfound freedoms tendered by the Fifteenth Amendment, ratified on February 3, 1870, ostensibly giving blacks the right to vote.

That was an important occasion for two minorities in Kent County: members of the African American community and the county's Republicans of whatever race.

The former wanted all the rights that went along with their newfound freedom. The whites in the latter category saw it as a way, by adding the black male vote to the voting pool, of shoring up their scant showing in local elections (and nationally, buttressing a slow but steady decline).

There were several events in Kent that resulted from the constitutional amendment.

On May 19, 1870, as many as three thousand African Americans from throughout the region visited Chestertown for a peaceful celebration of the passage of the new law. The day started with a parade with flags, banners, colorful wagons and bands.

The gathering coincided with similar activities throughout the nation, one of the largest of which was in Baltimore the same day. There, Frederick Douglass was the keynote speaker.

As with the Baltimore celebration, the parade in Kent was followed by a rally. It took place in an area of "woods" in or near Chestertown, where speeches were given by local and visiting proponents of the amendment.[21]

Among them were Henry Highland Garnet, ardent abolitionist and former slave, born near Chesterville, who attained freedom when he escaped from Kent County with his family in 1824:

> *Some bitter things are reported to have been said, but the main effort was to impress the colored people with the idea that it was their duty to vote the radical ticket, which of course was perfectly natural, as that was the only object had in view in making them voters.*[22]

Race and the Hill Murder Trial

The first election in the county that the amendment affected was in May of that year. It was the election of new Chestertown town commissioners. In the chartered municipality, a law was in place—approved by the legislature two years earlier—that attempted an end run around any effort to allow blacks to vote:

> *The white male citizens of Chestertown in Kent county, of twenty-one years of age and upwards, the owners of real estate in said town in their own name or in the right of their wife, and who have resided in Chestertown or the precincts thereof one whole year next preceding the day of the election, shall annually, on the fourth Monday in May, elect seven persons of lawful age, each of whom shall be the owner of real property in said town in his own right, or in the right of his wife, and shall reside therein, commissioners for said town, and the persons so elected by the name of The Commissioners of Chestertown, are hereby declared to be a body politic with power to sue and be sued, and use a common seal and the same to alter at their pleasure.*[23]

The new federal law put an end to using race to limit voter eligibility, and while the state legislature approved the change in the town's charter, it was vetoed by Democratic governor Oden Bowie. Fellow Democrats, no doubt, perceived him as a traitor.

The veto made national news, and at least one urban paper, the *Philadelphia Evening Telegraph*, was not shy about expressing its opinion that Maryland's Eastern Shore was populated by racist, uneducated hayseeds:

> *The beneficial results of the fifteenth amendment are beginning to show themselves already. The Democratic, fire-eating, and Copperhead Governor Bowie, of Maryland, has accepted the situation, and has vetoed an act incorporating Chestertown, in Kent county, because the persons entitled to vote under the provisions of this bill are described as "white male citizens." There will be weeping and wailing and gnashing of teeth on the Eastern Shore when the news of this veto is received at the cross-road groceries that are the centres of intelligence in that benighted region, and curses both loud and deep will be bestowed upon Bowie, Congress, the "niggers," and all parties concerned.*[24]

Other aspects of the local law, including the requirement that voters own property in town, were not addressed or remained in effect from previous legislation.

Injustice on the Eastern Shore

Few black men in town owned property. One who did was fifty-year-old Isaac Anderson, a carter and fisherman who lived and worked from the small riverside lot and home on the east end of Water Street that he had inherited from his father.

On May 4, when it was clear that the Democratic majority would take the Chestertown commission election because most of the potential black voters didn't own property, Anderson sold a piece of ground, about four feet square, to forty-four black men, who together paid fifteen dollars total. Since those forty-four men were officially property owners, they were eligible to vote and did so on May 23. With the extra voters, the election favored the Republicans, who beat their Democratic opponents.

This also became a national news story, with the spin based on the editorial slant of the paper.

After the land buy but before the election, the *Belmont Chronicle* of St. Clairsville, Ohio, ran a report from the *New York Tribune* that lauded the move:

> *The negroes of Maryland are showing themselves very apt scholars in the political school. Although so very recently enfranchised, they already appear to be almost as smart at little political games as white folks. It seems that the Legislature of Maryland (entirely Democratic) at its last session enacted that only those shall vote for Town Commissioners in the ancient and respectable borough of Chestertown who are the owners of real estate in said town…These wise legislators in their worthy efforts to maintain the aristocratic character of the government of Chestertown, strangely omitted to state the extent or value of the real estate necessary to constitute an elector.*[25]

The *New York Herald* wasn't as kind in its comments after the election, describing the little land sale as a "mean Radical dodge to catch the negro vote":

> *At a recent election for Town Commissioners in Chestertown, Maryland, the negroes carried the day by one of the meanest species of fraud that the Fifteenth Amendment has yet produced. According to the charter of the town all voters at a town election are required to be freeholders. Out of the one hundred and fifty darkeys who desired to march to the polls not more than two or three could point to a foot of land they possessed…It happened that there was one negro in Chestertown who owned a small and worthless patch of land adjacent to the river. This he divided into lots of one-foot square*

and made deeds of it to his fellow colored would-be voters. As a consequence one hundred and fifty negroes, representing just one hundred and fifty feet of land, went to the polls, and claimed and secured votes as freeholders, and elected their ticket….Naturally enough the bona fide *freeholders of Kent county are highly indignant at the outrage, but there appears to be no help for them, and they are obliged to look forward to the day when a "white man will be as good as a nigger" in reality.*[26]

With freedom, however ponderous its forward momentum, African Americans were less inclined to accept being slighted in what, to many, would have appeared an obvious miscarriage of justice. Thomas Campbell was murdered at McWhorter's oyster saloon; someone had to pay the price. That was the law, the same in theory for black or white. For Dr. Hill's errant autopsy, punishment wouldn't be meted out by a constable or judge.

HILL SETS UP HOUSE IN MILLINGTON

Dr. James Heighe Hill was the son of Samuel Hill, a farmer of modest means in Locust Grove who came to Kent County from Odessa, Delaware, in 1857. Samuel Hill was the tenant, for a while, of Margaret B. Polk[27] on her 277-acre States Adventure farm, on the south side of the main road from Kennedyville to Locust Grove.

It's uncertain what the relationship was between Hill and Polk. Both were from Cantwell's Bridge, near Odessa, in Delaware's St. George's Hundred.

In 1872, Samuel Hill purchased a shop and residence on the four corners of Locust Grove from William O. Shallcross, another surname common to Odessa. At the time of the purchase, the shop was being used as a restaurant run by tenant James Pennington.[28] It was converted to a drugstore by George M. Beasten, no doubt related to a prominent Delawarean of the same surname.

In his later years, Samuel Hill was described as a man of small frame who sported a white goatee.

His wife, the doctor's mother, Hester Showaker, was originally from Philadelphia, the daughter of Carl and Anna Reaver Showaker. The surname was German in origin; Carl Showaker, a cooper by trade, was the son of Johan Schauwecker.

Samuel J. Hill was originally a carpenter, according to the 1850 census. He married Hester in 1849, and the two started their family at Cantwell's Bridge. It's uncertain what compelled them to move to Maryland seven years later.

Race and the Hill Murder Trial

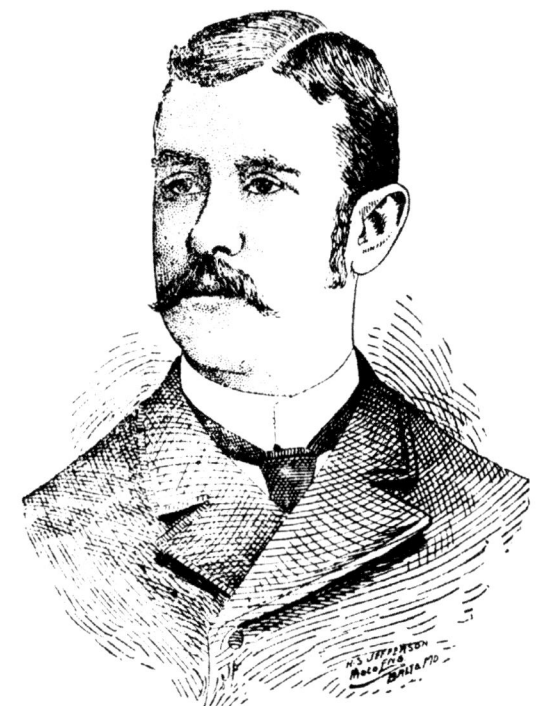

Right: Dr. James Heighe Hill, from a woodcut in a local newspaper. *From the* Kent News, *May 7, 1892.*

Below: The Locust Grove store as it looked about 1915. *Courtesy of Mark Newsome.*

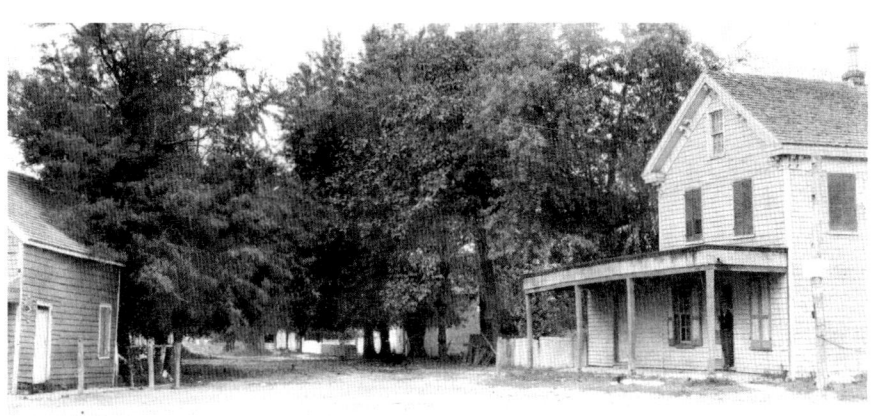

The doctor was one of their six children to grow into adulthood. Siblings, eldest to youngest, included Sarah (Sallie), Charles, Harry, Walter and Maggie, an accomplished organist. Heighe Hill was the youngest—"the baby."

Heighe was born on May 20, 1862, and he either chose the career of medicine early on or it was chosen for him. It was in his name, which was

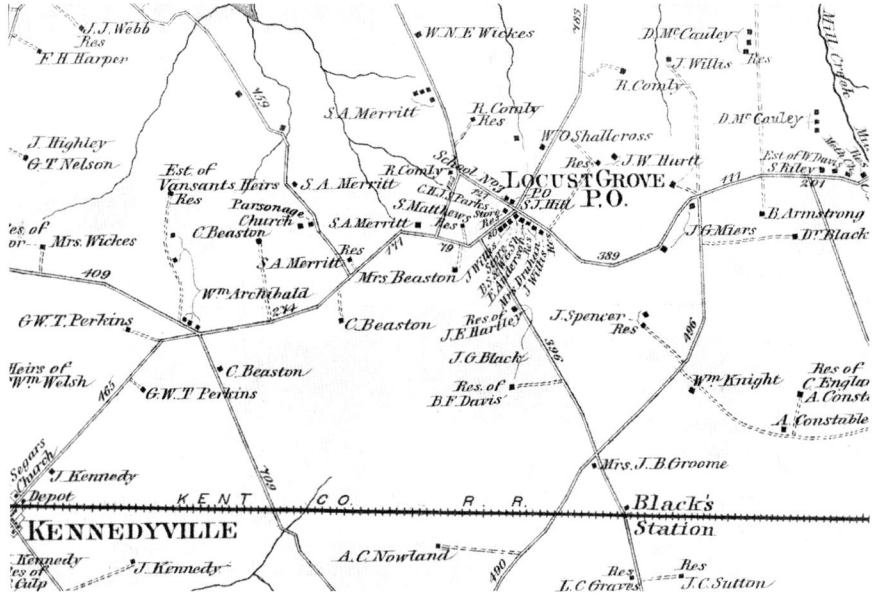

Samuel Hill's store is noted at the four corners in this 1877 map of the district with Locust Grove. *From the* Lake, Griffing & Stevenson Atlas of Kent and Queen Anne Counties.

derived from Dr. James Heighe, a popular and successful Kent doctor, one of those who tended to the victims of an 1851 mass murder near Galena. Dr. Heighe, who was the Hill family doctor, died in 1871, and his wonderful manse just north of Galena became an academy for young women.

Little Heighe Hill grew up around Locust Grove, so named about 1861 when the post office was established there. Ironically, this was the same name as the farm near Odessa owned by Mary Polk's father and might be the source of the name.

Locust Grove back then was a small, four-corners village that was a stop in the main east–west road spanning Kennedyville and Harmony Corner on the one side and Galena on the other. The intersecting road ran to Shrewsbury Neck to the north and south to Black's Station, located just south of Black's Crossroads, the closest railroad stop. Beyond that in that direction, the road took the traveler on to Chesterville and on to Millington.

Today, there are no traditional shops in Locust Grove. The post office was closed in 1918. The school closed in 1936, and the building was moved in 1985. The church building, sold by the surviving trustees in 1950, eventually fell into ruin.[29] Samuel Hill's old "storeroom" remains as a craft shop/residence.

Race and the Hill Murder Trial

While a student at the one-room village schoolhouse in Locust Grove, the young Heighe Hill also worked in Beasten's drugstore. They became related by law when Beasten married Hill's sister Sarah.

Beasten must have regaled his little brother-in-law with many stories of his days fighting for the Confederacy as a private in the First Maryland Cavalry.

Hill wanted to be a druggist, following in Beasten's footsteps. He initially attended the Philadelphia College of Pharmacy, the first college dedicated to the study of pharmacology in the nation.

His interest soon migrated to medicine. He began attending the University of Pennsylvania in 1883, graduating with his medical degree in April 1886. The ink on the diploma was barely dry when he returned to the state and county of his birth that summer. He began his doctoring career in Sassafras, on the county line north of Massey, setting up his practice there. That's where he met his future wife. Although her connection to Sassafras is unclear, they met while she was on a visit there.

By 1887, the doctor had a busy private practice.

Also that year, he became the official "surgeon" for the Kent and Queen Anne's Railroad, taking over from Dr. Britton D. Evans, who left to take the job as assistant medical director at the Maryland Hospital for the Insane in Baltimore[30] and, later, medical director of a New Jersey insane asylum.

That spurred Hill's move to Millington.

He purchased Evans's drugstore and took on Evans's patients along with the railroad appointment. At first, he rented a room at Mallalieu's Hotel. He ran an ad in the *Transcript*:

> *J.H. Hill, M.D.*
> *Millington…Maryland.*
> *Office and Drug Store on Cypress street.*
> *May be found at Mallalieu's Hotel at night.*
> *A supply of Medicines carried for out-of-town patients.*[31]

Hill was a handsome man, five feet, six inches tall and about 140 pounds. He had dark hair and eyes, a carefully cropped mustache and "close-cut English side-Whiskers."[32]

On Wednesday, September 25, 1889, he married the dark-haired, dark-eyed, nineteen-year-old Arrelee Bond, the daughter of Benjamin Franklin Bond and Sarah J. Bond of Patapsco Neck, Baltimore County.

Injustice on the Eastern Shore

She was the eldest of three daughters in the family and grew up on the outskirts of Baltimore. Her father, a gardener, was born in Maryland, while her mother was from Delaware.

Arrelee was described as "a very pretty woman," "small in stature but well molded," with nice features and a pure white complexion.[33]

The wedding took place at the Reverend B.F. Devries's parsonage, at 310 Bank Street in Baltimore County. After the ceremony, the newlyweds took the 12:45 p.m. train from Union Station to New York City.

Upon returning from their two-day honeymoon trip north, a "sumptuous" party celebrated the happy couple's nuptials. When the party ended, they were left alone in their new home on Cypress Street in Millington.[34]

Their abode near the railroad tracks was closer to the hardscrabble lots in Sandfield than to the high-class and roomier Victorians that were springing up on the west end of town. The couple rented one side of a double house, possibly from James Edwards. The house, along with the whole block, and much of the town's commercial center burned in the 1904 fire.[35]

The *Lake, Griffing & Stevenson Atlas of Kent and Queen Anne Counties* shows a small double house on the site. After the fire, the lot was purchased by John Ahern, who sold it, in 1920, to Isaac Hollins for a department store called The Hub. Farmers Bank purchased the lot in 1974.

The Hills' side of the double house had two furnished bedrooms, one of which held a featherbed, bureau and washstand. As with most houses of the day, there was a sitting room, dining room and kitchen. A privy and stable were out back. A large clock dominated the sitting room. There were several rocking chairs, perhaps brought in so Arrelee could rock her babies when and if the family grew.

Hill apparently had an office in the house, too. It was furnished with a set of fifty medical books, a "manikin," a looking glass, a desk and two chairs.[36]

The Hills of Millington quickly fit in to the upper-class social life of the bustling municipality. They frequently attended dances and other functions.

Along with his busy practice and the railroad position, the doctor ran the drugstore he took over from Evans. This was the building rented from James Edwards, who owned the property near the four corners. It was a common practice among doctors of the day to peddle the drugs they prescribed.

A bill from one of Hill's suppliers offers some insight on the types of things that made up his inventory. Items included extract of lactuca, a sedative; quinine; saltpeter; antimony; and yarrow, the latter used as a coagulant. Among the manufactured items were Castile soap, Warner's Safe Cure and Pisos Cure.[37]

Race and the Hill Murder Trial

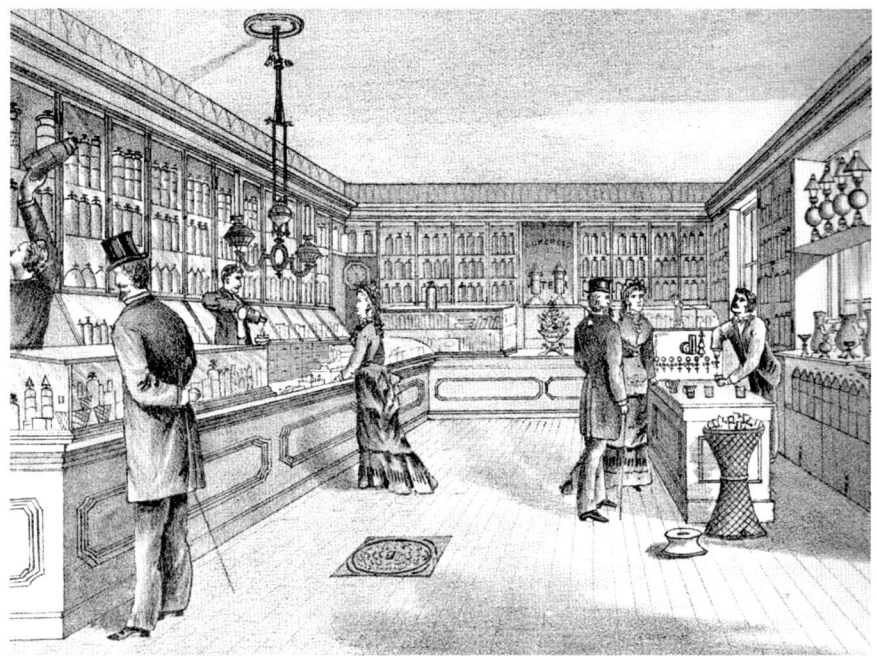

The classic drugstore of the late nineteenth century is depicted in this drawing. The artist made the image after visiting Stam's Drugstore in Chestertown. *From the* Lake, Griffing & Stevenson Atlas of Kent and Queen Anne Counties.

Like many drugs dispensed in the late nineteenth century, Pisos Cure would be illegal today. Originally made with opium, that component was removed in the 1880s, but the formula that Hill sold contained cannabis. It was touted by the manufacturer, E.T. Hazeltine, as a cure for consumption (tuberculosis). The federal government forced that claim to be dropped in 1906 after the company name was changed to the Piso Co.

Given the formula of this and similar "tonics," it's not surprising that they became top-selling items and the druggists who sold them familiar faces in the community.

Hill also became an active member of local civic organizations, joining the Epworth League, where he was vice-president of the Christian works committee; and Algonquin Tribe No. 80, Improved Order of Red Men. The Millington chapter of the venerable club that dated to George Washington's time had formed only two years earlier. He was also a member of the board of trustees of the Asbury ME Church, the larger of two white Methodist churches in town, the other being Trinity ME Church South.

Why two Methodist churches in such a small town?

Injustice on the Eastern Shore

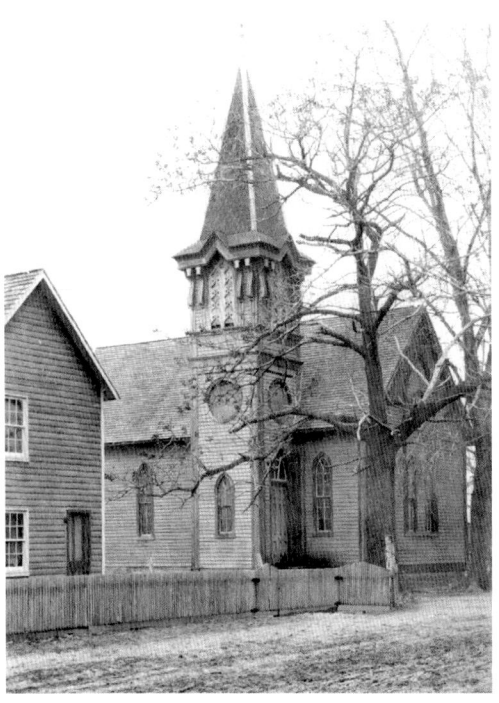

The Locust Grove ME Church, seen in this postcard image about 1910, was sold in 1950 and eventually fell into ruin. *Courtesy of Mark Newsome.*

The ME Church South, as an organization, was an outgrowth of the schism in the Methodist establishment on the issue of slavery and having African Americans as part of a church's congregation. It was where religion and institutional racism collided. The rift in the church began in the mid-1840s.

It wasn't long before the split affected the churches in Kent County, whose plantation economy was maintained substantially by black laborers both before and after emancipation. The dichotomy lasted long beyond the Civil War, and in 1872, the heirs of John Cacy sold a small parcel of land on Sassafras Street in Millington for $200 to the trustees of the ME Church South.[38]

Construction was completed soon after. The Millington church became part of a circuit that included Chesterville and Sudlersville. The church in Millington was the northernmost bastion of the splinter organization, which remained in existence until it merged with the Methodist Church in the 1940s. A vestige of the Millington church remains in the form of its former Sunday school building, which is now a residence.

By contrast, the Asbury ME Church, named for one of Methodism's first bishops, dated to the early nineteenth century, when Methodism began to replace Quakerism as the dominant religion in town. The building on Cypress Street where the Hills worshipped was relatively new, built by Millington native Horace M. Stuart. It was the replacement for the original church, a thirty-four- by forty-four-foot brick building constructed in 1837, once located where the town cemetery is today. The old one was demolished when the newer building was mostly completed in 1871. It was dedicated the following year.[39]

Race and the Hill Murder Trial

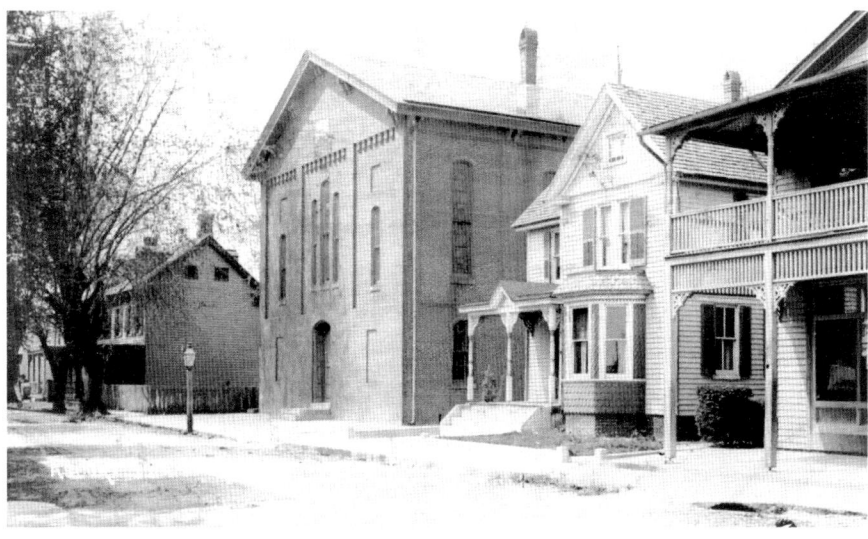

Hill was a member of the board of trustees of the Asbury ME Church in Millington, seen here in an early twentieth-century postcard image. It hasn't changed much since it was built in 1871. *Courtesy of Mark Newsome.*

It's uncertain why the Hills selected the Asbury Church for their religious needs. It may simply have been an extension of Dr. Hill's association with the church in his native Locust Grove and had nothing at all to do with the lingering debates associated with Civil War–era racial politics. Suffice it to say that there was competition for the souls of Millington since churches rose and fell on the size of their congregations. At the time the Hills were beginning their residency in Millington, the Asbury Church had the larger following.

Their little baby girl was baptized there.

There is nothing to indicate that the Hills had any children before blue-eyed Ethel, her first name possibly derived from Arrelee's younger sister. She was born in February 1892.

That was a cold month. Children continued to skate on the millpond well into the middle of the month, and a large number of floating, paralyzed fish found in the Chester River was attributed to the cold. But March would usher in better weather, a hint of spring heralded by perch fishing, for the white and yellow varieties, which commonly make the run up the Chester in the first couple weeks in March.

Was Hill a good doctor? It's hard to say. A doctoring kit in those days often included hardware seemingly more fitted to a blacksmith's shop. Fortunately, during his day, medicine was rapidly modernizing. Bloodletting, for example—the treatment responsible for George Washington's death—was by the late 1800s considered "quackery." But leeches were still a common treatment for some ailments.

Hill's cases frequently involved victims of trauma. For example, on February 20, 1887, he was summoned to John Goldsborough, in Sassafras, who had been bitten and stomped by a berserk colt. Goldsborough probably lost a finger. Hill extracted a bullet from John Manor's elbow two months after the Golts man was accidentally shot on November 4, 1889. The doctor was summoned because the wound became infected. A week after Hill extracted the bullet, Manor died of "blood poisoning," another common result of trauma cases in the day. Hill treated James Mannon for a cut to the leg in December 1890. He began treating Emma Thomas in February 1890. She died one month later, probably of advanced cancer. However, he successfully treated his own mother's illness that same year.

It's a case log that seems average for a country doctor. There is nothing to indicate that he was superlative or particularly bad at his trade. He treated whites and blacks in a time when not all white doctors catered to a diverse clientele. It was clear he took his job seriously, had a good bedside manner and was responsive to his patients. Had it not been so, he might have lived much longer.

A HOUSE CALL

On the evening of Saturday, April 23, 1892, Arrelee Hill was not feeling well. She was convalescing from what was described as a serious illness. After tea, the doctor read to her for a little while and then, tucking her into bed, kissed her and little Ethel goodnight, leaving the house about nine o'clock.[40] He told Arrelee he wouldn't be gone long. He then crossed the street to his drugstore, which was being tended by his clerk, fifteen-year-old Watson Spear.

Spear, who lived near Massey, had replaced Thomas Holliday the year before as Hill's clerk. Holliday may have been a friend of the family or at least a friend of Hill; he was a guest at the Hills' wedding. Holliday left to start a drugstore in Philadelphia. Things might have turned out differently had it not been so.

Hill's store, like most in Millington, stayed open late on Saturday nights, sometimes as late as midnight. This is when farmers, who worked their fields throughout the week, flocked into town to take care of all their purchases, since the stores were required by county ordinance to be closed on Sundays. After checking in with Spear, Hill walked a couple doors down to the home of William M. Johnson,[41] the same man who had worked out the ratio of doctors to undertakers.

Johnson was the local magistrate and justice of the peace, an office he had held since 1883.[42] He was no friend of African Americans, having taken it upon himself to cure local "rowdyism" and stating his determination "not to allow drunken negroes to entirely over-ride the town." His actions led to a near riot on July 6, 1889.[43]

Injustice on the Eastern Shore

The ordinance that accompanied the town's incorporation in 1890 not only gave him the right to enforce town laws but also mandated that he do so. Section 161 read:

> *And be it enacted, That the justices of the peace resident in said town are hereby declared to be the conservators of the peace of said town, and it shall be their duty to order the arrest of person or persons found breaking the peace or disturbing the quiet or order of the town, or violating any of the ordinances made by the commissioners for securing the safety, health, property or lives of the inhabitants of said town, and shall have power to require any person so offending to give security to keep the peace, or in default thereof, may commit said person to the county jail for not more than ten days, and in addition thereto may for the commission of said offense impose a fine on such person of not more than five dollars; and such in default of payment thereof may be committed to the county jail for a period of not more than ten days…*

There's no doubt that Johnson had a strong personality with a ration of flaws. The *Kent News* noted in Johnson's obituary that he was "a very warm friend…although he had his glaring faults."

He was also the town clerk.

But as a justice of the peace who had once practiced law, he took his job seriously as his magistrate's docket demonstrated. His dedication wasn't limited to blacks, whatever his prejudices; it seems he meted out his brand of justice to each and all as equally as the times permitted. For example, in June 1890, he charged Frank Bottomley with assaulting Sam Corrigan. Bottomley, a well-known white grocer who had a store near the four corners, was fined $1.00 and had to pay court costs of $2.63.

As with most local magistrates, the majority of the cases were about money, often seemingly insignificant amounts, such as for store tabs, which were far more common in days of old. Even Dr. Hill was compelled to go after his customers with Johnson's aid. He sought restitution in 1889 against Charles Cacy for $11.80 and against Thomas Stevens for $89.57.

On this occasion, Hill went to Johnson's place for the charter meeting of the local Cleveland Club, to support Grover Cleveland, one of the Democratic candidates for president. Such organizations were springing up all over the county since many of the county's Democrats supported Cleveland over the alternative. The local papers even touted the clubs in an effort to increase local support:

Race and the Hill Murder Trial

Kent may be "sold for Cleveland without clubbing," but the Cleveland Democrats should see to it that each and every district in the county has a Cleveland club, composed of pure and unadulterated Cleveland and Tariff Reform men.[14]

In Johnson's office that night, you can almost imagine the "here heres" and the "hoorahs," a consequence of the political fervor, shouted out by the dozen or so attendees. Who knows how the black man who was peering through the window interpreted the to-do or whether he cared a wit about Grover Cleveland and the upcoming election. His malevolent thoughts were far removed from the realm of politics.

Hill was elected as the club's chairman. But the meeting was cut short when Spear interrupted with the message that James Shaw, one of the doctor's clients, had sent a message that his sick daughter had taken a turn for the worse.

Shaw, twenty-eight; his wife, Annie; and their children lived on Clarence Hurlock's farm about two and a half miles north of Millington just south of Massey. Hill had been treating Shaw's daughter Eva and had told the farmhand to let him know if her condition deteriorated. The ailing tot was about two years old.[15] Shaw sent his wife's brother, eighteen-year-old John Reese, who lived with them, to deliver the message about nine o'clock and left the message for Hill with Spear at the drugstore, apparently just after the doctor had left for the Cleveland Club meeting.

The doctor wasted no time. Leaving the meeting a few minutes after ten o'clock,[16] he gathered up his

Grover Cleveland. *Library of Congress.*

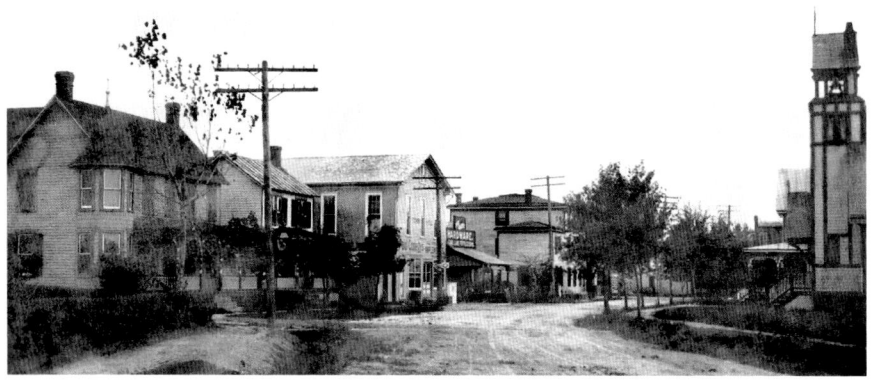

This image of Sassafras Street dates to 1910. The street would have looked similar at the time of the murder. *Courtesy of Mark Newsome.*

wooden medical box and went to his waiting dogcart, a small, light, open, two-wheeled carriage that Watson had already hitched up to the doctor's sorrel mare.[47]

Then he started up Sassafras Street. The street was probably shelled those days within the new town's municipal boundaries. But beyond the town's line, it was simply a dirt lane that became the Millington–Massey road. Other than the composition, it was little different from today's Route 313. The soft thud of the mare's hooves would have been swallowed by the still night. The sun had set more than three hours earlier, and the stars burned bright.

Knowing he didn't have far to go, he didn't bring a coat; indeed, after a cold and meteorologically unpredictable early spring, the weather was only just becoming pleasant. It was a balmy sixty degrees with a light breeze whispering from the northwest—a perfect evening.[48]

He always told his wife when he was going out on a call, but this time he failed to alert her to the unanticipated house call. She was sick, and maybe he didn't want to disturb her.

FORD'S HILL AND DESTINY

Ford's Hill, named for the family that once owned the London Bridge farm next to it, is a little less than three-fourths of a mile north of Millington.[49] Massey is three miles farther north.

It's not much of a hill. Approaching from the south, it's a gentle incline that precedes the still gentle but slightly steeper drop to Long Meadow Branch, where the road takes a slight turn a few degrees closer to due north. The "branch" is a small stream that parallels the road most of the way until it jogs east and crosses under the road, at a place sometimes called Ford's Hollow. The stream empties into one of the millponds that supplied water and power to Jarman's old mill, so called because Wesley Jarman had owned it for about a dozen years before his death in 1890.

A little wooden bridge, maintained by the county, spanned Long Meadow Branch. The bridge, the hill and the stream beyond would have been dominant geographic elements in an otherwise flat landscape squared off into cornfields planted only a week or two earlier. Peach trees, in neat rows, may have broken the otherwise even horizon. They would have been carefully pruned to the most productive size and shape, mostly by black laborers, and would have only recently shed their pretty pink and white flowers to start the fruit growing.

With neither streetlights nor headlights to cut the dark of the moonless night,[50] Hill would have been guided only by local knowledge and the lantern lights and shifting fireplace flames peeking from the windows of the occasional farmhouse.

Injustice on the Eastern Shore

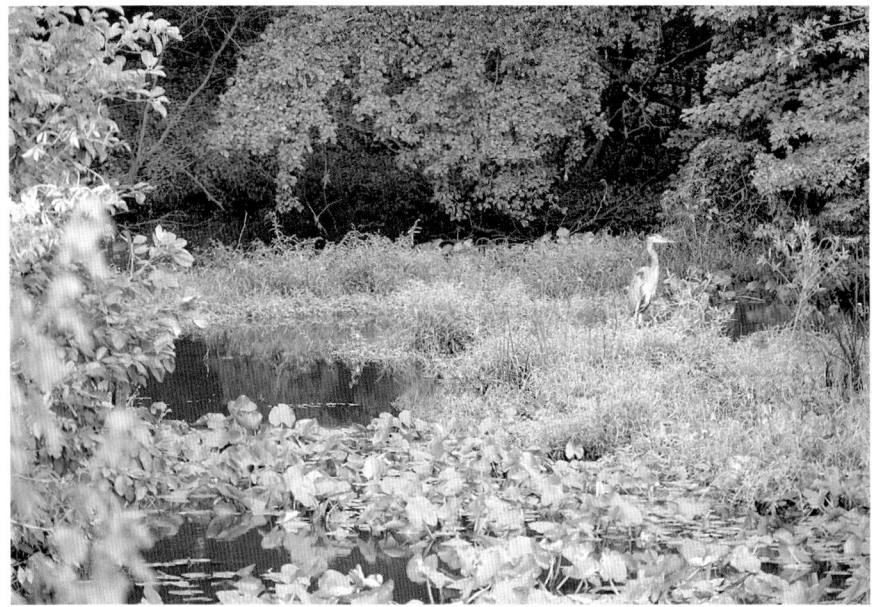

A heron relaxes on Long Meadow Branch, just north of the road from Millington to Massey. *Photo by Kevin Hemstock.*

But he wasn't the only one out and about. It was Saturday night, and people were returning from an evening of shopping in town or still lingered outside their homes enjoying the fine spring evening. At the house of Stephen Cooper and family, who lived on the Hendrickson property on the other side of Long Meadow Branch, an "oyster treat" was underway.[51] There were several carts and wagons on the road, and at least two teams passed a group of about a dozen black men and boys who had congregated in the vicinity of Ford's Hill. Some among the group had been drinking.[52] They raucously called out to the passing teams.

At the road's rise, a dozen yards or so south of the murmuring branch, Hill encountered the group at about 10:30 p.m., according to later testimony. It was the beginning of the end of his life.

And it all happened quickly.

The sorrel mare, whose name is now lost to history, was pulling the dogcart at a steady gait, and as Hill pulled up on the group, he slowed but didn't stop. One of the revelers cried, "Hold up!"[53] and when Hill continued, two of the elder members of the group, Charles "Buck" Brooks and Fletcher Williams, who were standing in the middle of the road, reached out and grabbed the horse's bridle gear. The horse veered to the right bank of the road, turning the rig at a right angle to the direction of travel.

Race and the Hill Murder Trial

"Hold on, Doctor, I want to see you on business," Williams reportedly said.[54]

Brooks called fifteen-year-old Perry Bradshaw and Frisby Comegys to help hold the horse.

Hill, sensing the group's malevolent intent, told them to go ahead and take his money. He said, "Don't hurt me, boys. I've not done anything to injure you."[55]

It was too late. Someone grabbed the doctor from behind. Brooks then came from behind and, wielding a rock the "size of a duck's egg," bashed it at least three times against Hill's right temple, jolting the doctor and knocking him backward. Hill shouted, "Oh!" as he fell back in the cart, but he did not fall out of the cart by most accounts. It was probably his last instant of consciousness. Williams then reached over and grabbed Hill's head, pulled it back and stabbed him in the neck with a long, ten-cent folding knife.[56]

Williams then exhorted the others to "come up and do something," such as stab Hill or beat him so that all could have a vested interest in the crime. Moses Brown and sixteen-year-old Lewis Benson, wielding penknives, allegedly "pricked" Hill in the head, possibly where he had been bludgeoned. It was moot—the doctor was done if not dead.[57]

The accounts of those of the group who chose to talk generally agree on what happened next at the scene, if not by whom. Brooks, Williams, Bradshaw and Brown arranged Hill, whom they thought was dead, back in the cart. Williams forced the doctor's head between the shaft and the iron rod on the underside of the shaft on the right-hand side of the cart, with his inert form lying down where one would normally place one's feet while driving the cart. Both feet were placed out of the way of the wheels on the left side of the cart. They put his hat on his head.[58] Then, Bradshaw pulled the horse around onto the road, and someone either slapped the horse or "chirped" to start it back on the road, moving north as before, at a fast trot, with the unconscious, mortally injured doctor wedged awkwardly in the cart's framework.

The agitated, excited or otherwise stirred-up attackers then "fussed and cursed among themselves," Joshua Baynard, one of the participants, later recalled. Certainly, if there were some in the group, particularly among the younger ones, who had not anticipated the violence, they would have been stunned. There they stood in their hand-me-down clothes, the dregs of poverty, on the wrong side of a gaping racial divide, with the blood of a prominent white doctor on their hands.

When the shock wore off, they celebrated, at least outwardly. Several reported that they danced on the bridge and then took some time to coordinate their stories, no doubt a tale dictated by the three eldest among them. Then they dispersed. Several made their way to the Coopers' house for the oyster feast, where they were well known and welcome and, it was later alleged, where they cleaned off the evidence of the crime.[59]

Meanwhile, Hill's horse continued on her seemingly appointed task, heading for Massey at a measured pace with the cart's inert passenger.

Clip-clop, clop-clip, clip-clop.

She passed the oyster feast at Cooper's house on Gus Hendrickson's property, the old Ringgold farm, on the left. The property, a piece of the old thousand-acre Partnership grant, was steeped in local history. It was once owned by Daniel Toaes. Major James Parker, a War of 1812 veteran, was probably buried somewhere on the property. But his was not among more than a dozen headstones in the family graveyard that formed a silhouetted, crook-toothed smile on nights when the moon was full. Colonel Elijah E. Massey, a Civil War veteran, was buried there, along with his wife, Mary, and a number of their children. But since there was no moon, the stones would have faded into the nighttime shadows.

The horse quickly came up to the Spear plantation on the right, where Spear's Lane shot off into the lonely fields, but she took no turns. The plantation once belonged to James Spear and his son of the same name, the latter a Confederate veteran who died six years before the sorrel mare passed his lane.

Hill's hat flew off at about this point, and investigators later found the beginning of a blood trail here.

On went the sorrel mare, passing Spring Lane and then the lane named for the walnut tree that stood at the intersection with the Massey road. It's now called Walnut Tree Road, but the tree is long gone. Then the horse passed the late Colonel Richard C. Johnson's old spread, owned by the colonel's daughter and son-in-law, Mary and Dr. Enoch G. Clark. Stanley Road, which shot west from here, would one day be named for Clark's son Carroll. Here, the cart and horse might have paused. But she quickly moved on straight north on the road to Massey.

The rig passed sixteen-year-old Walter Roe riding a horse. Roe reported seeing a man, whom he thought was drunk, lying in the foot of the cart. Roe said that as it passed, he heard the sound of something striking the wheel. The man in the cart had his arm dangling very near the road.[60] The youngster later found Hill's hat. Was he involved, as some would later suggest?

Two men who were riding a milk wagon toward Massey later testified that a dogcart passed them with "a man with his hand hanging down." Roe noted that he saw the milk wagon near Hendrickson's gate.

Race and the Hill Murder Trial

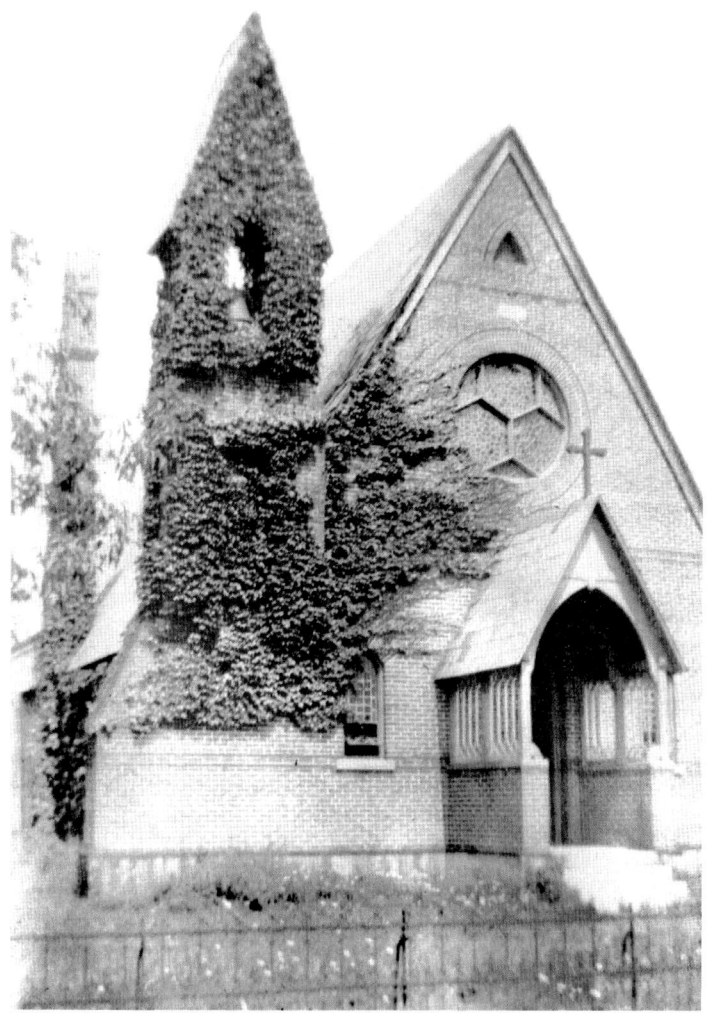

St. Clement's Church, in Massey, as it appeared about 1916. *Courtesy of James Edwin Spear IV.*

On went the sorrel mare, *clip-clop, clop-clip*, past the Hurlock farm on the left, where the Shaws fretted over their sick child. Then it passed the old Cacy farm. Then the cart went through the Massey crossroads and over the railroad tracks on the north side of the burg.

More of a little village, home of St. Clement's PE Church, a substantial stone building constructed less than ten years earlier, it was the best example of a town-that-might-have-been given the chance. The village was at a crossroad of the Kent and Queen Anne's and Delaware Railroads, and a business boom commenced at the completion of the iron horse intersection in 1871. Great things were expected, and one pundit suggested it would become the New York City of Maryland. Two hotels and new dwellings quickly rose during that decade.

But the growth—and the plan for the little apple—was cut short by a fire that gutted the village's commercial core in 1888. That blaze took out nine houses, three stores and one of the hotels. One of the stores was that of Adam F. Huey, just across the east–west tracks. It must have been quickly rebuilt because, four years later, that was where Hill's horse stopped.

Merchant Huey, from Pennsylvania, moved to Kent sometime after 1870 and started a farming equipment business, using the warehouse for storing his inventory. Several years later, he would open up a "carriage emporium" and spend his last days in the little village. His remains are buried in St. Clement's shaded, well-manicured cemetery.

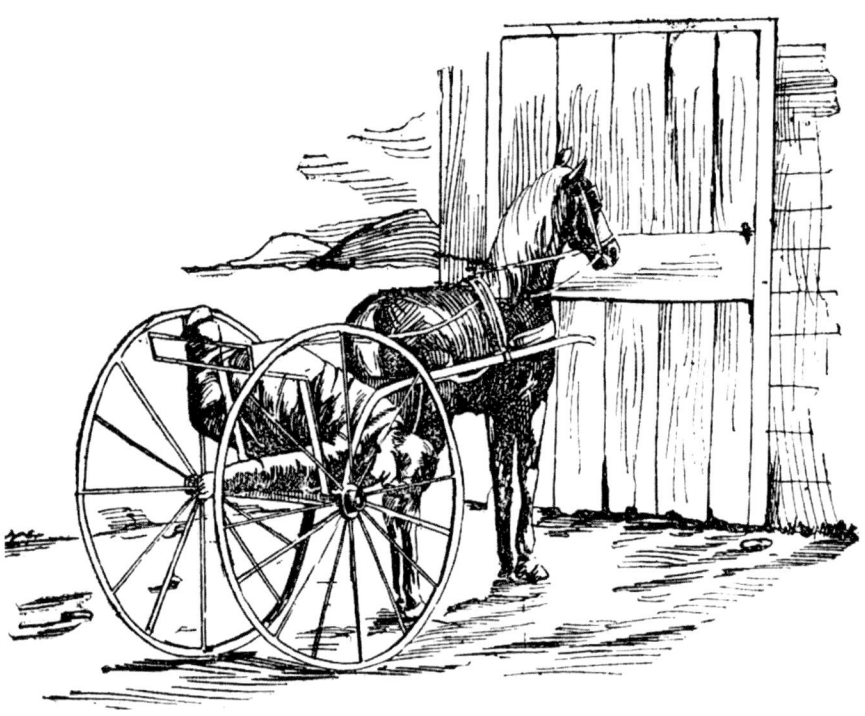

Philadelphia newspaper reporter Paul Winchester arrived in Millington the day after the victim's death. He drew this picture of Hill in the dogcart for his and other newspapers. *From the* Kent News *supplement, May 7, 1892.*

Race and the Hill Murder Trial

He was the one who found two large pools of blood by the warehouse, which he later pointed out to searchers, and then noticed that it appeared the horse had pawed at the ground there. The horse and cart, it was determined, must have remained at that place for several hours.[61]

In the early hours of the morning, the horse started in the opposite direction, no doubt seeking her cozy berth at the stable in Millington. When the wheel tracks were followed later, it was seen that the horse, after entering the town, went around by Dr. Edward J. Power's house, onto Back Street and past the depot, which was an "unusual route for the doctor's horse to go," according to fifty-one-year-old shoemaker William J. Porter.[62] But there was no account of the cart being seen or heard in town on the return trip, until about three thirty on Sunday morning, when Arrelee Hill heard the horse and cart enter the yard.[63] She went to the back window and in the dim light could barely make out the outline of the horse standing at the carriage house door. She thought her husband was unhitching the horse so wasn't immediately worried.

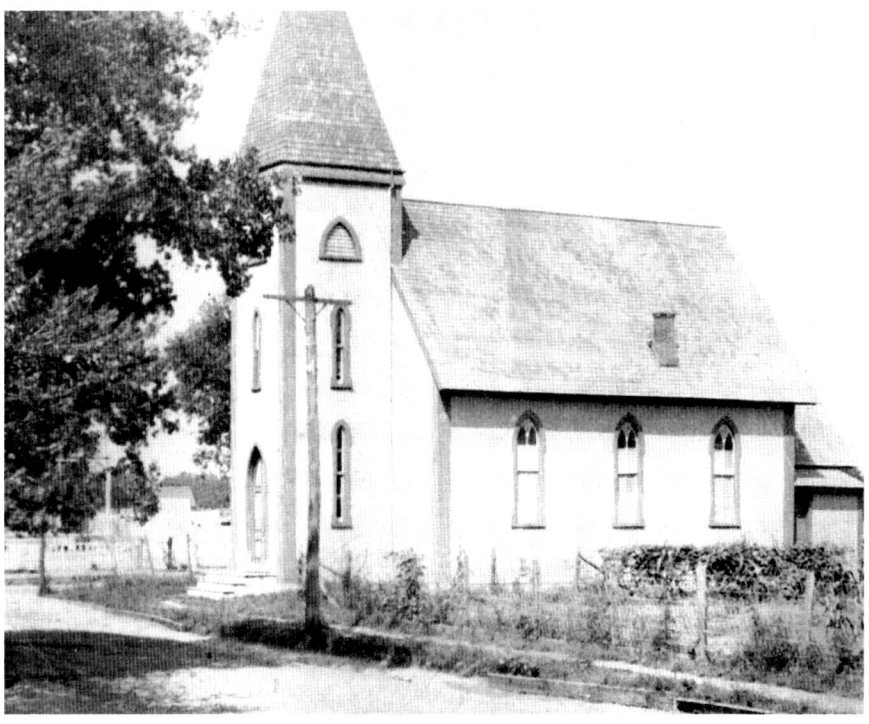

The Holy Cross Episcopal Chapel was located on the southeast corner of Sassafras and Back Streets. Hill's dogcart would have turned here to get to the back of his house. *Courtesy of James Edwin Spear IV.*

She waited about ten minutes before becoming concerned, she later testified.[64] Then she looked out the window again, and things didn't look right.

"I immediately put on my slippers and wrapper and went down," she recounted. What she found horrified her: her husband lay at an odd angle in the dogcart seat, head toward the front, wedged under the shaft, and feet to the rear, the right one near the spokes of a wheel. One hand was dangling. He was unconscious and bleeding from the head, neck and foot. There were three puddles of blood near the shed door.[65] A groan came from somewhere deep inside him.

She spoke his name, but he didn't answer. She lifted his head a little, but it dropped back.[66]

How Hill was found in the dogcart near the shed was depicted in a drawing by Paul W. Winchester of the *Baltimore Evening News*. The horrifying graphic was carried by the *Kent News*.

Arrelee Hill was stunned. It was a sight that could have seemed only a waking nightmare. It was a visual that would no doubt remain with her for the rest of her life. She went around to the front of the double house and frantically knocked on neighbor John Ahern's door, waking his wife, Clorinda, who in turn woke her husband. Arrelee breathlessly tried to describe the incomprehensible scene. She then ran to alert Justice Johnson across the street. He looked out the window when he heard her knocking.

"The doctor has been killed—murdered—and is all doubled up in his carriage!" she shouted tearfully.

Ahern told officials that he found Hill with his head wedged in the frame of the cart, his body "half reclining on the left side, the face being toward the rear of the cart." The injured man was breathing laboriously, and "his tongue was sticking out."[67]

Ahern and Johnson had a difficult time extricating the doctor. He was a dead weight; his body was stiff and was literally wedged into the seat's undercarriage and the cart's shaft work. Porter, who lived nearby on the north side of Cypress Street next to the Quaker burial ground, had heard Mrs. Hill shouting for help and came to assist. A black man named Lambden also helped.

As they disentangled the doctor from the cart, Arrelee approached, but Ahern told her to go back into the house because he didn't want her to see them working on him in his "mangled condition," he later testified.

While this grisly task was underway, Mrs. Ahern took Arrelee from the scene.

Once they pulled the doctor from the cart, they carried him to a settee inside. Ahern said that Hill, at that point, was "breathing heavily but slowly," not more often than two or three times a minute. Doctors were summoned immediately. First on the scene was forty-year-old Dr. Todd, who was renting the home of Dr. Clark on the west side of town. It was a three-minute brisk walk away. He soon found the cut on Hill's neck that was surrounded by abrasions; the whole right side of Hill's face was swollen, indicating a blow to the right temple. A portion of his right foot, which had been rubbing up against the wheel spokes as the cart made its way all the way to Massey and back, had been worn off. That's probably the noise that Walter Roe heard when he passed the cart earlier in the night.

Todd quickly sewed up the wound in Hill's neck.

Soon, Dr. John W. Latimer, thirty-eight, arrived from Galena. Then, forty-one-year-old Still Pond doctor J. Horton Kelley arrived.

Latimer was the Hill family physician, and he had recently tended to Arrelee Hill "in a severe illness." He testified that Hill had cold, clammy skin and an extremely weak pulse. Hill's tongue, ragged from Hill having bitten it, protruded from his mouth. Latimer said he was sure that the main trouble was from a concussion.

Dr. J.K.H. Jacobs, of Kennedyville, arrived a little later to assist.

The four doctors worked on their colleague through the morning and into the afternoon—to no avail. It must have been difficult, as they worked futilely, knowing that they could do nothing within the limits of the medical procedures of the time to replace the life force that had dissipated during the long night. They would have known long before his last breath that the spirit had long departed the anatomical enclosure. Hill died about three thirty that Sunday afternoon without ever having regained consciousness.

After his death, Kelly and Todd performed a postmortem examination. They were each paid ten dollars by the county for their labors. Examining the skull, the doctors found no fractures, but there was "an effusion of blood" on the opposite side, caused by concussion. Several blows might have been received in the same place, the doctors surmised.[68]

Dr. William Maxwell Jr., of Still Pond, wrote in his diary, in which he noted weather information and current events, "Dr. James Hill of Millington was found this morning in his dogcart with his throat cut and head mashed. He died this afternoon. He was called to see a patient and was attacked on the road."

The first act in a macabre melodrama was over. The second act would soon begin.

IT WAS NO ACCIDENT

As the local magistrate, William M. Johnson was the first judicial arbiter—and sometimes the last—in an area between Millington and the Delaware border, including Golt's Station. Kent had one or two dozen justices of the peace at any given time, covering the five districts, in the later half of the nineteenth century. It was a judicial system for petty crime that wouldn't be changed until 1930 and ultimately eliminated in favor of the district court system in 1971.

Born about 1825 in Delaware, Johnson was a farmer and later a miller, in addition to practicing law, just north of Townsend near Noxontown Lake. He moved to Massey about 1870 and then to Millington, where he ended his days.

In May 1883, he was appointed as justice of the peace to replace William Blackiston.

By Sunday morning, the assault on Hill had been broadcast by word of mouth, if not by telegraph and telephone, all over the community. At first, it was uncertain what had happened; no one was ready to suggest that a popular young white doctor had been murdered. But it was soon determined otherwise. And it wasn't long before suspicion about the assailants began to grow.

Even as Hill lay dying, the sixty-seven-year-old magistrate set out on foot, just after first light on Sunday morning, to retrace the doctor's path to and from Massey. It was a fairly long walk—a testimony to Johnson's fitness in his later years. On his way, he was joined by Charles E. Comegys, a twenty-year-old drug salesman whose father was a physician. They must have seemed an odd pair making their way north along the road—a young man and an older one, stopping and stooping here and there to examine this print or that and various articles along the way.

Both men were well acquainted with Hill. Johnson, a Cleveland Club associate and Hill's neighbor, had indeed, only a few hours before, extricated the dying man from the cart, and Comegys, a pharmaceuticals salesman, had probably sold goods to the doctor for his drugstore.

Johnson later testified that he checked the imprint of the hooves of Hill's mare and could make out the horse's tracks on the road. The two found a heel from one of Hill's shoes; they compared it to the other shoe, about a mile and a half north of Millington, near William Rolph's place.[69]

They weren't the only ones to conduct an investigation that day. Shop owner William H. Price and undertaker Thomas M. Britton drove a buggy along the route from Millington and found the place where Hill's cart had gone off the road about twenty feet before the crest of Ford's Hill. They counted several sets of foot tracks. They could also see where the cart had stopped near Dr. Clark's field; it appeared, Price said, that another cart had stopped next to it. But there was never a determination that someone in another cart had stopped to examine Hill. Was it the milk wagon?

This was also where the first blood was spotted.

Clark was a prominent doctor who built a fine house in the early 1870s on Cypress Street in Millington. He and his wife eschewed "city life" in 1881, moving to the farm belonging to her father, Colonel Johnson, who died just two months before Hill was attacked. During his time on the farm, Clark apparently rented his Cypress Street house, first to Dr. P.S. Downs and then to Dr. Todd. Clark returned to the town in 1893, rekindling his medical practice and moving back into the attractive home that he modernized. The house is there today.

Price and Britton continued following the trail all the way to Huey's, where they found the two large pools of blood.[70]

More significantly, on their trip, they ran into Fletcher Williams riding along the road on horseback with Joseph Lamden. Williams had Hill's hat in his hand. Britton asked him where he had gotten it. Williams said he found it and thought it belonged to Joe Coburn. Price took the hat and gave it to farmer Thomas J.F. Smith.

Smith was one of the first ones on the road that Sunday morning. His son measured the track at Ford's Hill and compared it to that of Hill's mare, confirming they were one and the same.

But these were just locals playing at being sleuths, and they probably destroyed as much evidence as they discovered. Soon, the pros would arrive, and the arrests would begin.

All of this, however, took place on Sunday before it was officially determined that Hill was a homicide victim. By Monday, it was clear that Hill's death was no accident. Still, the local newspaper next to publish—the *Chestertown Transcript*, which came out on Thursdays—seemed hesitant to raise the cry of murder. In the April 28 edition, on page three, where most of the local news landed in four-page "broadsheet" papers, it asked: "WAS IT MURDER? Dr. J.H. Hill, of Millington, Dies Under Most Distressing and Suspicious Circumstances."

But the same edition contained a "special" update to the main story, indicating that the first story had been typeset and the "special" added just before printing on Wednesday night at the paper's headquarters, located then in the old church building on the north side of today's Fountain Park in Chestertown:

> *Mr. Paul Winchester, of the* Baltimore News, *swore out warrants before Squire Johnson at 1 p.m.* [Wednesday] *for the arrest of Charles Brooks, Charles Emory, Perry Bradshaw and Henry Hurtt, all colored, on suspicion of knowing something of the murder of Dr. Hill, and sheriff Plummer left at 2 p.m. to make the arrests.*

Harvard-educated Winchester, the *Baltimore News* man, would later take the helm of the *Easton Democrat* and other local papers, form the Journalists' Club in Baltimore and write and speak his political analyses until his death in 1932. He was the same man who made the drawing of the dogcart. He and Wilbur Bates of the *Philadelphia Press* were the first wave of an invasion of city reporters who would cover the case, demonstrating that a new sensation-driven media fueled by technology—i.e. first the telegraph and then the telephone—had evolved to feed the urban frenzy for hard news. The two were pioneers in the realm of pushy media types who used bluster, the power of persuasion and, when necessary, subterfuge to get the story and get it transmitted to their offices quickly (and preferably before their competition). In this case, they would go a step further and become actively involved in the investigation. In fact, Winchester and Bates started out doing the same thing that Johnson, Comegys, Price and Britton, and dozens of Millington residents, had done two days earlier. They followed the route, asked questions and formed opinions from which they developed a draft scenario based on the information they gathered.

Bates recalled that his editor told him, "Bates, go to Millington, find who killed Dr. Hill, and catch the men that did it."[71]

The *Transcript* didn't have a scoop; the story was coursing around the nation by April 27, when the *New York Times* ran a front-page piece headlined, "Mysterious Maryland Murder," indicating that Fletcher Williams, Frisby Comegys and Phillip Mander had been arrested. A headline in another New York State paper stated in its head and subhead: "A Cowardly Crime. Dr. James H. Hill Murdered near Millington, Md."[72]

The *Times*'s competitor in Philadelphia, the *Record*, had the story on Tuesday, April 26. The *Record*'s headline read: "Dr. Hill's Throat Cut," with subheads "The Horse Trots Home with the Physician's Dead Body" and "Vengeance of the Negroes."

The urban dailies had turned the news around quickly, and for all practical purposes, the accounts in both were accurate. Additionally, there seemed little question about the motive even in the early stages of the case:

> Dr. Hill was called to examine the wounds of the dead man, and in his evidence said that they did not appear to be of a character to have caused the man's death. The Coroner's jury dismissed the case. The colored people were much incensed, and swore vengeance on the whites.[73]

It's uncertain what the local news editors knew or whether they had received any of these news accounts by the time they were ready to go to press. When *Kent News* editors William B. Usilton and his sons, Fred and William Jr., broke their story on Saturday, April 30, there was no question that a "murder most foul" had taken place because one of those involved, Josh Baynard, had, in back-alley police parlance of the day, "spilled his guts."

The official inquest, begun on Monday, April 25, at Johnson's office, was also underway, and it started at Hill's home. Members of the jury of inquest included Coroner Robert K. Pippin and the foreman, Millington blacksmith Charles P. Loper. The rest of the panel comprised Henry S. Cook, Enoch J. Moffett, Benjamin P. Morgan, Richard W. Comegys, William H. Ford, James Edwards, William F. Russell, William O. Dugan, C.L. Gill, James C. Moore, Amos B. Kelley, W.F. Collins, Benjamin F. Vansant, John McWhorter and newspaperman Frederick G. Usilton. The report, finalized in Chestertown on May 3, stated that the members of the jury of inquest *who being sworn to inquire on the part of the State of Maryland, when, where, how and what manner the said Dr. J. Heighe Hill came to his death, do say upon their oath that on the 23d day of April, 1892, on Foard's* [sic] *Hill, a section or spot of ground on the public road, between Millington and Massey's, in said county, one Frisby Comegys, one Charles Brooks, alias Buck Brooks, one Perry Bradshaw, feloniously stopped and held the horse of Dr. J. Heighe Hill, while on his way to visit a sick child, and that the said Charles Brooks, alias Buck Brooks, struck the said Dr. Hill with a stone, and that one Fletcher Williams stabbed the said Dr. Hill with a knife, inflicting mortal wounds, of which the said Dr. Hill died the following day, Sunday, April 24th, 1892, and the said Perry Bradshaw, Frisby Comegys, Fletcher Williams and Charles Brooks, alias Buck Brooks, then and there feloniously killed and murdered the said Dr. Hill against the peace and dignity of the State of Maryland.*[74]

Harrison Vickers, as special counsel for the state, was appointed to investigate the case for the prosecution. State's attorney William Slay was occupied with other cases.

On Monday, April 25, Vickers questioned Williams, Brown, Bradshaw, Hurtt, Baynard, Frisby Comegys, Charles Emory and Brooks and interviewed numerous witnesses. The testimony elicited the general narrative of the crime, due to secondhand testimony given by George Bell that another witness, Phillip Mander,[75] had told him that Baynard had described the assault. Mander and other "witnesses" were jailed along with the suspects on Monday and Tuesday. It was not unusual to take the witnesses into custody, especially if they were thought to favor the accused or it was felt their safety was in jeopardy. This was to prevent them from leaving the area. However, Mander was also thought to be a suspect.

Baynard may have told Mander, but he didn't say anything to the investigators for several days.

It was "detective" Bates, as one paper described him (meaning the newspaper reporter), who approached Baynard when the lad was waiting in a crowded room on Thursday at "Mallalieu's Hotel," located on the southwest corner of Cypress and Sassafras Streets. Sam Mallalieu, a native of England who had been part owner of Unicorn Mills, had managed the hotel and the associated livery stable since 1889.[76]

Baynard was waiting to be transferred from Millington to the jail in Chestertown. Bates told him that Mander had given him up. Queen Anne's County constable C. Sydney Jump, who had arrived on the afternoon train

Race and the Hill Murder Trial

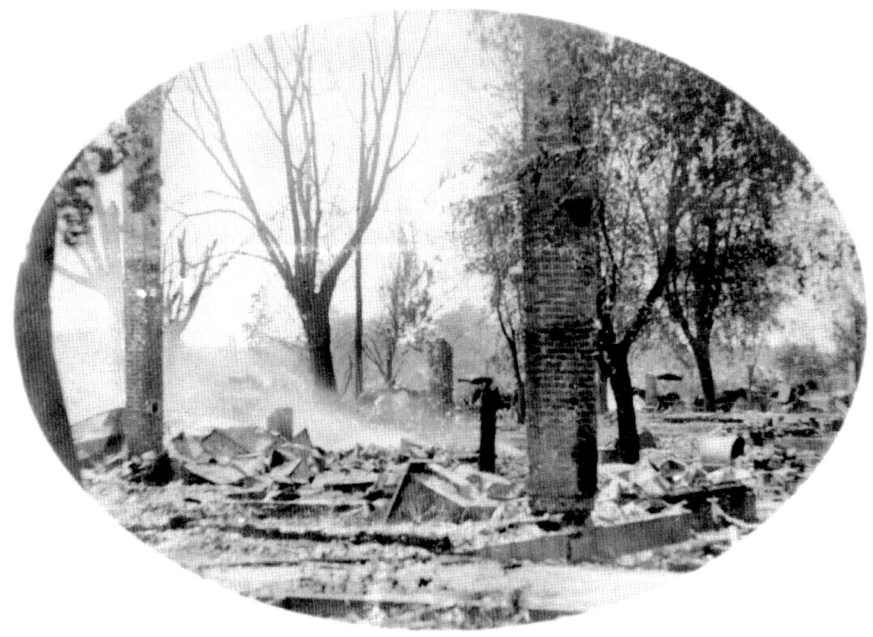

Maxwell's Hotel was burned in the 1904 fire. By then, it was known as the Bailey Hotel. This rare image was taken for a postcard before the smoke had cleared, probably the day after the fire. *Author's collection.*

with Queen Anne's County sheriff Frank Seward, also questioned Baynard. They had jurisdictional qualifications, too, because Millington was—and still is—half in Queen Anne's County.

What they got was the general description of the assault. Baynard left out anything to do with premeditation; in fact, he said he didn't know who the victim was until after the incident. When he gave his confession, transcribed by a *Transcript* reporter, the crowd in the room became so agitated that Baynard was moved to another room.[77]

Soon after, he was placed in a wagon with Coroner Pippin, Pinkerton detective James Nevins, deputies Amos B. Kelley and William O. Dugan and a correspondent from the *Sun*.[78] He was then transferred to the county jail in Chestertown.

The participation of Jump and Seward led to a little territorial drama about who should get credit for bagging the suspects up to that point. Seward, in an April 29 letter to the *Baltimore Sun*, claimed credit for solving the "Millington Mystery." The immodest accolade to himself was quoted in the paper:

Injustice on the Eastern Shore

> *Constable Jump and myself are the men who drew out everything that was given away by the negro Baynard. No one else did this but Constable Jump and myself. The jury of inquest has been discharged. The negro was at large when we arrived. He made the confession to us, and we are the men to whom the credit belongs of solving the mystery, and to no one else. We want the facts made known to the readers of the* Baltimore Sun.

The *Transcript* of May 5 had a different version:

> *Messrs. Seward and Jump are evidently in error in their understanding of the situation when they arrived at Millington on Thursday. While the coroner's inquest had succeeded in eliciting nothing of a positive nature during the day, the case had been carfully* [sic] *worked by the Kent authorities assisted by Detective James Nevins, of the Pinkerton force, and Detective Bates of Philadelphia.*

Nevins, hired by the county with part of the $1,000 budgeted to Vickers, brought an air of professionalism to the investigation the likes of which Kent had never seen in a criminal case. The son of Irish immigrants, the thirty-seven-year-old shoemaker turned policeman was a member of the Pinkerton National Detective Agency of Philadelphia.

Bates, of course, was not a police detective. Nor is there any indication that the county hired him to investigate, as it had done with Nevins. It's more likely that one of the locals thought he was associated with Nevins or the paper simply got it wrong. The *Transcript* got it wrong several times.

However, he was a private investigator of sorts at one time.

He certainly had the mindset for one. Born in Boston in 1863, the son of a cooper, Bates, at the age of eighteen, was listed as a "private detective" in the 1880 census in East Boston. Career-wise, his life would be one adventure after another. He became a reporter for the *Boston Herald*, where he worked for about three years, moving then to the *New York World*. He then became a reporter for the *Philadelphia Times* for a brief spell before moving on to the *Press*. While he would be a reporter for the *Press* for only a brief spell, he always gravitated to jobs in the field of communication. Soon after the Hill murder suspects were incarcerated and about the time of their trial, he entered show business.

And then there were those the doctor left behind—friends, acquaintances and loved ones.

Nothing brought the case into sharper focus throughout the county than Hill's April 26 funeral, which began at his house, where the walnut casket was on display. The funereal procession then moved to the Asbury ME Church and ended about nine miles away at the cemetery of the ancient Shrewsbury Church near Locust Grove, nearly within view of his parents' home.

The venerated church, constructed about 1834, is the third building on the site; the first was built in 1692. Revolutionary War general John Cadwalader is buried there. Two years before Hill's remains were deposited at the ancient cemetery, a remodel added a crenellated tower, among other improvements.

Closer to the doctor's Millington home, members of the Asbury ME Church were particularly distraught. Hill was not only a member of the congregation but also had been on the church's board of trustees for more than two years.

A resolution passed by the board expressed its sadness:

> *Whereas our brother Dr. J.H. Hill has been taken from us by death at the hands of wicked men;*
> *Whereas he was a good citizen, a good man & a member of this board of trustees;*
> *Therefore be it resolved*
> *1. That in the death of Dr. Hill, not only the church & community, but this Board of Trustees sustain a loss…*
> *Resolved 2nd, That we tender to his sorrowing wife our deepest sympathy & pray that the God of Infinite Mercy & love who withholds no good thing from the upright, will grant her the needed consolations of his grace.*[79]

While the public resolution was benevolent, the minutes of the trustee meeting at which it was approved made it clear there was no doubt among the trustees about the guilt or innocence of those who had been taken into custody:

> *Since our last meeting the Board having lost one of its members, Dr. J.H. Hill, who was murdered by a gang of negroes, while he was on his way to visit a patient, it was ordered that a committee on resolutions of condolence and sympathy be appointed to draft such as will appropriately convey our sense of sorrow and sympathy at his untimely death.*

On the day of the funeral, a Tuesday, business was suspended in Millington. About 350 people attended the ceremony, conducted by the Reverend E.E. White, who was assisted by the Reverends R.K. Stevenson of Smyrna, E.H. Nelson of Galena and Addison Weller of Millington. Henry

INJUSTICE ON THE EASTERN SHORE

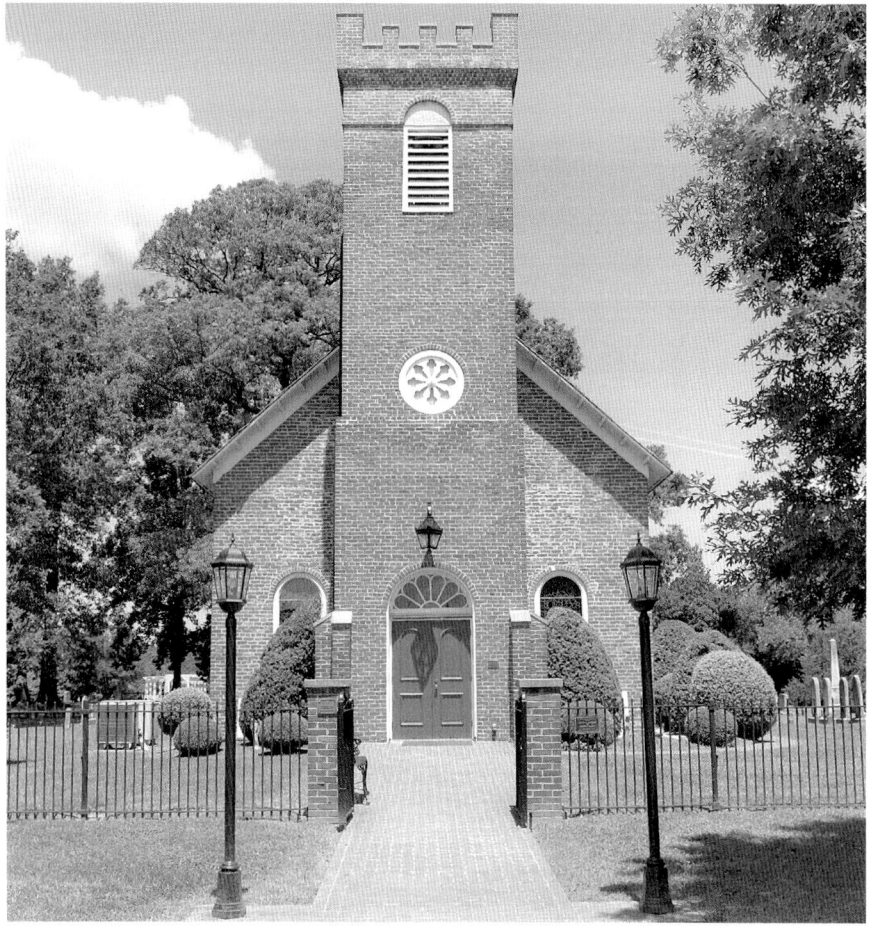

Shrewsbury Church, between Kennedyville and Locust Grove, is one of the oldest in Kent County. *Photo by Kevin Hemstock.*

Tonkin, the British immigrant school principal, led the seven-member choir, which opened with "Fade, Fade, Each Earthly Joy."

It seems safe to speculate that there wasn't a dry eye in the place.

The coffin was covered with flowers given by friends and family. Within the flowers was a pillow, added by Arrelee, with the words "My Husband" embroidered on it.

Reverend White began his address by noting that Hill was no longer a citizen of the town or a member of the church "but had gone to his reward; from the church militant to the church triumphant; from his little home here to his home above."[80]

Race and the Hill Murder Trial

The coffin was opened at the funeral for purposes of viewing, and the body's fatal injuries were apparent. When it was her turn to look, the distraught widow stood over the coffin for a length of time "gazing into the vacant face." Finally, tears streaming down, she cried out her husband's name and bade him a mournful farewell.

Lone Lee's poem in the February 1892 edition of *Godey's*, which Arrelee almost certainly would have read, probably best described her gloom:

> *In my soul's care-haunted room,*
> *Hushed and silent as a tomb,*
> *Sleeps the memory of a day*
> *Long since flown far away;*
> *Fair, sweet day, it cannot be*
> *Thou wilt come no more to me!*
>
> *When the dawn-kissed eastern skies*
> *Radiant grow with morning's dyes,*
> *And Bird carols wild and clear,*
> *Fall upon my listening ear;*
> *Fair sweet day I long for thee.*
> *Wilt thou never come back to me?*
>
> *Will thy laughing summer hours,*
> *All undimmed by shade or showers,*
> *Cast their golden glow no more*
> *On me, as they did of you?*
> *Fair, sweet day, it cannot be*
> *Thou art gone for aye with me.*
>
> *Like a voice heard in our dreams,*
> *Or the murmuring of streams*
> *From the portals of the Past,*
> *Thy reply doth come at last;*
> *"Heart bereft," thou answerest me,*
> *"I will come no more to thee."*

The choir ended the ceremony with "Meet Me Again When Life Is O'er."
Afterward, a funeral procession followed the hearse, probably driven by Millington undertaker Thomas M. Britton, to Shrewsbury Church for the

Injustice on the Eastern Shore

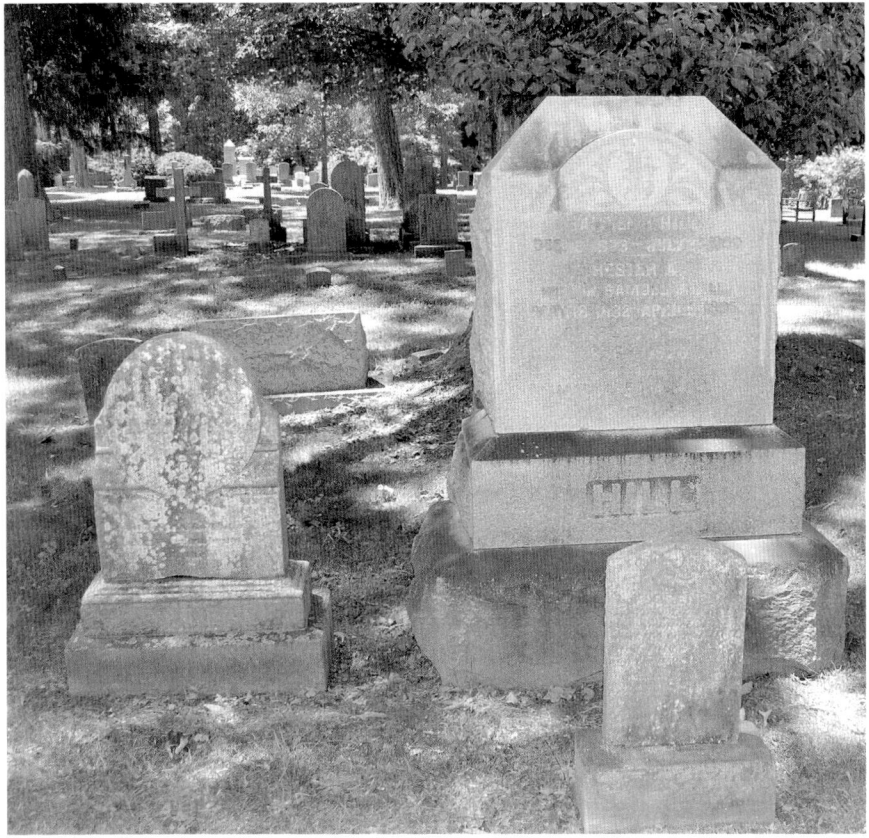

The gravestone of Dr. J. Heighe Hill in the Shrewsbury Cemetery, in the left of this photo, has deteriorated to the point of being unreadable. It sits next to that of his parents. *Photo by Kevin Hemstock.*

interment. The most likely route would have been up Sassafras Street to the Chesterville Road and then north along the Locust Grove Road. Britton made all the arrangements, including supplying the casket. His charge was seventy-five dollars. He didn't take care of digging the grave, which Frank A. Emory arranged for three dollars.[81]

The pallbearers were mostly town residents and included three members of the Algonquin Tribe of Improved Order of Red Men (IORM), a secret, whites-only organization of which Hill was a member. They were John Ahern, Henry S. Cook and J.C. Vansant.

The IORM traced its beginnings to colonial times and claimed affiliation with the Sons of Liberty, whose members tossed tea overboard during the Boston Tea Party. One of the benefits listed in the society's bylaws included a funeral service. For example, the bylaws of the Toghwogh Tribe, the branch in Chestertown, read in part:

> *All members of this Tribe who are not in arrears except those suspended for cause other than non-payment of dues shall be entitled to funeral honors, and on the death of a brother in good standing, the Chief of Records shall notify the Sachem, Senior Sagamore, Junior Sagamore, Prophet, Keeper of the Wampum, Guard of the Forest to attend the funeral (and shall also attend himself) in carriages provided at the expense of the Tribe.*[82]

The rest of the pallbearers were Joseph Mallalieu, Richard W. Comegys and dentist Dr. Frederick A. Walls.

The mournful rites of death, the vision of the wife exercising her grief at the casket and the cross-county procession lent a more intense pitch to the community's outrage and fed the frenzy for quick justice. Not everyone in the small, close-knit county had confidence in the court system's ability to mete out justice equitably or quickly. There was some talk of putting a new judge on the case: "Judge Lynch."

LYNCHING PREVENTED

Forty-year-old Sheriff Edward J. Plummer was a farmer by trade and had all the inborn savvy of a man raised for and by the land—and Kent land at that. Of medium build, he was balding but had a lush handlebar mustache that was the style of the day. He also enjoyed the occasional picnic and dinner party.

Enforcing the law was as much in his blood as the Kent soil. His grandfather Eli, born in the county the year the great rebellion against King George began, was a justice of the peace and carried the sobriquet "Esquire" to the end of his days, which came about in 1843.

His father, also an Edward, like himself a good Democrat, was a constable and held the post of sheriff, presumably living in the previous jail/home, from 1874 to 1875.

Edward J., born in March 1852, was the product, along with a number of siblings, of his father's second wife, Sarah. James H. Plummer, half of the publishing team of the *Kent News*, was his half brother.

In March 1875, the sheriff married Eliza J. Prettyman, whose family had roots among those of the same name in Sussex County, Delaware.

Democrat Plummer became Kent's top lawman, having been duly elected by the county's voters in 1891 in a feisty race against his Republican opponent, William H. Lambert. Plummer won the election with a 276-vote majority. But it's interesting to note that Lambert led in the two Chestertown districts in the November 5 election. Plummer took more of the rural, conservative vote. One factor: almost all of the black voters in Chestertown were Republican, the "party of Lincoln."

Race and the Hill Murder Trial

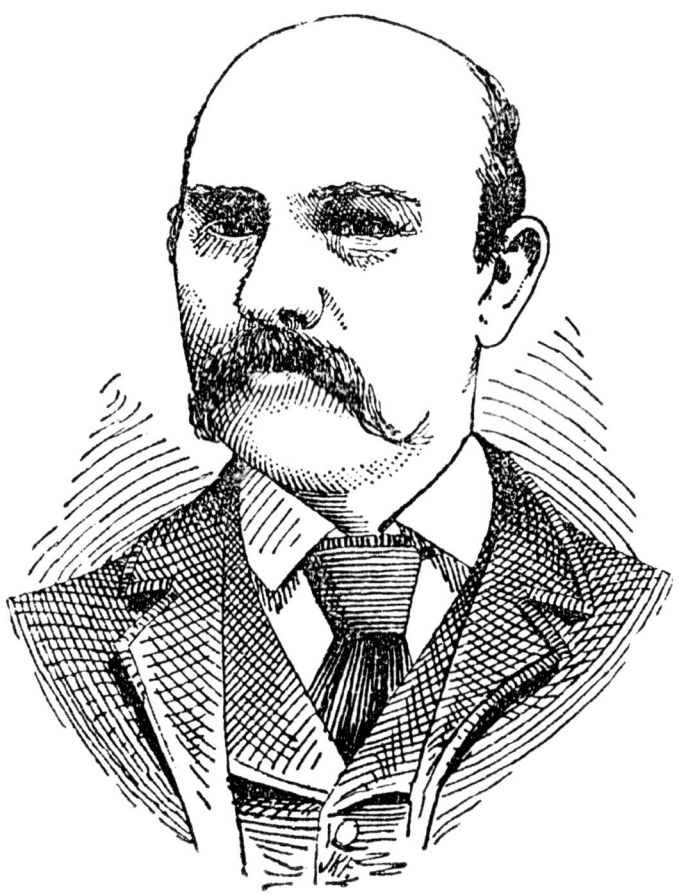

A woodcut of Kent County sheriff Edward Plummer. *From the* Kent News, *January 30, 1892.*

After the election, Plummer moved into the town's relatively new jail with his wife and family members, as was the custom and responsibility; the position of sheriff included the post of jailer and executioner if that grim task were required. He was also responsible for the safekeeping of his incarcerated charges. He took that responsibility seriously.

The Hill murder suspects appeared to be safe and sound in the Chestertown jail. But there were few sounds coming out of the suspects' mouths, and whether they were safe was questionable. There was talk among the increasing crowds milling around town of taking justice into their own hands.

Injustice on the Eastern Shore

The two-and-a-half-story brick Kent County jail was located in Chestertown next to the courthouse between Cross and Court Streets, the latter lane also commonly referred to as "Lawyer's Row." Designed by prominent Baltimore architect J. Crawford Neilson,[83] the jail had just been completed in 1885 by local builder Horace M. Stuart—the same man who built the church in Millington—to replace an aged and dilapidated building nearby that dated to the eighteenth century.

Use of the new building began on February 24, 1885, when the sheriff of that time, John W. Parsons, marched three white and eight black prisoners from the old prison to the new. Five weeks after that cold march, on April 5, John Pierce, jailed for stealing a beef hide, escaped out the window of the bathing room (a room separate from the "water closet"). The window was secured by iron lattice, not bars, and the prisoner separated the rows of lattice by wedging a piece of flooring into them in what must have been a time-consuming effort.

"The prisoners in the upper cells are not kept under as close confinement as those in the lower cells," noted the *Transcript*.[84]

Once Pierce got through the window, he employed the classic method of fashioning his blanket into a rope and slipped to the ground and his freedom. The paper said the townspeople were astonished by the escape, not because it should have been impossible in a brand-new jail, but because of the normal lethargy of the prisoner.

"Pierce is a shiftless, vagabondish sort of individual, and it would not be supposed that he had energy enough to steal a beef hide let alone break out of jail," the paper opined.

Three months later, two men escaped by prying a corridor door open with a bed rod. The *Transcript* sarcastically noted, "The new jail does not seem to be a tower of strength."

As part of a regular routine, the grand jury of each term of circuit court had among its duties the requirement to tour the jail to evaluate conditions. For the April term in 1892, the grand jury, under foreman William B. Usilton, "found the prisoners comfortably provided for" and "found the jail and premises in a fair sanitary condition."

The grand jury report for the October term had a glowing review. "They have visited the jail and found it in exelent [*sic*] condition and the prissoners [*sic*] comfortably provided for."

In 1908, the Reverend Jesse O. Stutsman described the building as a "brick mansion" from the outside.

The facility was also the sheriff's residence, with the larger jail attached to one side, like a snail to its shell.

Race and the Hill Murder Trial

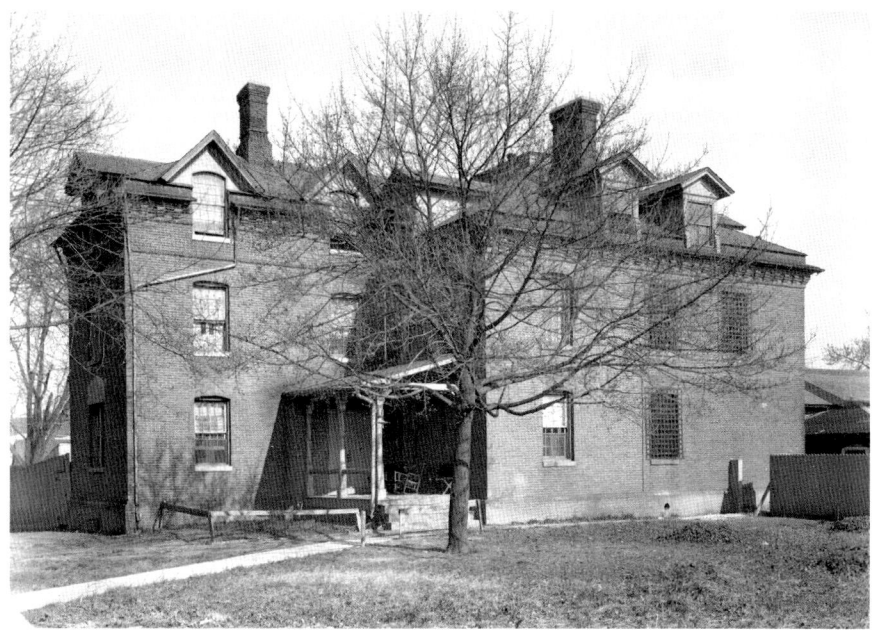

This early twentieth-century photo of the Kent County jail by Colonel John M. South shows the main entry on the south side. *Historical Society of Kent County.*

Stutsman evaluated it:[85]

> *One very noticeable feature of the jail is the proximity of the jail to the actual living quarters of the Sheriff. It is not possible to get a prisoner up to the second tier without taking him through the living quarters. The corridor in which the worst criminals are congregated is within constant sight of the Sheriff's dining room and chief hallway of the Sheriff's residence.*
>
> *There are two distinct sections of cells in the prison proper—one on the first floor and one on the second. A corridor 8 by 50 feet is the approach to the four cells on the first floor. This corridor is well ventilated and sufficiently light in the day, but the entire section has but one electric light for night. This section is the weak point in the jail. A single-barred door is all that prevents escape. The prisoners are allowed free use of this corridor in daytime, and with concerted action all could escape. I regard such an arrangement as exceedingly dangerous of the jailer.*
>
> *The cells in this section are about 8 by 10 feet and are lighted through the door which leads from the corridor. There is a hollow ringing echo in them which makes their occupancy doubly disagreeable. The doors are of*

unchilled bars. The only commode or running water on the section is in one of these cells, which is used by all. Buckets are used when the men are confined in the cells at night.

The upper section is composed of four large cells and a bathroom. This bathroom is equipped with a fair bathtub and a commode for general use. The cells are much larger and lighter than those of the other section. Each is about 10 by 14 feet in dimensions, and is lighted by windows about 2½ by 5 feet. The windows are double-barred and secure, except that they are easy of communication from the yard at the rear of the jail. Two of these cells are securely lined with sheet steel. Two are of ordinary brick walls, which have been recently white washed. The floors of the latter, as well as those on the first section, are of concrete, and the door of the steel-lined one are of three-ply wood.

There does not seem to be much system about the classification of prisoner. All the time I was in this section a colored female prisoner was sitting on the floor of the corridor in front of the door leading into one of the large cells playing cards with three colored men who were confined in one cell.

The beds are of iron, with mattresses and double blankets. They are clean as could be expected.

Due to a series of escapes, improvements were undertaken in October 1887. They included lining the ceiling and walls of two cells with boiler iron, to which Stutsman would later refer; the windows were grated, and iron doors and jambs were installed. This was done as an alternative to building a wall around the entire jail property, seen as a greater expense.[86] It's unlikely that there was an electric light until 1899, when the Chestertown Electric Light Company came into existence and signed a contract with the town. The commodes—one in the sheriff's residence and the other in the jail—were novelties added in 1889, prior to which a water closet with a bucket provided the same function for the prisoners and a privy served the sheriff's household.

Beefing up the cells couldn't prevent all escapes, of course. In January, just a few months after the 1887 improvements, thirty-year-old oysterman Frederick Bolsom tried two ways of getting out of jail after he was incarcerated for stealing a watch. First, he tried to hang himself with a large handkerchief. A week later, he broke out of jail when his cell door was accidentally left open. He sprinted to College Avenue with only one shoe before being nabbed by three deputies.

Race and the Hill Murder Trial

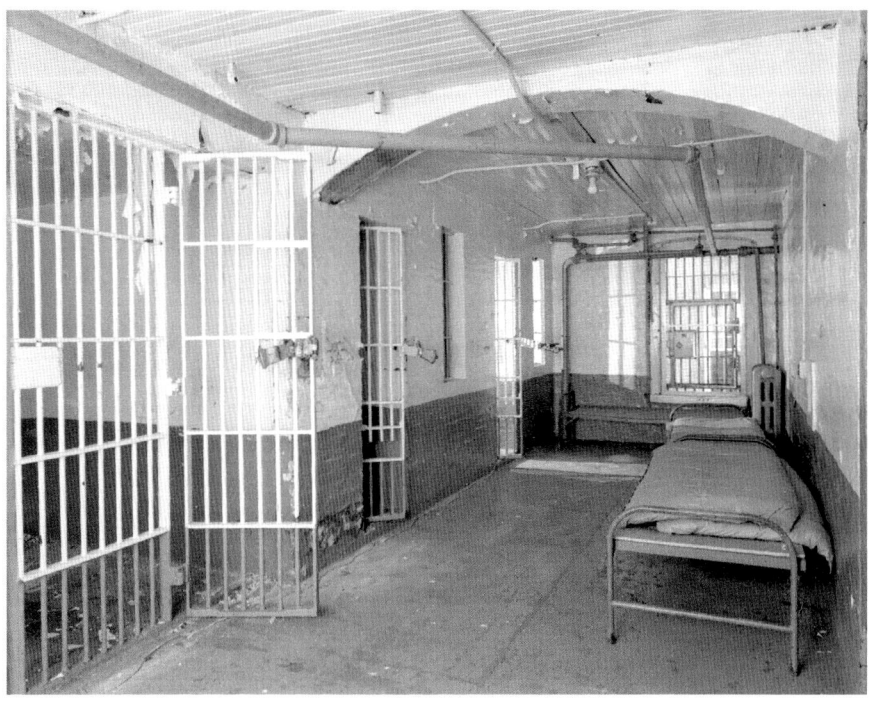

The inside of the Kent County jail as it appeared after it was abandoned. *Courtesy of Tyler Campbell.*

The Hill murder suspects and some of the witnesses were held at the jail while the inquest continued. They may well have been more concerned about how easy it was for others to get into the jail rather than the ease of escaping.

On Thursday, April 28, the day Baynard confessed, it was rumored that 250 lynchers were in town.[87] But there was no attempt that night to raid the jail. It was a tense moment. One report said that a group of African Americans was prepared to violently prevent a lynching, demonstrating the racial volatility.[88] Had there been a real interest in shortcutting justice that night, then sympathy for Sheriff Edward J. Plummer's ill wife, Eliza, must have put the scheme on hold. The sheriff, however, decided to take no chances since the mood of various crowds showing up early Friday was ominous.

Just before two o'clock that afternoon, the four main suspects—Comegys, Brooks, Williams and Bradshaw—handcuffed, chained and supervised by the sheriff and accompanied by Nevins and Bates, were ushered out of the jail's main access on the northeast side to waiting covered carriages and transported to the train station, located at the time on upper High Street

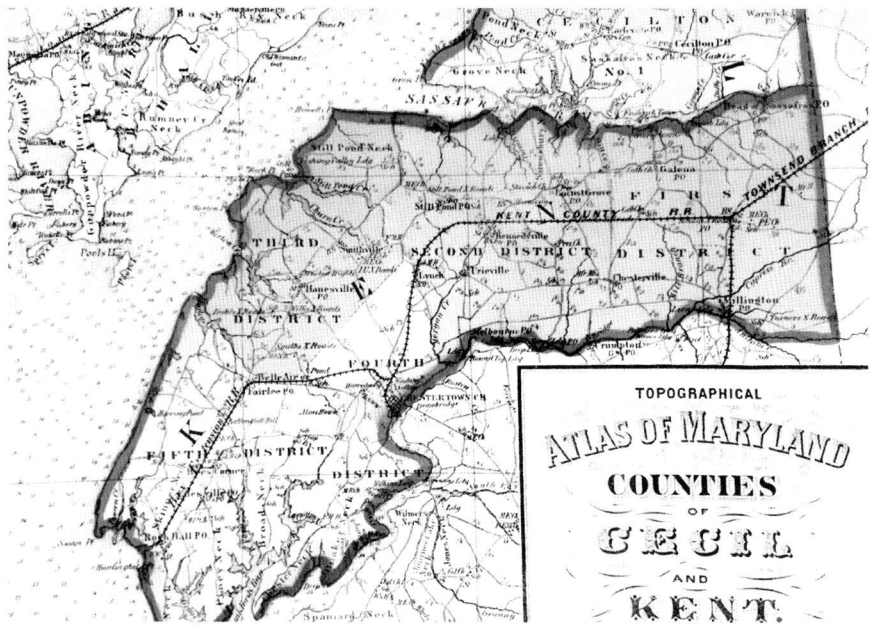

The railroad connections in Kent County are clearly indicated in this 1873 map. *From the Topographical Atlas of the State of Maryland.*

near what is now Dixon Drive.[89] The lawmen each had a pistol and a Winchester rifle.

It's uncertain the route Plummer and his charges took to the depot, but the likeliest way to avoid detection would have been via Church Alley to Queen and Princess Streets, over to Cannon Street and then up to Kent or Mill Street and thus back to High Street. Whichever route was chosen, they evaded the milling crowds. At the depot, an engine with a single passenger car waited. They boarded the train and left town for Baltimore. It would not be an uneventful trip.

In that era, rail service, begun twenty years previous, was from Chestertown courtesy of the Baltimore & Delaware Bay Railroad Co., through Kennedyville, Blacks Station, Lambson Station and on to Massey—in the exact opposite direction from Baltimore. Since the Chesapeake Bay couldn't be crossed, the route went up and around the head of the bay. From Massey, the tracks crossed the Delaware state line to Townsend, where a southern spur led to Clayton and a northern track veered to Newark, thence across the state line again to Elkton and across the Susquehanna River to the western side of Maryland. The train schedule at that time apparently required a diversion to Clayton, another turn in the wrong direction. It was a circuitous route allowing ample time for drama.

Race and the Hill Murder Trial

The travelers arrived in Clayton, where they had to change trains. They waited for about forty-five minutes. As they waited, a crowd began to grow. People were probably alerted by telegraph or telephone that the prisoners were there. By the time their train arrived, the mob, grown to about one hundred strong, wanted to see the suspects "stretched up" right there and then.[90] The sheriff was very careful to quickly lead the prisoners across the platform, and there was no attempt to rush the passenger car. However, the incident in Clayton well demonstrated the regional indignation that the crime manifested.

The prisoners were safely installed in the Baltimore City jail that night. Plummer was so pestered by newspaper reporters after getting the prisoners situated that he gave orders to the desk that no one be shown to his room.

The prisoners were now in the capable hands of the Baltimore police, under the care of Warden Daniel Constantine. They were put to work the next day scrubbing floors in the basement cells. The investigators from Kent County returned to Chestertown to question more suspects.

On April 30, Hurtt denied complicity in the murder. But it was Moses Brown's testimony, given on May 1, that firmed up the details and the players. The way Brown's testimony was extracted added yet another sensational element to the crime's saga.

Newspaper reporter Bates, the interviewer this time, claimed that he read Brown's mind. He described his talk with Brown to a reporter four years later.

He said he told Brown, "Moses, whenever a man commits a crime God has so fixed it that a photograph of what he does is taken on his brain and a voodoo man can look into that man's eyes and see a picture of what he has done. I can see a picture of what you did, and I am going to describe to you exactly what was done to Hill and the part you took in it."

Brown was mesmerized. Bates then grasped the man by the throat and yelled, "What did you do with that knife you held in your hand?"

At just that point, owing to the dynamic of their proximity, the suspect's chair fell backward while Bates maintained his grip on the man's throat. Demoralized, intimidated and frightened, Brown grasped, "I threw it into the branch," meaning Long Meadow Branch.

Afterward, according to Bates's story, Brown gave a complete confession: "The confession of Brown, on Sunday afternoon, May 1, it is said, was extracted from him by Bates, successfully pretending to be a mind-reader."[91]

In some circles, due to this incident, Bates was credited with solving the crime. Several months later, the *National Police Gazette* of New York described him as the reporter "who recently worked up the Hill murder and landed the guilty one in jail."[92]

Because of Brown's confession, Detective Nevins, on May 7, had Long Meadow Branch diverted and used a rake to search for a knife or other evidence in the creek bed.[93] He found nothing related to the case.

AFRICAN AMERICAN DELIBERATIONS

Hill's murder was racially motivated, and it's clear that his death and the subsequent related and unrelated events widened the area's racial chasm. But prominent African American leaders in Millington and Chestertown sought early on to distance themselves from those responsible for Hill's death.

On Thursday, May 5, at a meeting in Chestertown at Janes Church, then located where today's Cross Street becomes Quaker Neck Road across from Wilmer Park, area blacks held an "indignation" meeting to denounce the crime and express their wish for quick justice for the perpetrators.

The Reverend Benjamin A. Queeley called the meeting to order, and William Perkins, a prominent African American politician and businessman who made his mark as the proprietor of the Rising Sun oyster saloon in Chestertown, was chosen as "president" to conduct it.[94]

Perkins was a fixture in Chestertown and could arguably be termed the African American ambassador to the white community in the county. He knew how to work the press; he advertised in the papers, and periodically in his long career as an oysterman and confectioner, he favored the editors of the *Kent News* with samples of his popular ice cream and cakes. Usilton and Plummer returned the favor with coverage of his various activities. The coverage wasn't always positive, however. The paper took aim at Perkins when it came to his ardent Republican politics.

Perkins was politically involved early in his life and stumped for equal rights for African American citizens. He was a speaker at the May 19, 1870

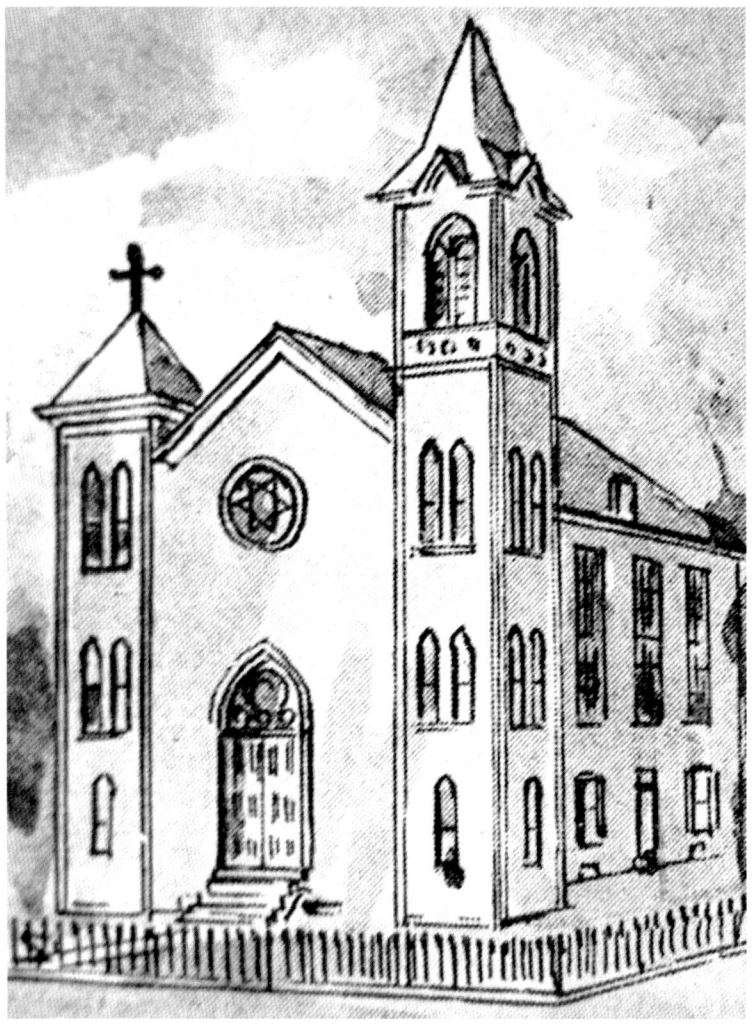

Janes ME Church was located across from what is now Wilmer Park. It burned down in 1914 and was replaced with a new building at Cross and Cannon Streets. *From the* 1907 Birdseye View of Chestertown. *Historical Society of Kent County.*

Fifteenth Amendment rally with General Robert Clay Crawford and Henry Highland Garnet. Perkins Hall, next to the Rising Sun on Maple Avenue in Chestertown, was named for him, and it was used as a focal point for entertainment, political gatherings and African American civic functions. His most notable efforts were aimed at greater educational opportunities for African Americans, and he lobbied for more funds for black schools.

Race and the Hill Murder Trial

While his fame, fortune and influence had declined with his advanced age by the time of the Hill murder, Perkins, seventy-two, still enjoyed some notoriety as a messenger in the customhouse in Baltimore. It was a minor position of political favor to which he was appointed by port surveyor Captain William D. Burchinal, prominent Kent County Republican, for his efforts in supporting the party. Perkins still called Kent County home and remained an authority in the administration of Janes Church.

Other officers included the Reverend John H. Accooe, Philadelphia-born pastor at Millington, as first vice-president; J.P. Henderson, second vice-president; and Perry Frisby, secretary.

Perkins praised the sheriff's courage, resolve and ingenuity in circumventing a possible lynching. Accooe said the African Americans of Millington deeply regretted Hill's death and "have no sympathy with those involved in the attack." Among those present at the meeting were Samuel Comegys, Frisby Comegys's father, and Samuel Emory, Charles Emory's father.

The meeting was finalized with four resolutions, including the denunciation of the actions of the guilty parties; commendation of the officers "in preventing the enraged white citizens from taking the law into their own hands"; condolences to the family of the victim; and the denunciation of the use of liquor in the community, "inasmuch as the use of such intoxicating liquor is damaging to us as a community, and was a means to the end of the committal of this dreadful murder which we deplore."

The document containing the resolutions ended with:

> This is to certify that we the law-abiding colored citizens of this neighborhood do not agree and are highly incensed with the murderers of Dr. Hill. We, with wishes of peace and happiness, have strove [sic] hard to bring such desperate characters in good society, but in vain, and we earnestly hope the white citizens of this county will not frown at this neighborhood on account of the actions of the guilty. In regards to Dr. Hill he was a good citizen, faithful in discharging the duties of his profession, whose kindness will never be forgotten by me and was greatly appreciated by a great many of our people.

It was a curious slip of the author of a group document to lapse into the first person singular.

Their sincere and sensible efforts to temper the simmering race relations cauldron, always ready to boil over, became a footnote in futility ten days later in a case that had nothing at all to do with the death of Dr. Heighe Hill.

UNPREVENTABLE LYNCHING

Just after breakfast on Sunday, May 15, 1892, on a farm outside Kennedyville, a bright, delicate flower of a girl named Nellie Silcox, who would turn eleven in October, was raped in the kitchen while her father was in the carriage house greasing carriages and her deaf mother was skimming milk in the cellar. Her attacker, Nellie said later, told her to keep quiet or bad things would happen to her and her family. It was only later in the afternoon that white farmer John Silcox and his wife, Sallie, determined that something was very wrong with their firstborn daughter.

The victim identified an African American man, twenty-four-year-old James Taylor, a part-time farm laborer from Pondtown in Queen Anne's County, as her assailant. He was nowhere to be found that day. That night, Taylor was found by a gun-toting posse of the farmer's friends at a house at Segar's Bottom near Kennedyville. He was quickly trundled off to the jail in Chestertown, where he was locked up in a cell with Moses Brown.

When the word spread through the county that a black man had been charged with raping a ten-year-old white girl, community outrage grew to a level that was simply beyond measure—and beyond control.

The next day, as more people heard the facts and fantasies of the case, the community's indignation mounted even further, and Sheriff Plummer received clear, unambiguous intelligence that Taylor would be lynched that night. As with the Hill suspects, he spirited Taylor out of the jail, this time placing the intended target on the steam launch *Gracie*, which he commandeered when he heard it whistle for the bridge as it was making

Race and the Hill Murder Trial

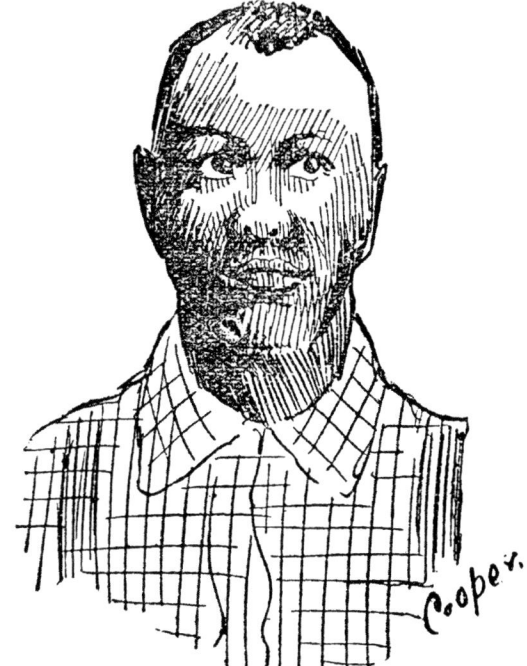

Right: This drawing of James Taylor was titled *The Negro Fiend*. From the Chestertown Transcript, *May 21, 1892.*

Below: Gracie, used to protect rape suspect James Taylor, was no doubt similar to *Chester*, a riverboat used for passengers and freight in the same era. *Courtesy of Mark Newsome.*

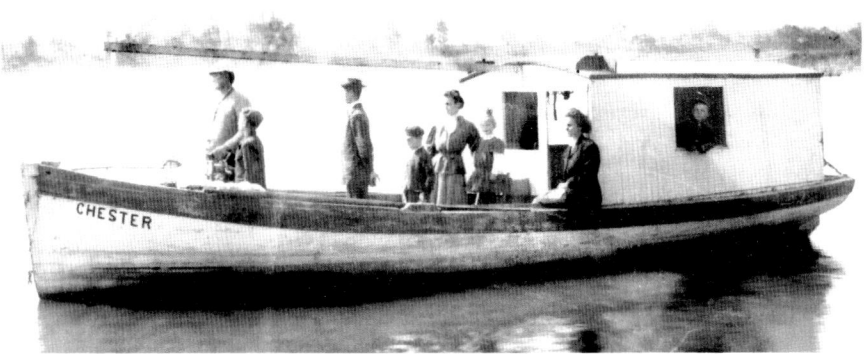

its way to berth at Joseph Turners's boatyard in the vicinity of what is now Scott's Point.

Gracie was about fifteen to twenty feet long. It likely had a single cabin on it, like a number of vessels that plied the bay and its tributaries, and could probably carry about a dozen passengers and crew. For Plummer's purposes, it was good enough for the security of his charge. The vessel steamed a relatively short distance downriver to Wilmer's Wharf on the Queen Anne's County side. There, the captain and the prisoner waited out the night.

Injustice on the Eastern Shore

The sheriff's concerns were not misplaced. About eleven o'clock, an angry mob of white men, numbering as many as eight hundred, broke into the jail and ransacked every cell looking for Taylor. They also went through the sheriff's home but were prevented from searching Mrs. Plummer's bedroom.[95]

Moses Brown, still considered just a "witness" in the Hill case, was also taken on the boat chained to Taylor; the sheriff was concerned that Brown would be mistaken for Taylor or simply be lynched as a surrogate. Brown later said he was frightened but enjoyed the respite from jail.

Plummer returned the prisoners to their cells about five o'clock the next morning, thinking that the passion for retribution was spent. He was mistaken.

About nine o'clock that evening, a similar crowd, armed with weapons of all sorts, showed up at the jail led by a group of masked men. They broke down the door with a sledgehammer and shoved aside Deputy Sheriff Frank Plummer, the sheriff's younger brother, and several others on guard. Paying little attention to Brown, who had requested a cell on the first floor out of fear,[96] they snapped up the terrified, shoeless Taylor, who was in a second-floor cell. A rope was placed around his neck, and he was rudely towed by it down the stairs, out of the jail and across the street, between the Rockwell House and the Armstrong Hotel, where he was hanged by the rope after it was tied to a small tree. And so he died, found guilty by "Judge Lynch," across the street from the county courthouse.

If the community was incensed by the alleged crime of rape, it was nauseated by the sickening manifestation of vigilante justice that resulted. The May 19 *Transcript* ended its report:

> *The lynching of James Taylor, on Tuesday night last, is the first case of lynching that has ever taken placed* [sic] *in Kent county as far back as the oldest citizens can remember, and we hope it may be the last. Whatever may have been the provocation, the stigma will rest upon our county for many years.*

Taylor's lynching had nothing at all to do with the Hill case. No one in the community thought it did. The only true connection was bad timing.[97]

Did the lynching of James Taylor satisfy the white community's frothing bloodlust whipped up by Hill's murder? The incident certainly was a scandalous embarrassment for the town, the county and the state. The *Transcript*, which seems to have had a slightly less racist leaning than the *Kent News*, spent more time defending the community against big-city newspaper

RACE AND THE HILL MURDER TRIAL

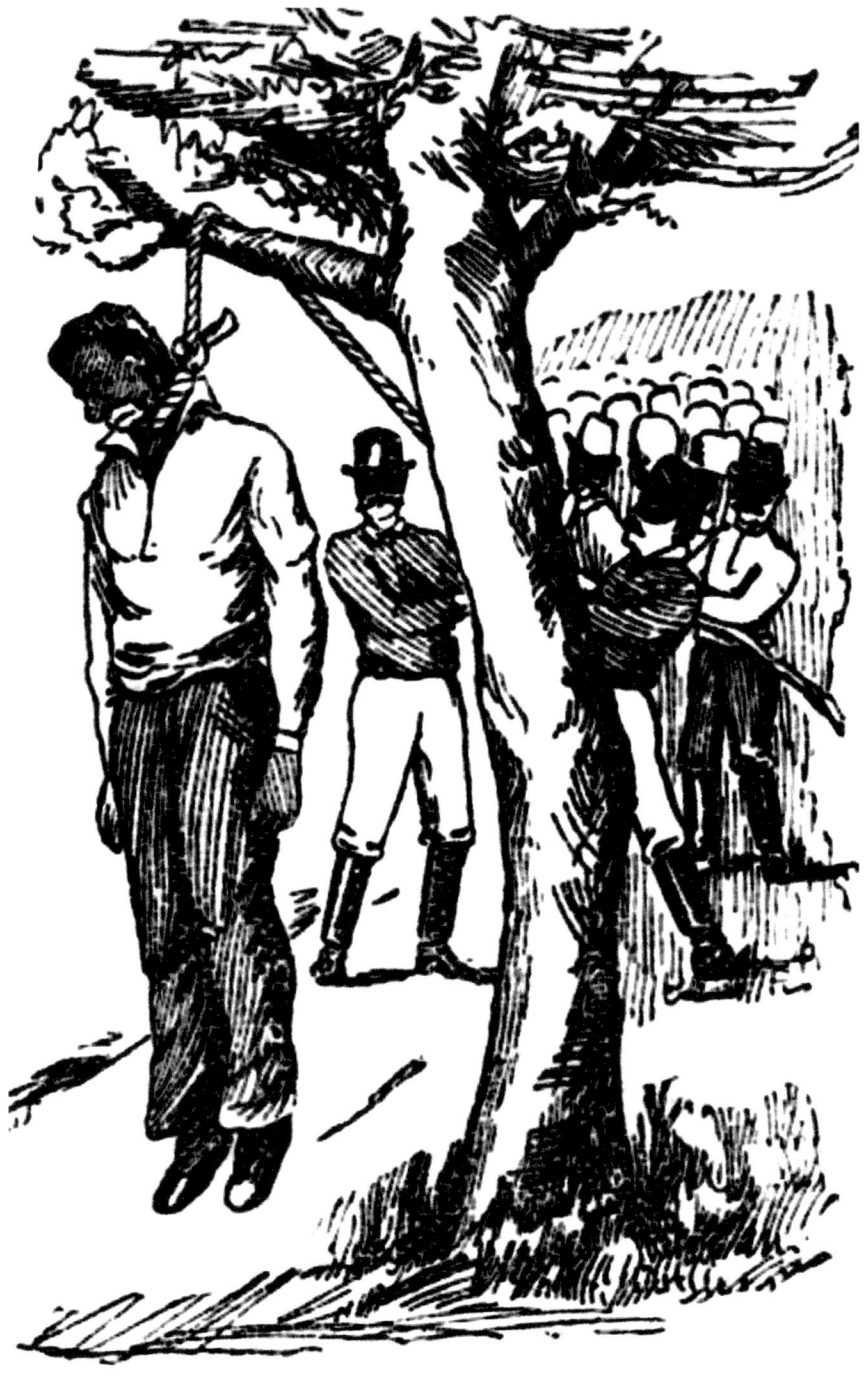

This gruesome drawing was published following the lynching of James Taylor. *From the Kent News, May 21, 1892.*

claims that an innocent was hanged than soul searching. There was, in fact, another suspect, who was white.

Local African Americans again tried to diffuse the racial tension. Soon after the lynching, a meeting of prominent members of the small black community of Morgan Creek was held, and as before, resolutions were passed to underscore their feelings:

> *Whereas, We desire to manifest to the public, by word and action, that prejudice, retaliation and threats are not the dominant spirit of the intelligent and Christian colored citizens of Kent county.*
>
> *Resolved, That we assure Messrs. Medders and Justis, and all others, that we are humane and in accord with whatever promotes the welfare of the people and the protection of property.*
>
> *Resolved, That we carefully admonish the wayward ones of our people (the minority) and assure them that we assent to nothing that manaces* [sic] *our social quietness and Christian excellence.*
>
> *J.T. STRYCKNING*
ISAAC CAULK
FRED TURNER.[98]

While the lynching may have been an extension of the community's ire over the Hill murder, there's a good chance Taylor would have been lynched in any case. The scenario was played out many times on the Eastern Shore before and after the Kent County incident. In fact, Taylor's lynching was presaged by a very similar occurrence just a year earlier in Queen Anne's County.

In that case, an African American, Asbury Green, was accused of breaking into the Kent Island home of a white woman, Mary A. Tolson, on the night of February 28, 1891, while her husband was away and beating and raping her. Green was arrested on March 12 and tried before a jury during the May term by the three circuit court judges, Joseph A. Wickes, John M. Robinson and Frederick Stump. The jury found him guilty of the assault. Stump, the only judge present for the sentencing on May 11, gave him twenty-one years for what was normally considered a hanging offense.

He gave the lighter sentence, he said, because the victim's description of the attacker was sketchy. Also, Green had a fairly strong alibi; several people testified that he was someplace else at the time of the incident.

Concerned about the rumblings in the community, it was decided that the prisoner would be transported the next day from his cell in Centreville to the penitentiary across the bay.

Race and the Hill Murder Trial

But he didn't get another day.

Knowing that there might be a problem, Sheriff T.B. Turner had increased the number of guards at the jail. But it wasn't enough. About one o'clock on the morning of Tuesday, May 12, a crowd of about sixty men, some toting guns, axes or farm tools, arrived at the jail.

The sheriff met them at the door, and when he refused to give up the keys to Green's cell, they pushed him down.

They then forced the guards to open the cell. They placed a rope around Green's neck and dragged him by the rope out of the cell and about three hundred yards just outside town, where they hanged him from a peach tree. It was later thought he died while being pulled along, before he was hoisted up into the tree.

The case nearly caused a race riot.[99]

Some African Americans threatened to burn down the town, and local white residents claimed the lynching party came from out of town.

For many decades, the Eastern Shore would set the unwholesome standard in cases of white vigilante justice aimed at black suspects or those convicted. Instances included Isaac Kemp in Princess Anne, June 8, 1893; Matthew Williams in Salisbury in 1931; and George Armwood in Princess Anne in 1933, to name a few.

Such incidents, however, were not limited to the eastern side of the state.

George Briscoe was strung up from a tree by a group of fifteen or so hooded white vigilantes at New Bridge, about fifteen miles from Annapolis, on the night of November 26–27, 1884. His alleged crime? Burglary. But he was accused of so many burglaries and robberies in the area that the community was incensed.

The *Evening Capital* opined in favor of the savage act because, the paper said, it was "the only way to rid the community of so desperate a character as this negro had proved himself to be." And, "while we do not approve of lynch law, yet there are some instances where it is justifiable."[100]

A case in Baltimore County a year later sorely tested the institutional racism of the judicial system, then beginning to fracture, as the new black freedoms started coming into play and into question in the state's courts.

As with this and other lynching cases of the era, there were no repercussions for those who took the law into their own hands.

Kent's dominant white community seemed to develop a case of collective amnesia when it came to the Taylor lynching.

The grand jury report of the October term stated:

They have summoned 9 respectable persons of Chestertown and vicinity to testify if they knew of any persons who aided or abetted or counseled the lynching of Jas. Taylor and to each and every question each and all answered that they were there but did not aid, abet, counsel or encourage the lynching nor did they know any of the persons violating the law, and they endeavored to prevent by counsel and persuasion the commission of the act, but went no further knowing full well that it would have been futile to join their force against such a body of men…The Grand Jury as a body deprecate and denounce the lynching of Jas. Taylor as a violation of the law and against the good government and peace of society and should not be tolerated by the community especially as the party was in the hands of the law and inside of a prison from which no prisoner could escape.[101]

"Judge Lynch" would be recalled at length and with contempt once more by one of Kent's favorite sons. But at the time, there was a ready-made diversion: the Hill murder case was working its way through the county's legitimate justice system, and it would keep tongues wagging, reporters writing and lawyers, judges and politicians pontificating for months to come.

THE LONG SUMMER

While the suspects languished in separate jails, ripples of the murder, investigation and trial continued, with the needle on the gossip meter bouncing back and forth at every point.

In Millington, Dr. William M. Pippin, of Easton, bought Hill's drugstore, and the business continued with a new face behind the counter. In the meantime, Arrelee Hill and her infant daughter moved in with her in-laws at Locust Grove. Witness Stephen Cooper, whom some claimed entertained some of the suspects on the night Hill was attacked, was released from jail on $250 bond, posted by his employer, Augustine "Gus" Hendrickson.

Moses Brown's level of involvement was still in question, despite Bates's "hypnosis." On May 14, the *Kent News* reported that a blind inmate recalled overhearing a jail cell conversation between Brown and Henry Hurtt. The conversation went something like this:

> *Brown: Henry?*
> *Hurtt: Well what do you want?*
> *Brown: Is that you, Henry?*
> *Hurtt: Yes, what you want?*
> *Brown: What did you tell for?*
> *Hurtt: I had to.*
> *Brown: No, you didn't.*
> *Hurtt: Yes, 'deed I did. I was afraid they'd get me into it.*

Injustice on the Eastern Shore

Brown: Well, take it back. I told too, but I took it back, and I'm going to stick to it. You do it too.[102]

On June 1, Sheriff Plummer and watchman John Greenwood fetched the four main suspects—Brooks, Bradshaw, Williams and Comegys—from Baltimore, returning them to their cells in Chestertown. The prisoners didn't like it because in Baltimore they had been given work details, allowing them to breathe some fresh air and actually make some money. In Chestertown, they were chained in their cells to prevent escape from a facility that was well known for its escapability. The reason for the prisoners' return was that the threat of lynching had apparently subsided.

The June 9 *Kent News* noted:

> It is believed that the excitement in this community has sufficiently subsided to make it perfectly safe, for the commissioners think the people now realize that it would be a crime to lynch these men, and are fully resolved to let the law deal with them. This is the only proper view to take of the matter, not only for the sake of our county and our State, but for the family of Dr. Hill who want the whole affair investigated. Another thing will be brought to light, that is whether this crime was the result of race feeling or personal feeling against Dr. Hill and if these men did not have a trial this would never be known. The men are securely chained to the wall in their cells, and pass most of the time sleeping and sometimes in reading.

However, it's far more likely—the article alluded to it—that the expense of keeping the four in Baltimore was more than the county commissioners cared to expend. Ultimately, the Hill murder case would be the most expensive ever tried in the county to that point, and the bills were mounting. The time the prisoners spent in Baltimore was just a budgetary footnote to the grand cost picture of the investigation and trial. It was $59.99 to transport the four prisoners and an additional $82.50 to house them at the Baltimore City jail. It cost an additional $15.50 just to take testimony in Baltimore.[103]

By the middle of June, the number of suspects had begun to grow, and in some cases there was little distinction being made between some of the witnesses and those accused of direct participation. Five were arrested on June 20, including John Potts, Frank Baynard (Joshua's brother), Walter Roe, Henry Hynson and John Harrison. Four of the five were apprehended in Millington. Hynson was arrested at Tilghman's in Queen Anne's County.[104]

Race and the Hill Murder Trial

This meant a total of sixteen people had been arrested in the case: Williams, Brooks, Comegys, Emory, Bradshaw, Joshua Baynard, Benson, Brown, Cooper, Harrison, Hynson, Roe, Frank Baynard, Potts, Phillip Mander and Hurtt.

Cooper, as noted, had been bonded out. Not long afterward, he received a threatening letter advising him to leave the county. It was signed by the "White Caps and cross-bones," and at the bottom were drawings of a dirk, knife, pistol, crossbones and coffin. The letter had been sent from Millington.[105]

Did such a group exist? Was it actually some spinoff of the Ku Klux Klan, whose nineteenth-century incarnation had gone defunct? It's uncertain. But a group referred to as the White Caps had been causing trouble for several years in Kent County.

In a curious report, the *Kent News* stated on January 19, 1889, that the "white caps are about," but people who abide by the law shouldn't be concerned. "If…outlaws do come their reception will not be gratifying."

But then the *Transcript* reported a couple weeks later:

> One of the citizens of Chestertown was accosted on the street on Tuesday night by three of the Kent county order of White Caps. The command was given to "halt," which was several times repeated, followed by shells which were thrown by the caps. Notwithstanding the spectral appearance and determined commands of the nocturnal intruders upon the serene meditations of the citizens addressed, he claims to have been "the noblest Roman of them all," and stood his ground undismayed, it has been suggested, however, that possibly the powers of locomotion of our friend was somewhat interfered with by the unexpected guest, or in other words he was so badly frightened that he couldn't move.[106]

In that same paper, Locust Grove correspondent "J.I.C." noted that the White Caps were around and acting as a sort of morals police:

> The White Caps have put in an appearance, and are running things to suit themselves. One of our young men has been notified that he must forsake home and friends and take his departure within ten days, and forget the girl he leaves behind him.

Three years later, perhaps as a result of the Hill murder and racial tension, a whites-only "law and order league" was formed in Millington about the same time a similar organization was established in Chestertown. Its focus

INJUSTICE ON THE EASTERN SHORE

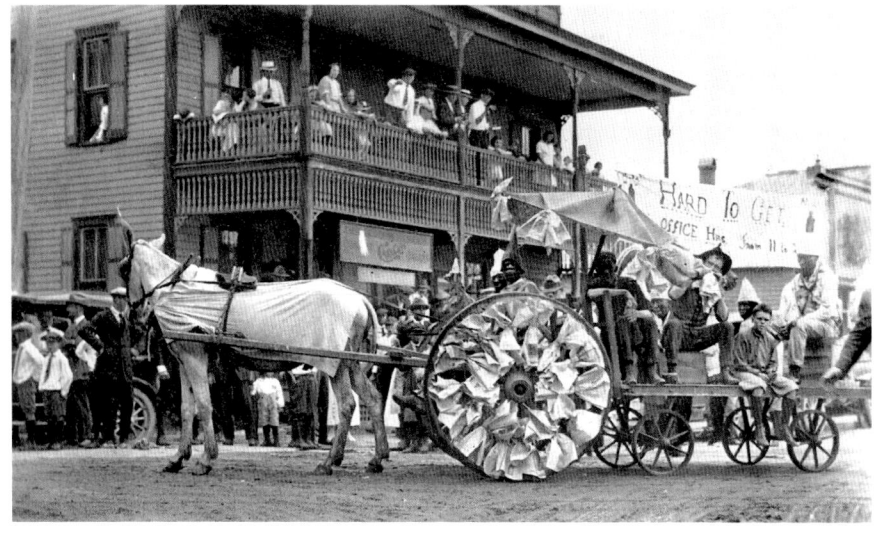

This entry in the 1922 Independence Day parade in Millington passes in front of the Central Hotel. Some of the passengers sport black or white cone-shaped hats, and "blacks" are white men and boys in Al Jolson–style blackface. *Courtesy of Betty Lockwood.*

was shutting down illegal liquor sales. In one instance, the Millington group hired a detective to determine whether Thomas Pratt's pear cider was actually beer. The verdict was that it was beer, and he was forced to get rid of it.[107]

Another "law and order society" was organized in Millington in the 1920s. Benjamin Jones remembers seeing members wearing white cloaks and pointed hats, à la the Ku Klux Klan, during the funeral of his cousin Margaret Vansant.[108] While the group had been trying to emulate the Ku Klux Klan, they were not affiliated with that feared and denounced national organization as far as can be determined, although there was Klan activity in Kent in that period and a known chapter in Cecil County.

Nonetheless, as the summer of 1892 dragged on, interest in the Hill murder case subsided since little seemed to transpire as the days ticked off until the trial, scheduled for the October term.

The county was bustling with distractions. There were balloon daredevils performing at the amusement park in Tolchester. Several injuries were reported. Local and regional baseball was becoming a more popular diversion, with nearby communities often becoming friendly and sometimes not-so-friendly rivals. Sheriff Plummer bought a new bloodhound in Pennsylvania. At six months old, the "pup" was already one hundred pounds.

Race and the Hill Murder Trial

Plummer kept him chained outside the jail. Bicycles were all the rage. The weather was unusually hot, leading to a shortage of ice; the two-year-old Nicholson ice factory, in the upper part of Chestertown, was completely unable to keep up with the demand. And the Millington creamery began operation in August.

On September 7, Dr. Hill's widow had a stone erected on her husband's tomb at Shrewsbury. The stonework was done by A.J. Hynson on Vermont marble. Inscribed on it are the words: "Dr. J. Heighe Hill, May 20, 1862; April 24, 1892." And on the base: "I thank my God upon every remembrance of thee."

One item of murder news stood out. A report said that a "detective" had been in Millington, and the arrest of high-placed white men, alleged conspirators in the case, was imminent. The man who started the erroneous rumor—a "crank," as the local newspaper called him—was chased out of town.[109]

County residents looked toward October with a growing sense of anticipation for two reasons: one was the 400th anniversary of Columbus's discovery of America. It was a big deal locally and on the national level. President Benjamin Harrison would proclaim the first official Columbus Day holiday.

In Kent, however, it would be followed by the trial of the century. Businesses were gearing up. The local newspapers were already getting commitments for more ads than they could possibly carry in their four-page regular editions. And the Hill murder suspects were starting to get nervous.

COLUMBUS DAY

James Alfred Pearce and state comptroller Marion deKalb Smith didn't draw lots to be chosen as the defense attorneys for the nine main suspects charged in Hill's murder, but they certainly had the stature for the case. The two high-profile Kent lawyers, both heavily steeped in local and state Democratic politics, were appointed by the court in the arcane system used in those days (there was no public defender's office). They probably put their names in the running since either side of the case would bring notoriety to the lawyers involved. And both were lightning rods to public attention and acclaim. They both knew the business of capital crime, each having served as Kent's state's attorney at points in their careers.

That's not to say it would be an easy case; they were between the proverbial rock and hard place. They had to please justice in the court and the court of public opinion in the county, which provided them with their more consistent and generally more profitable business of estates, real estate transactions, civil suits and such. And they were the second choice of those to be tried.

They were appointed after failed attempts to get prominent Baltimore defense attorney Thomas C. Ruddell to represent the suspects.

Ruddell, an Irish immigrant, had a varied list of clients and cases, but it's uncertain whether he ever defended against murder charges. And it seems most of his time was spent representing clients in appeals. Nonetheless, he wanted $600 for the job, and the defendants couldn't afford him. Donations were sought from throughout the two-county area, and fundraisers were held, including an oyster dinner in Centreville. But it was too little too late.

Race and the Hill Murder Trial

"Unless some lawyer is retained by them, the court will have to appoint an attorney for the defense," said the *Baltimore Sun* on October 18.

Getting locals on defense made people in Kent, including the victim's father, feel a little better, but perhaps for the wrong reasons.

Pearce, fifty-two, was the scion of a deep-rooted and wealthy Kent family. His father of the same name was a U.S. senator who died in 1862. Though of lesser stature in politics, James Jr. excelled as a lawyer after graduating from Princeton. He was admitted to the bar in 1864 and ran a successful campaign for state's attorney three years later, serving two terms. He was a longtime former member of the Chestertown commission and a member of the school board for many years.

He lived with his wife, the former Eunice Rasin, in the stately house on the corner of Front Street (Water Street) and Maple Avenue.[110]

Pearce was also firmly entrenched in the white

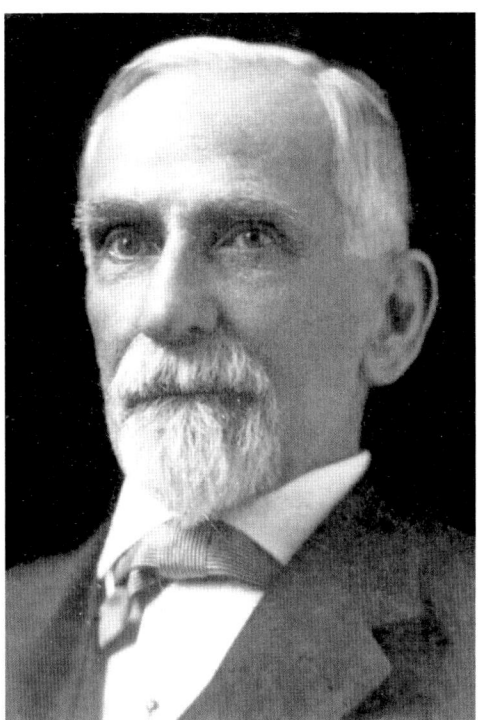

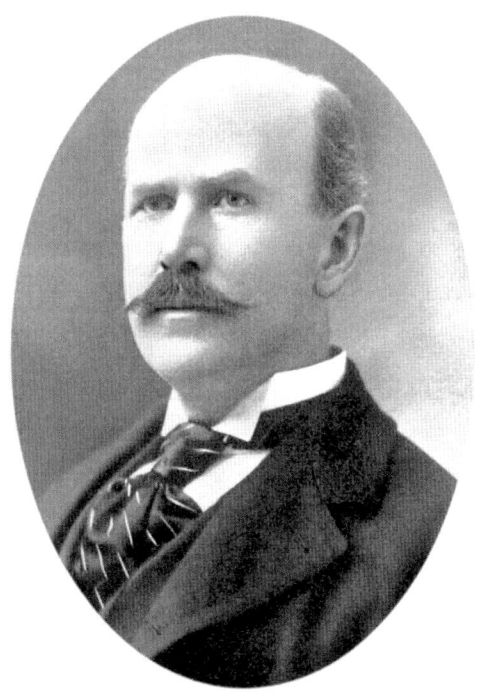

Top: James Alfred Pearce Jr. *Historical Society of Kent County.*

Right: Marion deKalb Smith. *Historical Society of Kent County.*

INJUSTICE ON THE EASTERN SHORE

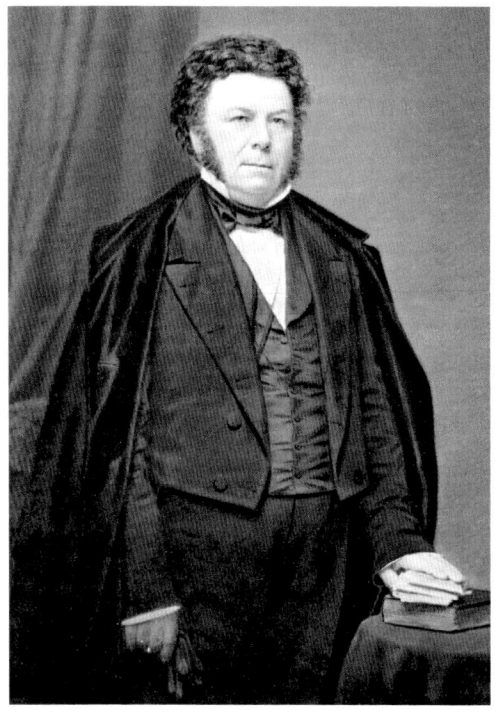

Senator James A. Pearce. *Library of Congress.*

supremacist social scheme of Kent County and the rest of the Eastern Shore. His father had been one of the largest slave owners in the county[111] and had fought earnestly and loudly as a senator to preserve the institution of slavery. Pearce Sr. even went so far as to express support for the mob of genteel whites that tarred and feathered Quaker abolitionist James Bowers in an incident that received national attention in 1858.

After the Hill murder trial, Pearce Jr. would go on to become a circuit court judge. He would later also purchase and arrange the placement of a granite Civil War memorial near the High Street side of the courthouse. The monument makes no mention of the four-hundred-plus black veterans of the war, a community error of omission that was not corrected for seventy years.

Smith, thirty-one at the time of the trial, was the son of James Smith, a Kennedyville farmer who owned slaves.[112] The family moved to Chestertown in 1858. Smith was only twelve when his father died. The grandson of prominent Millington-area farmer Jesse Knock, the youngster attended Washington College, graduating in 1870. Smith got his start in law in the office of Richard Hynson and was admitted to the bar in 1873. In 1883 and again in 1887, he was elected as state's attorney, and in 1891, he was elected as state comptroller. He would have been in mourning when Hill was murdered; his mother had died only four days earlier.

Smith and Pearce knew each other well and sometimes worked together. They were both involved in the establishment of the Chestertown Bank and briefly served side by side on the new bank's board. They were both members of the board of visitors of Washington College. And they sometimes faced off in the courtroom.[113]

Race and the Hill Murder Trial

The stature of these local legal giants obscured what surely existed in both, based on their upbringings: a strong racial bias. The *Transcript* praised their appointment and said that Pearce and Smith—whose legal ethic, said the paper, was "beyond reproach"—would ensure that there would not be a change of venue, avoiding outrage among Kent's white citizens:

> *The appointment of Messrs. Pearce and Smith to take the cases in charge, immediately produced a feeling of relief throughout the community, assuring [sic] as it did, that the prisoners would be defended by two gentlemen whose eminent ability and high standard of legal honor will insure [sic] to the friends of the murdered man, a trial of the case purely upon its merits, and at the same time giving a guarantee to the prisoners and their friends, that a strong and conscientious defense of their cases would be made. All feeling of apprehension was at once dispelled, as it was conceded on all sides that the trials would not be removed, but would be tried at the present term of court, thereby removing all danger (if danger ever existed) of lynch law or violence. This was, of course, a relief to all parties.*[114]

The locals also figured that since the defense attorneys were longtime locals, representation with an aim to acquit would be less than stellar.

And then there was the prosecution.

Harrison Wilson Vickers, born in 1845, was the ninth of eleven children of U.S. senator George Vickers—a lawyer's lawyer—and Mary Mansfield Vickers, the daughter of a prominent Chestertown builder and property wrangler. Both parents were descended from a long line of successful and prominent English colonial families, the Vickers clan having arrived in Kent in the late seventeenth century.[115]

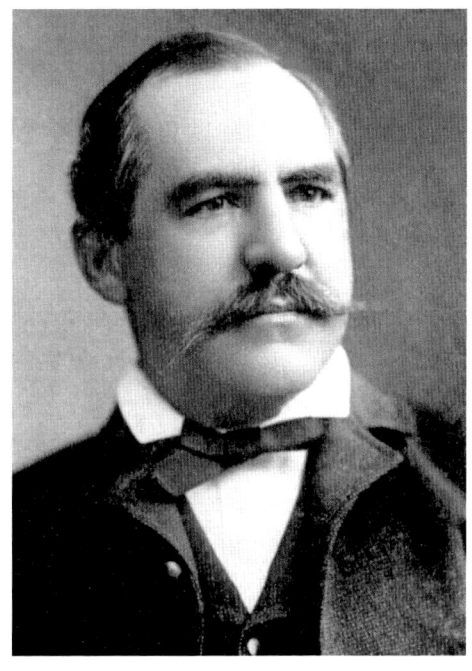

Harrison Vickers. *Historical Society of Kent County.*

Harrison had a comfortable upbringing, growing up around the streets of Chestertown, frolicking on his father's country farms and sleeping comfortably in a High Street town house and, later, a grand mansion at High and Mill Streets across from the Methodist Episcopal church.

Several of the senator's five sons who grew to adulthood were not altogether the bright lights in Daddy's eyes. Harrison, however, carried the reins well, inheriting the senator's legal and political acumen along with his receding hairline. After being admitted to the bar in Kent County, under the tutelage of his father and Judge Joseph A. Wickes, he was elected state's attorney for two terms, from 1875 to 1883.

By the time of the trial, he was married to Jennie B.Y. Shemwell, and they had six children. The successful barrister lived outside Chestertown in a wonderful but oddly architecturally eclectic manse called Lauretum. Designed by Baltimore architect E.G. Lind and built by premier builder Robert K. Pippin in 1881, the odd dwelling survives to the present day as a bed-and-breakfast.

Vickers's forte and preference was criminal law.[116] He was good at it, judging by his case histories. He didn't seem to care which side of the aisle he was on, and he was well respected in his chosen specialty. And it's clear in the Hill murder case that he had taken the lead, both as investigator and prosecutor. He was the state's appointed representative on the case, for which he was ultimately paid $600 by special legislation.[117]

State's attorney William M. Slay had a very different upbringing than his prosecutorial cohort. He wasn't a "native" of Kent County like most of the county's legal gentry, such as Pearce, Smith, James Ricaud, Wickes or his contemporary Vickers.

Born in 1847, he was the son of a Delaware farmer and merchant. His mother died when he was a tot, and he was educated in local public schools and, later, a private school in Dover, Delaware. In 1865, he advanced to Yale University, graduating in 1868 with honors. He then moved to Chestertown, taking a position as a teacher, while studying law with his brother and George Vickers, which is no doubt where he first encountered his co-counsel. He was admitted to the bar in 1872 and thereafter focused almost exclusively on equity cases.[118]

While his background had less of the home-grown luster than that of Vickers or Pearce, he made up for it by marrying into the local legal aristocracy. In December 1885, he was joined in wedlock with Augusta Hynson, daughter of Richard Hynson, one of the highest-caliber lawyers in the community and, as noted, Smith's mentor.

Race and the Hill Murder Trial

Slay and his wife lived with his sister in the old Burchinal House on the southeast corner of Queen and Maple Streets. His law office was located in the Masonic Hall, in the same room where George Vickers once located his own office before the statesman moved to Court Street.

Slay ran for and won the race for state's attorney on the Democratic ticket the year before Hill's murder, though he would hold the position for only a single term.

One person who was slated to help with the prosecution didn't materialize for the trial. That was Attorney General John P. Poe, who was expected to consult with the local prosecutors but was a no-show. Did the governor ask him to stay away?

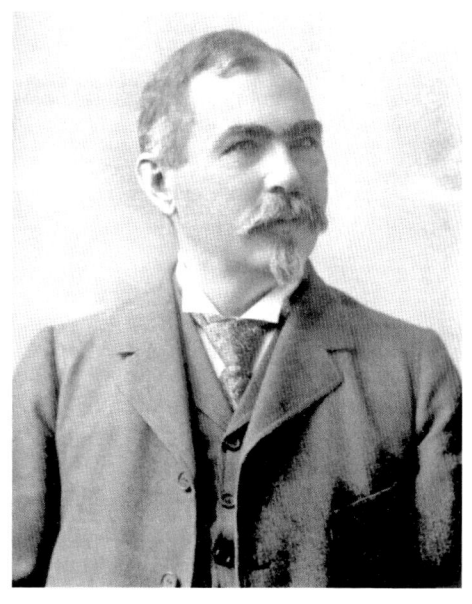

William M. Slay. *Historical Society of Kent County.*

Poe, a Princeton graduate, was a second cousin of Edgar Allan Poe and later supported failed legislation that would have disenfranchised black voters.

And the jury of their peers?

There would be no jury, with or without peers. In those days, no black man or woman was tried before a jury of his or her peers, with a racially diverse selection of jurists chosen from a broad segment of the population. It would be years before blacks would be permitted to sit on a Kent County jury.

There was a chance for equal treatment, back when that "representative of the Fifteenth Amendment" tried to buy that orange. In March 1875, an off-session Congress approved a Civil Rights Act that would guarantee blacks equal treatment by the law, by commercial entities and with government services. Section 4 of the law said that no one could be excluded from a jury because of race:

> *That no citizen possessing all other qualification which are or may be prescribed by law shall be disqualified for service as grand or petit juror in any court of the United States, or of any State, on account of race, color, or previous condition of servitude; and any officer or other person charged with any duty in the selection or summoning of jurors who shall exclude*

or fail to summon any citizen for the cause aforesaid shall, on conviction thereof, be deemed guilty of a misdemeanor, and be fined not more than five thousand dollars.

Emory would no doubt have been pleased to know, and perhaps he did, that Charles Sumner, for whom he was named, introduced the bill. That may explain how and why he got his name.

But in 1883, that law was struck down by the Supreme Court, which held that Congress could not pass a law that favored one race over another. That, the court determined, should be left up to the state. According to the majority opinion:

> The statute of 1875, now adjudged to be unconstitutional, is for the benefit of citizens of every race and color. What the nation, through Congress, has sought to accomplish in reference to that race is what had already been done in every State of the Union for the white race—to secure and protect rights belonging to them as freemen and citizens, nothing more. It was not deemed enough "to help the feeble up, but to support him after." The one underlying purpose of congressional legislation has been to enable the black race to take the rank of mere citizens. The difficulty has been to compel a recognition of the legal right of the black race to take the rank of citizens, and to secure the enjoyment of privileges belonging, under the law, to them as a component part of the people for whose welfare and happiness government is ordained.

African Americans did not benefit from the court's decision, and it paved the way for Jim Crow laws, varying from state to state, which often used subterfuge to deny blacks the rights brought about by the Fourteenth and Fifteenth Amendments. In some cases, literacy tests were required for voters unless they were able to vote before 1865. That meant that a former slave could not vote, but an illiterate white man who voted before 1865 could.

It also meant that states such as Maryland need not include African Americans in jury pools.

Challenges were rare and ineffective until 1931, when Euel Lee (alias Orphan Jones) was tried for the murder of a white family of four in Worcester County. His attorney, Bernard Ades, won a new trial in 1932 based on a number of challenges that included the failure to include blacks in the pool of people from which the jury was chosen. It didn't do any good; Lee was found guilty and ultimately hanged.[119]

Race and the Hill Murder Trial

In 1885, long before Euel Lee faced a jury, William George Weld and A. Robinson White, attorneys for Howard Cooper, charged with rape in Baltimore County, sought a higher court's review on the basis of whites-only juries.

They claimed their client's civil rights were violated because there were no blacks in the jury and that the law failed to allow for blacks in the selection process.

State law, at the time, required the circuit court to draw names for a jury from several lists, one of which was "the white male taxable inhabitants of the county." The circuit court ruled against the lawyers because another list—that of eligible voters—included blacks. The court's logic went thus:

> 1st. That the confining the list of taxables to those only who are voters, taken together with all the provisions of the law, does not operate as an obstacle to the free selection of colored persons as jurors.
>
> 2nd. That if the list of taxables were the only source from which jurors could be selected, the objection that a discrimination was made against colored persons as jurors would be well founded; but as the poll books are likewise furnished on which the white taxables also appear under the more comprehensive classification of voters, together with all the colored voters of the county, practically the distinction appearing on the list of taxable is merged or lost.
>
> 3rd. That the possibility that there might be colored tax-payers who would be selected because of their intelligence, "sobriety and integrity," for the juries, if on the list of taxables, who are not on the poll books, where every male entitled to vote presumably, is, and therefore are excluded from jury duty, is to[o] remote and conjectural to support an allegation of exclusion of colored persons from jury duty, because of race and color, by the laws of Maryland.
>
> The circumstance that a jury may be composed entirely of white men, is not in itself a violation of the rights of colored men. Their constitutional right is, not be kept off the jury because they are colored men.[120]

Even with juries being a whites-only club, and even if the alleged perpetrator were African American, it could be difficult seating a jury in the Victorian age, as was so clearly demonstrated in Kent County only two years before Hill was attacked. This may have influenced the trial.

On Thursday night, November 7, 1889, twenty-seven-year-old Frank Harris, son of a Cross Street oyster peddler, decided to have a night out. He and three friends drank three half pints of whiskey before moving on to Perkins Hall, at the corner of Bridge (Maple) Street.

Injustice on the Eastern Shore

In the hall, where many in the African American community had celebrated holidays; enjoyed entertainment and political speeches; seen tributes; and gathered for parties, weddings and funerals, Harris got into a spat with two men, Alfred Trusty and Edwin Brown. The motive was never really clear, but it is thought that a woman was involved.

When the argument escalated to violence, Harris pulled out a large-caliber pistol that he had "borrowed" from a trunk on the steamer *Emma A. Ford*, where he worked. He pulled the trigger three times: *boom, boom, boom!* And when the acrid stench of gunpowder smoke had cleared, Trusty and Brown were dead on the floor, and the twenty-three other people in the room were shocked beyond belief.

The sheriff soon had Harris in custody, and the wheels of justice quickly moved the case along to trial.

Joseph A. Wickes was on the bench. State's Attorney Smith prosecuted, and Hope H. Barroll—whose mother had grown up on the same street in Millington where the Hills lived—and Richard Hynson defended.

But when the trial started on the second floor of the Kent County courthouse on April 28, 1890, the jury pool was quickly exhausted. Many, according to one local paper, were excluded because they objected to capital punishment. Others had formed well-defined opinions about the accused's guilt or innocence. Finally, twelve talesmen, all white, were selected from the crowd of bystanders, and the jury was empanelled.

The next day, after closing arguments were made, the jury deliberated for twenty minutes and returned a verdict of guilty on the charge of second-degree murder.

Harris was sentenced to a combined eighteen years for the two murders.

Not surprisingly, the local papers missed the opportunity to opine on capital punishment and the endemic prejudicial judicial system. But they didn't miss the chance to rail against guns and whiskey, with a little racial zinger thrown in for good measure:

> *This case, concluded this week in our county court, serves a wholesome lesson to every one, but more especially to the colored people. Pistols and whiskey were brought permanently to the front. Harris indulged in both. He carried a bottle and flourished a revolver. The result is two men shot dead without a moment's warning, and the perpetrator goes to the State prison a convict, to endure many years of degrading servitude. The results are horrible to contemplate. But they are no more than may be expected from such loose and vicious habits. "None but cowards*

and murderers," it is said, "carry deadly weapons." If this saying be true there must be a great many cowards and murderers among certain classes as it is well known that many make a practice of carrying pistols and razors. Such a practice every brave and honorable man should discountenance. It is not only disreputable, it is dangerous, as was so fearfully shown in the case above referred to. Let the colored people quit it, and the white people also if there are any who indulge in such barbarian habits. Officers alone should carry weapons. Other people are justified only in keeping pistols at their homes to repel burglars, thieves, and like trespassers. The law justly stamps crime upon the brow of Harris, and he doubtless feels the weight of his woe, but it can never bring his victims back to life. They both went suddenly into eternity—because this man carried a pistol![121]

All of that was moot in the Hill case.

In fact, the nine charged with the murder of Dr. James Heighe Hill were not tried before a jury of any kind after being indicted by the grand jury. The nine black men and boys accused in the murder of the prominent white doctor would be tried together and judged by three stuffy old white men who had grown up in an era of slavery, racism and discrimination.

That's not to say they were dishonorable men or that they had any doubts about their stations in the theater of local jurisprudence.

Joseph Augustus Wickes of Kent County, John Mitchell Robinson of Caroline County and Frederick Stump of Cecil County composed the three-judge panel that would hear the case, reach a verdict and decide a penalty if the verdict was guilty.

Their resumes were well known on the Eastern Shore.

Wickes was the scion of a Kent family tree that had roots dating to the seventeenth century. Many of his forebears were lawyers and doctors before him, often bearing the same given names. The eldest of the three judges, he was born on September 27, 1826, the son of Colonel Joseph Wickes, a veteran of the War of 1812, and Elizabeth Caroline Chambers.[122] He was the nephew of the late Ezekiel Chambers, a prominent Kent judge, former U.S. senator and rabid supporter of slavery in his day.

Wickes grew up in Chestertown and attended Washington College, like his father before him. He had an abbreviated term there before matriculating to Princeton, where he graduated with honors in 1845. He studied medicine at the University of Maryland, graduating in 1848. He then moved on to study law with his father.[123]

Injustice on the Eastern Shore

Judge Joseph A. Wickes. *Historical Society of Kent County.*

He was admitted to the bar in 1852 and began a practice in Chestertown. But he also jumped into the tumultuous political fray. That year, he was a Democratic presidential elector. However, he changed his pace in 1854 by moving to Cumberland, Allegany County, and began a practice there. A year later, he was elected for a term to the Maryland House of Delegates. Health problems prompted his return to Kent County, if not for the better climate then for proximity to family. After the Civil War, he was involved in rewriting the state constitution, helping to shape new judiciary guidelines. In 1867, he was elected, along with Stump and Robinson, to a first fifteen-year term as a judge in the second circuit. All were elected to second terms in 1882.[124]

Judge Wickes married Anna Maria Tilghman, who died in 1864 after producing five children. It was a difficult year for him—the same year his illustrious father died.

The judge's second wife was Ann Rebecca Wickes, a cousin. They lived in the grand brick manse on the corner of High and Water Streets built by Samuel Wallis or another of his family in 1769 and acquired by the Wickes family in 1831. It is to this day called the Wallis-Wickes House and stands as a noble sentry to a cluster of homes dating to the town's colonial era.

His second wife died in 1889, but it's unlikely that left him a lonely man in the sunset of his life. He was socially visible and as connected as the imprint of his family—denizens of the county for two centuries—could be.

Wickes was also involved in town politics at one time or another as a commissioner and was a board member of the Second National Bank, appointed in 1890. For many years, he was president of the board of visitors and governors of Washington College. He was a former slave owner[125] and had served as a lieutenant in the militia but apparently did not actively participate in the war.

In November 1891, Wickes handed down the death sentence for Thomas Thompson, a black man found guilty by a jury of the murder of another black man, William "Bully" Adams, on August 22 of that year.

Wickes was sixty-five at the time of the Hill murder; however, whatever his early health problems, he would live well into the twentieth century, giving up his final breath at the age of eighty-nine.

John Mitchell Robinson was the son of Peter and Sarah Mitchell Robinson, born in 1827 in Tuckahoe Neck, Caroline County. At the age of sixteen, he started at Dickinson College, graduating in 1847. Afterward, he read law in the offices of Carmichael & Brown in Centreville.[126] In a rapid rise in the legal realm of the Eastern Shore, in 1851, he was appointed deputy attorney general for Kent and Queen Anne's Counties by Attorney General Robert J. Brent.

In his first year in that role, he prosecuted Kent County's most sensational murder case up to that time: the Cosden case, in which William Cosden; his wife, Mary Ann; her sister Rebecca; and his sister Amanda were murdered. The outrage, in February of that year, was perpetrated by four bounders—Abraham Taylor, William Shelton, Nicholas Murphy and Stephen Shaw—who teamed up on a rampage to rape and plunder.

According to James A. Pearce, writing about Taylor's trial many years later in a report for the Maryland Bar Association, Robinson

> *thought it his duty to take the leading part in the trial, and he prosecuted the case so ably and fearlessly as to excite the admiration of the people, and to establish at once a reputation for which years are often required…So thorough had been the presentation of that case, and so general the belief that the verdict was correct, that it foreshadowed the result in the other two cases, though they all denied guilt to the last.*

Robinson was subsequently elected as Queen Anne's County's state's attorney. He was elected a judge of the Third Judicial Circuit in 1864.

He was sixty-five at the time of the Hill case.

Judge Frederick Stump was fifty-five at the time of Hill's death. He lived at Perry Point, the Cecil County abode that his parents and grandparents inhabited before him. They were all descendants of a Stump who had come to the area in 1700. At one point, he was part owner of the *Cecil Democrat*.

He was also a graduate of Princeton, class of 1859, and was admitted to the Cecil County bar in 1861. He was one of ten children.

His brother was on the Supreme Bench of Baltimore City, and another brother was a doctor.[127]

In later years, he would be referred to as "one of the most popular men on the bench in Maryland."[128]

All three were sage men who had seen many cases, both mundane and complex, and had worked together on numerous occasions even before their judicial nominations. Wickes served with Robinson as early as 1863.[129]

The Kent County courthouse was fairly new compared to venerable abodes of justice in nearby counties. It was the third courthouse to be located on the site. The first one was likely built sometime after Chestertown was established in 1706. It was burned down in 1720. The burned structure was replaced with a new building that cost fifty-five thousand pounds of tobacco, the smokable leaf being the legal tender of the day and valued at about two pennies to the pound. That building was updated about 1846. The Martenet Map of 1860, complemented by drawings, shows a rounded-end structure. But by 1859, when the surveys were undertaken for Simon J. Martenet's Baltimore mapping firm, it was thought to be beyond repair, and the legislature authorized $12,000 for a new one. That fine brick structure is now the western half of the current courthouse. The newest section was built in 1969 over a portion of the old town graveyard.

The "old part" of the complex seen today, the 1860 courthouse, includes the district court upstairs—the courtroom of 1892—and land records and the register of wills on the main floor of the building. There is also a basement where the court commissioners meet, but it is otherwise used for storage. An attic provides additional storage space.

The interior of the courtroom was modernized in 1888, with a railing running crosswise through the room's center enclosing the bench and jury box. Another rail separated the jury box from the bar. The changes were just a few of those requested by judges, attorneys and officers of the circuit court, presented in a petition earlier that year by lawyer Charles T. Westcott.

The courthouse grounds had a tree-shaded "green" on one side, where children often played and which at least one clerk, in the 1860s, made every attempt to beautify with plantings.

At the time of the trial, the "front" faced west, toward High Street and what is now Monument Plaza. The Cross Street side was catty-corner to the county jail, the forced habitat of the nine to be tried.

Race and the Hill Murder Trial

In the week before the trial, Chestertown was bound up in the weeklong pomp of the celebration of the 400th anniversary of Columbus's great discovery. It was one of the biggest celebrations in the nation, and Kent Countians were no slouchers at marking the quadricentennial.

Wednesday, October 12, the actual holiday, started the festivities with a bicycle parade, organized by the Chestertown Cycling Club, and activities continued throughout the week with banners flying from every public building, school functions and a reading of the presidential proclamation.

Unfortunately, the *Kent News* and the *Chestertown Transcript* were unable to report all the Columbus Day activities. The *Transcript* apologized. That news was being forced out by the quantity of reporting on the Hill case. In Kent County, as excited as the locals were about the great mariner, they knew it was just the opening act for the real show coming up at the courthouse.

THE TRIAL

The fall term of the circuit court was called to order on Monday, October 17, presided over initially by Judge Wickes. It began with the selection of the grand jury, whose purpose, among other things, was to pass down indictments. Cornelius J. Scott was chosen as foreman. A prominent surveyor of Galena, he had held several offices in Kent, including county commissioner, judge of the orphan's court and school commissioner. He filled all of the offices with fidelity, and he was highly respected. At the age of seventy-one, he was one of the last alive who had served on one of the Cosden murder trial juries.

Also on the panel was Adam F. Huey, who owned the shop where Hill's dogcart had stopped in Massey. And there was George B. Westcott—not the prominent Chestertown banker who had died several years before, but his relative and namesake, son of Nicholas G. Westcott. The others included William Morris, Benjamin F.H. Caulk, Joseph Turner, Daniel E. Jewell, John A. Groves, J.M.J. Byron, William T. Maslin, Frank H. Ruth, James B. Crowding, James P. Wickes, Charles S. Hill, Garrett Foxwell, William D. Pennington, James R. Jones, Thomas W. Skirven, Colin F. Taylor, William E. Keyser, George Beck, Samuel Todd and James L. Beck.

It's uncertain if the Charles S. Hill on the grand jury was the murder victim's brother, but it appears to be so. He is the only person by that name in Kent County listed on both the 1880 and 1900 censuses; if so, it would add an unquestionable component of bias. However, there is no indication, in news articles or the court documents, that this was considered in any way unusual.

Race and the Hill Murder Trial

Wickes instructed the grand jury's members:

> *Before you retire, gentlemen of the grand jury, it is my duty to direct your attention to those cases which you will be called upon to investigate and in reference to which you should receive the advice and instruction of the court. Ordinarily, it is only necessary to direct your attention to the rules which should govern your deliberations, as the cases before you are usually of a plain character the law applicable to them familiar to you…*
>
> *I am informed that eight or nine persons were present when the terrible deed was committed. How many, and who, participated in committing the act, either by striking the blows which caused the death of Dr. Hill, or who aided or assisted, or in any manner encouraged those who assailed him, you must determine, after a careful and patient examination of the witnesses who will be before you.*
>
> *To constitute the crime of murder, it is not necessary that the party charged should strike the fatal blow; but all who in any manner aid or assist or counsel or encourage the one who strikes the blow, are equally guilty. There is reason to suppose that a plot to murder Dr. Hill had been entered into, by those who assailed him, with others who were not present, when the terrible deed was committed. If such is the fact, if there are others—no matter how many—who entered into a plot or agreement to take his life, or who advised or counselled [sic] those who assailed him, they are guilty of murder, although not present when the fatal blow was struck. I charge you, gentlemen, to probe this matter to the bottom. Calmly and patiently investigate the facts and bring to light every circumstance connected with*

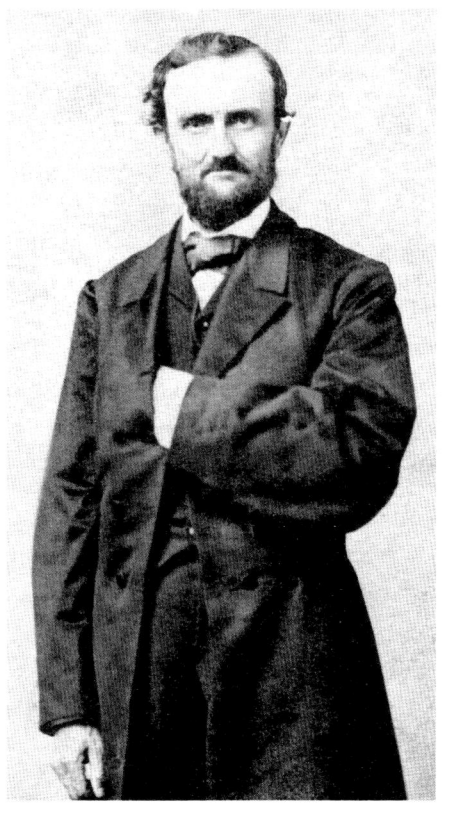

Cornelius J. Scott. *Courtesy of Mary Woodland Tan.*

that brutal murder. Let no guilty man escape, but let all who participated, directly or indirectly, in that terrible tragedy be punished.[130]

Wickes also used the opportunity and his lofty perch on the bench that day to rail against the "mob of disguised men" that had lynched James Taylor the preceding May. He described the act as an assault on the Constitution and the Bill of Rights, which, however heinous the crime committed, "declares that no man ought to be deprived of his life, liberty or property but by the judgment of his peers and by the law of the land." He also compelled the grand jury to bring charges against anyone who took part:

Lynching is a reproach to any community; it impeaches the adequacy of our institutions for the punishment of crime; it brutalizes those who participate in it and brings shame and disgrace upon our Christian civilization. It is my duty to say to you, that all who participated in committing that act are guilty of murder, and it is your duty to ascertain, if possible, who are the guilty parties and to indict them for the crime which they have committed.[131]

That would never happen. They found the sheriff blameless in that case and were unable (or uninterested in trying) to identify even one of the lynchers.[132]

After Wickes's preamble, the grand jury considered several cases that were outstanding, including a shooting, a bigamy and another case about whiskey sales, all of which would have been interesting to court watchers had not the Hill murder proceedings so dominated everyone's attention.

One of those lesser cases stood out, at least as a jocular counterpoint. That was the bigamy case.

It was taken up on Tuesday, the state versus Joseph Goff, who brought a "razzle-dazzle" show, operating out of a flashy wagon, to Chestertown's market plaza in August. While in town, he married Ida Cooper. It was later determined that he was already married to Lizzie Cross, whom he had wed in 1879 in Pennsylvania. The matter reached a boiling point when wife number one, with children in tow, arrived in Chestertown looking for her husband.

Hell hath no fury like a woman scorned, particularly when she has hungry children following along. She filed a writ.

Goff claimed the first marriage hadn't been properly certified. At the trial, the jury would have none of it, and after hearing the case for twenty minutes, its members found the flim-flam man guilty. He was sentenced to five years in the penitentiary, which, in all likelihood, helped neither wife.

Race and the Hill Murder Trial

This and the other minor cases were dispatched by October 19, and the case that had everyone's attention was set to begin the following day with the assignment of the attorneys.

With all the sensation—Columbus Day, the upcoming presidential election and a trial of national relevance—it is surprising that anyone had time to mark the partial solar eclipse that began just after noon and lasted for a couple hours on October 20. But the sky was clear, and the county was enjoying an Indian summer. The eclipse was watched by "many persons, and by means of smoke glass, beautiful views of the solar phenomenon were enjoyed," reported the *Transcript*.

On Friday, October 21, the grand jury quickly found "true bills" against the eight main alleged Hill murder conspirators. More important in the minds of many, John Potts was added to the list on Saturday, October 22. That hadn't been a certainty because the evidence against him was slim. But it was generally thought by "judge citizen" that Potts was the "most guilty of the guilty parties."[133]

Noted the *Transcript* in its October 26 "daily" extra edition:

> *The Potts brothers were considered two of the most dangerous negroes in the vicinity of Millington, and owing to the delay in removing the obscurity which for so long kept him in the background, it was feared that John Potts might escape altogether.*

At ten o'clock on Tuesday morning, October 25, 1892, the three dour, berobed judges made their way down the second-floor hall and into the "uncomfortably crowded" courtroom. It was the first day of trial. As they made their way down the aisle, the din in the courtroom died down—as it did throughout the community (the gossip was over, the guesswork was done)—and the process of justice was now underway. About ten thirty, Sheriff Plummer, assisted by Chestertown's police officer, a constable and four deputies, brought the nine defendants into the courtroom. They were:

- FLETCHER WILLIAMS, twenty-four to twenty-seven years old at the time of the attack. He is not readily found on the 1870 or 1880 censuses but is said to have been Charles Emory's half brother. He lived and worked for Charles Rolph in 1892. He is described as five feet, six inches tall but was probably slightly taller, based on the *Philadelphia Record* drawing made from John South's photograph. He was described as "dark skinned" or "copper-colored."[134] He was often referred to as the ringleader and was accused of stabbing Hill in the throat.

Injustice on the Eastern Shore

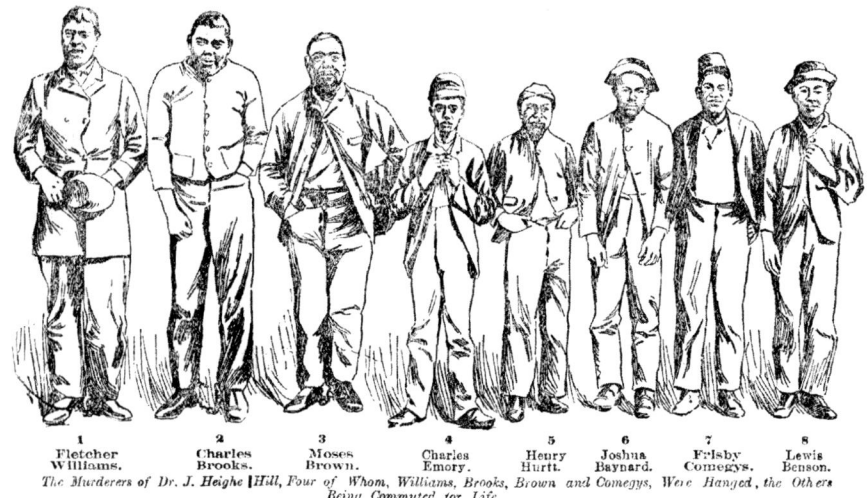

A drawing of the suspects in the murder of Dr. J. Heighe Hill. *From the* Philadelphia Record, *January 14, 1893.*

- CHARLES "BUCK" BROOKS, listed variously as twenty-one and twenty-eight years old at the time of the attack. He might have been the son of Walter Brooks, of near Crumpton, in whose household a nine-year-old Charles is listed in the 1880 census. That would have made him twenty-one at the time of the attack. However, in 1892, Brooks said his parents lived near Golts, so it's not certain his father was Walter. According to the *Sun*, he was twenty-seven.[135] He was described as five feet, four inches tall, but in the *Record* drawing, and in the picture from which that portion of the drawing was made, he is about as tall as Williams. Brooks was the leader of the Hill assault. If he was Walter's son, he might have had more of a motive for the attack since the Potts family may have lived nearby. Could there have been another, more racial element to his passionate attack on Hill? In 1881, a man named Frank Brooks attacked Samuel W. Aldridge, a prominent white farmer of near Chesterville, a Kent community with ample interaction with Crumpton and Millington. Aldridge, a former slave owner, criticized Brooks's work and, according to the laborer, was about to attack him when Brooks struck him with the handle of a pitchfork, knocking the farmer unconscious.[136] Brooks was found guilty of assault with intent to murder and sentenced to eight years in the penitentiary. "Frank Brooks" might have been related to Charles. Brooks was described as "copper-colored," with partly shaved hair with a tuft.[137] However, there is no "tuft" in his photo, which indicates that he removed it before the picture was taken. He said he lived with Thomas Donahoe near Golts at the time of Hill's death.

- MOSES BROWN, twenty-eight to thirty at the time of the assault. A nineteen-year-old Moses Brown is listed as a boarder with laborer Benjamin Warwick, in Kent's First District, on the 1880 census. A seven-year-old Brown and another named Samuel Brown are listed in the household of Augusta Camp, of Chestertown, in the 1870 census. Augusta was the widow of Colonel William Camp, who died in 1864. Augusta Camp owned ten slaves in October of that year. Among them were adults Emory Brown, Caroline and Laura Brown. Slave children included Milton and, in what seems to be a crude, slave owner–style jest, Stonewall J. Brown.[138] Moses Brown was not listed in the slave inventory. It is possible, however, due to the proximity in age, that Moses was actually the two-year-old Milton. Whether that's so, it seems likely that Brown was born as a Camp family slave. He was apparently the only one of the suspects who was married. He said his wife had had eight children, all but one of whom had died. In the photograph used for the *Record* drawing, he appears to be about three inches shorter than Brooks and Williams. He had a pencil-thin, manicured mustache. The *Transcript* described him as "stupid" but good-natured. The *Sun* described him as "black as night."[139] At the time of the murder, he lived and worked for William H. Ford.
- FRISBY COMEGYS, born about 1875, who lived most of his life in the Millington area. He was the youngest son of Samuel and Sallie Comegys. His parents are found in the 1860, 1870 and 1880 censuses in the First District. Comegys, whose first name was also spelled Frizby, was also called Fritz and Friz. He was accused, with Perry Bradshaw, of holding Hill's horse when the attack took place.
- CHARLES SUMNER EMORY, the only one of the suspects with a middle name, after the fashion of the white abolitionist senator, born about 1877. He was the son of Samuel Emory, a laborer of Millington. It's uncertain who his mother was; his father remarried about 1884. None of the family is found in the 1880 census in Kent or Queen Anne's Counties. However, Emory was said to be Fletcher Williams's half brother.[140] And the penitentiary log

indicates he was born in Queen Anne's County but was a resident of Kent. On the *Record* drawing, he is one of the shortest and slimmest of the eight prisoners. Emory lived with Molly Cacy in Millington early on in his life but then began living with Augustus Hendrickson five years before the Hill murder. He continued in Hendrickson's employ until his incarceration. He was five feet, two inches tall.[141]

- HENRY HURTT, thought to be the youngest of the group. He was said to be thirteen or fourteen at the time of the assault, but he told a *Kent News* reporter in January 1893 that he was sixteen. He was the son of George and Clara Hurtt, but his father, apparently, had died by the time of the trial since the youngster claimed only a mother living at Golt's Station. At the time of the incident, he lived and worked in the household of Dr. Enoch G. Clark on a farm between Millington and Massey. He said he also had worked for James Thompson; Lou Hayes at Galena; and at Joseph Peacock's. Hurtt said he attended school—probably at the AME church in Millington or Golts—for three or four years and could read and write. He was five feet, two and three-quarters inches tall.

- JOSHUA BAYNARD, whose parentage is uncertain. A seventeen-year-old Joshua Baynard is found in the 1880 census in the family of Daniel and Susan Baynard, but the age variation represents a large discrepancy since the suspect was said to be sixteen at the time of the murder. He said his father worked for John Reese. Baynard—the name was also spelled Bainard—worked for farmer William C. Rolph. Based on the *Record* drawing, he was of average build. He was five feet, two and a half inches tall.

- LEWIS BENSON, born about 1876, the son of George and Elizabeth "Lizzie" Benson. He lived on William Ford's farm. Little else is known about him. His parents lived for many years at Golt's Station, raising a large family. They are both listed on the 1910 census. An "S. Benson," possibly Lewis's brother Samuel, is interred in the Lee's Chapel cemetery at Golts. Curiously, in the *Record* drawing, it seems that Hurtt and Benson are switched around, based on the description of the January 1893 photo session from which it is likely that two photographic prints were used to create the drawing. If so, Benson would have been the shortest of the suspects, and this is borne out by Maryland prison records, which indicate he was four feet, eleven and a half inches tall.

Race and the Hill Murder Trial

- JOHN POTTS, suspected by many of masterminding the plot, born about 1855 near Long Marsh in Queen Anne's County. He was the third eldest of five sons of William—who was possibly a Civil War veteran—and Sarah "Sallie" Potts. The family moved to the vicinity of Blanco, a couple miles from Sandtown, between 1860 and 1870. A dilapidated Victorian-era farmhouse is still located on the property. Potts and his brother Joseph were involved in the Campbell affair, the motive behind the Hill murder.

The trial began with the reading of the pro forma indictments by Samuel G. Fisher, clerk of court, who stated that the conspirators, "him the said James H. Hill, then and there in manner and form aforesaid, feloniously, willfully and of their malice aforethought, [they] did kill and murder contrary to the form of the act of assembly in such cases, made and provided against the peace, government and dignity of the State."[142]

Then there was the business of calling the witnesses. Judge Robinson exclaimed that it appeared that the whole county "had been gotten" as witnesses.

In fact, the list of state's witnesses, without lawmen and experts, contained thirty-six names. The defense had an additional twenty names lined up to testify.[143]

Witnesses early on included those Millington residents, such as Johnson, Ahern, Porter and Price, who related what they saw in the hours after Hill was attacked. Other witnesses placed the various defendants in the timeline of the killing and described their movements afterward. Witnesses were paid "for their service" if they testified. It was a common practice then as now. It cost $426.69 for witness fees by the time the case came to a close.[144]

As the testimony was given, the prisoners sat in "sullen silence," according to the newspaper. In the meantime, the proceedings were watched this day, and throughout the whole trial, by Samuel Hill, the victim's father.

Arrelee Hill came over from her parents' home on the Friday before the trial began. She had apparently moved there after her husband's funeral. Samuel Hill told the *Sun* reporter that he was hopeful that his daughter-in-law would be able to get through the "ordeal" of the trial, "although her husband's death in such a horrible way was an awful shock to her nervous system."[145]

However, she did not testify, "owing to her delicate health." Slay asked her questions before the trial, and her written answers were submitted. They were primarily about when Hill left the house; she said about nine o'clock that night. And she noticed the return of the dogcart about three thirty the next morning.

INJUSTICE ON THE EASTERN SHORE

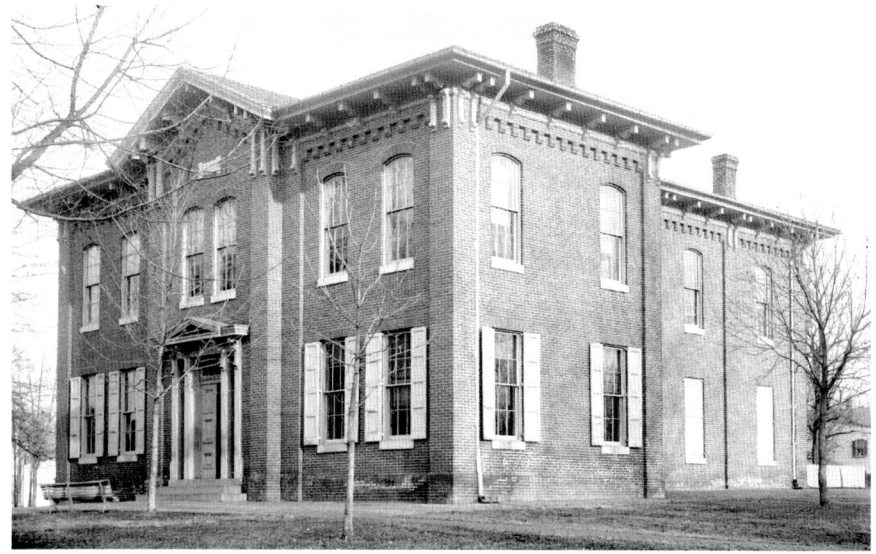

The Kent County courthouse as it appeared about 1900. The front entrance faced High Street. *Historical Society of Kent County.*

The doctors testified to the victim's condition, to their ministrations and to the cause of death.

Farmer Charles Rolph, with whom Williams and Baynard lived, said Williams had Hill's hat in his possession the day after the attack and claimed he had found it on the road and thought it belonged to a man named Joe Coburn.

Merchant Henry S. Cook said he saw Brooks, Brown, Baynard and Emory in his store on Saturday night about ten o'clock. They all left at the same time, he added.

Cook, who was forty-two at the time of the attack, was the proprietor of the small general store at the town's four corners, which he had purchased from McWhorter in 1890. He was McWhorter's brother-in-law, the saloon man married to Cook's sister, Martha. He lived in a fine new home on Cypress Street with his wife, Sally. The son of a butcher, Cook served terms as a Millington town commissioner both before and after the Hill murder and likely was among those involved in the Potts incident, at McWhorter's oyster saloon, when Campbell was killed.

Professor William P. Tonry, a Baltimore chemist, also testified.

An Irish immigrant who grew up in Canada, Tonry was a Union veteran of the Civil War who turned to chemistry as a career. He went into private practice in 1869 after he was fired from his job in the Surgeon General's Office.[146]

It wasn't the first time he had testified in Kent County; his testimony in the 1887 poisoning case of Deborah Bradshaw, who lived outside Millington, helped seal the conviction of her granddaughter for murder. His name was in the local paper long before that. He was mentioned in an article in the January 15, 1876 edition of the *Kent News* about a discourse at the Maryland Institute on the topic of improving the safety of kerosene.

His expertise, however, was poison and blood, long before blood typing[147] and DNA testing.

Tonry testified that he analyzed blood on the pants that Williams had worn the night of the attack. He said that bloodstains found in a pocket indicated that a bloody handkerchief had been placed there. He said that no blood had been found on Brooks's coat. Blood was found on the handle of Williams's two-bladed, ten-cent Barlow knife, but the witness couldn't identify the blood other than as being that of a mammal.

William Darrell said he saw John Potts standing near Johnson's office when the Cleveland meeting was taking place, but no one seemed to be able to place him at the scene of the crime. Darrell said he was out talking to James Spear and Charles P. Loper, at the four corners, when he saw the doctor leaving town. He started out over the same road about thirty minutes later. At Ford's gate, he claimed to have seen seven or eight black men, and one hailed him, but he thought they were calling someone else.

One thing that was never pinned down: how did the perpetrators know that Hill would be on the road? The original story was that John Reese, the messenger for Hill's patient Shaw, told Fletcher Williams that Hill had a house call. Reported the *Transcript* in June, "Williams, on his way to Millington about 7 o'clock, met Reese, the boy from Mr. Shaw's, who was sent to Millington for the doctor. The boy, while in conversation with Williams, told him that he was going for Dr. Hill, as one of Mr. Shaw's children were sick."

Reese later testified that he told only Willie Legg, with whom he left the message for Hill's clerk, Watson Spear. However, Reese said at the trial that there was an unidentified black man in Hill's store when he left the message.

Was young Reese lying over concerns that he would be blamed for Hill's death? Or was the doctor being spied on? If it's true that Reese told only Legg and didn't think the unidentified man heard him leave the message, could Legg have given out the information about the house call when Reese left?

Wheelwright Howard King, who lived with his wife in Power's house on Sassafras Street, said he saw "a crowd of negroes" and overheard one say, "If I get in one on him with this I'll fix the s[on] of a b[itch]." He said he recognized Williams in the group.[148]

After King's testimony, the court adjourned until the next day.

The following morning, people started filling the courtroom an hour before proceedings began, anxious to find out how the trial would play out and get a seat for the show. Many had no way of knowing whether there would be a verdict during this session. By 9:30 a.m., when the proceedings began, the room was packed.

The first up was Perry Bradshaw, who had turned state's evidence, being the first to detail, step by step, the account of the attack on Hill.

Born about 1877, he was the son of illiterate laborer Samuel Bradshaw and his wife, Harriet. The family moved around. In 1870, they lived in Sandfield. By 1880, the family had moved to Golts. Perry was described as a "coal black bullet-headed boy with two tufts of wool standing out like horns from his forehead."[149]

His statement would be damning. He testified that before the attack he had joined a group at Hilyard's store. They were "talking about killing a man," he said, but he wasn't sure whom they were talking about. He testified that Williams said, "I'm going to kill a man when I go out of town to-night."[150]

Bradshaw went over the details of the attack, playing with his hat as he testified. He said that they had met Hill's cart, that he and Comegys had held Hill's horse and that Brooks had reached down and grabbed something—he knew not what—and struck the doctor in the head with it. Williams, he said, stabbed the doctor with a knife.

Bradshaw said that afterward Brown and Benson left the group, and the rest went toward Cooper's house. Brooks, Comegys, Williams and Emory went in for a while. Comegys and Emory then came back out and went to Hendrickson's house. Brooks and Williams returned from Cooper's house, and the five of them—Brooks, Williams, Baynard, Bradshaw and Hurtt—continued up the road. During the walk, Williams found Hill's hat. Brooks found a cuff with a button in it. Bradshaw said he found a shoe. After that, Bradshaw testified, they split up, with Hurtt and Bradshaw catching a ride with Carroll Clark and the others heading off to Rolph's place.[151]

More than anything, Bradshaw indicated that the plot to kill the doctor was hatched as a conspiracy and that after the attack, they gathered to make sure everyone had their story straight.

Race and the Hill Murder Trial

What the fifteen-year-old didn't do was implicate Potts. He named the other eight (nine with himself) as those who were at Ford's Hill on the night of the attack. One reason that Slay and Vickers had given him immunity was for testimony that Potts was involved in the conspiracy. However, when the teen testified, he declined to implicate Potts.

In cross-examination, Bradshaw said he had gotten involved, held the horse and gone along with the coverup for fear that Williams would hurt him.[152]

The other defendants either testified or previous statements were read, including the confessions of Comegys, Benson and Baynard, which differed in only some of the details. Oddly, Benson confirmed his presence at the attack, even when the others indicated that he wasn't there.

Brooks's May 12 statement was given.

Williams denied being involved in the attack. He claimed that if there was any blood on his clothes, it was from a horse. He said he had seen Dr. Hill in Millington on the night of the murder but saw someone else's dogcart on the road.

Also read into the record was Brown's original confession, given to Bates in May, which he later recanted. He told Bates that Williams had hatched the plot, knew that the doctor had been summoned and wanted to kill him because of the Campbell affair. Brown said Williams told him, "Tom Campbell has been killed and no one has been found out, and I will kill the doctor, and will not be found out."

Brown said he thought that Williams was "funning." He also confessed to being the second one to "stick" Hill with a knife.

But he didn't testify to any of that during the trial.

Benjamin Benton, William Harrington, James Mannon and Charles Hurtt all testified that they had seen Potts looking into the window when the Cleveland Club met on that fateful night. However, there was no other testimony that connected Potts to the murder or put him at the scene of the attack.

The *Transcript* that was published the next day opined that Potts, "the arch mover in the crime," would probably get off. The paper also felt that a conspiracy had yet to be proven.

Court adjourned at three o'clock that afternoon, and Robinson announced that a verdict would be rendered the next day.

Because of that, by the time the proceedings began at nine thirty on Thursday morning, October 27, the courthouse had reached the point of bursting.

Long before the first crack of the gavel snapped the restive crowd to attention, witnesses, friends, relatives, the press and the curious, "from every section of Kent County" and, indeed, from other counties and outside the state, filled every available seat and then every available bit of space to set two feet together. Judges Robinson and Stump made their way with difficulty through the crowd and down the middle aisle to the bench. Wickes had to be helped over the railing. A. O'D. Hayward, the youthful reporter for the *Baltimore American*, and W.K. Richardson of the *Sun* had to be physically hauled over the shoulders of the crowd, mosh-pit style, to get a position close on the other side of the railing.[153] However, court crier John H. Greenwood told them that they would have to move when the judges appeared. And soon after, noted the *Transcript* reporter,

> *the surging mass of humanity which filled the courtroom when the judges took their places on the bench, was something unparalleled in the judicial history of the county, with possibly one exception, and that was when Thomas Hyer and Yankee Sullivan were tried for dueling at Plum Point in 1849.*

The attorneys had trouble getting seated, and Greenwood ultimately had to evict the newspaper reporters to standing room to make space for them.

Fifteen minutes after the judges were situated, the nine defendants were trundled into the room. They were all quiet. Brooks seemed to be unconcerned, apparently unaware of the gravity of the situation. Not so Williams, who "trembled visibly" when he entered the room. "It's very cold here," he said.[154]

All had been nervous the night before.

The reporter for the *Baltimore Weekly Herald* later reported that the younger defendants were talking and smiling at first.

After they were seated in the prisoners' "dock," bailiffs demanded quiet from the crowd, and Greenwood announced the opening of the court. Almost immediately, there was a "profound" silence.

According to the *Herald*, the judges then "engaged in a few minutes' earnest whispered conversation and then consulted a number of law books." Robinson, presiding judge on this day, then announced the verdict in "a clear calm and deliberate voice":

> *After having carefully considered all the evidence in the case, we pronounce Joshua Ba[y]nard, Louis Benson, Henry Hurtt, Moses Brown, Frisby Comegys, Charles Brooks, Fletcher Williams and Charles S. Emory, each is, and all are, guilty of murder in the first degree.*[155]

Race and the Hill Murder Trial

At this, there was some applause from the crowd while there was some surprise that the five younger prisoners were held accountable for the murder at the same level as the elder three. The noise of celebration from the audience was short-lived as Robinson expressed his displeasure at the outburst from the gallery.

The eight, who were now convicted murderers, seemed dazed and initially didn't realize that their futures suddenly had taken grim turns. They couldn't grasp the ramifications. There was no such question among the crowd; while the sentence would be delivered at a later date, there was no doubt what it would be. At this time, state law mandated the death penalty for a conviction of first-degree murder.

> *The prisoners did not seem to realize what was transpiring and the boys were unconcerned as ever. Of the three men Brooks was the most calm. Williams was very nervous and complained of feeling cold, while Benson was trembling all over. Every face was turned toward the prisoners and there was much commotion.*[156]

The crowd in the courtroom also expressed its outrage that Potts was not mentioned, and the bailiffs had to restore order before Robinson could continue.

Robinson tried to quickly douse the anger now brought into tight focus on Potts.

"There has been no evidence elicited by the prosecution to show any complicity of John Potts with the murder, and we declare him not guilty," he said.

Potts, described as "bright and intelligent," was initially relieved to be set free. He was free to leave, but he wasn't smiling as he realized he might have trouble getting away without a trial by "Judge Lynch." In fact, the rumors were already flying.

"If violence," said Robinson, "is to be thus offered, no man is safe, and the law becomes a dead letter. Anyone offering violence to the prisoner would be guilty of murder in the first degree."

Wickes added that he "hoped that the people and the county might escape the disgrace of having mob law thus exercised. When the majesty of the law is thus outraged, and summary punishment is administered by an infuriated mob, it was a situation to be most earnestly deplored."

Wickes warned that the grand jury had not yet been discharged and would be available if necessary. In other words, would-be lynchers should beware because they, too, could be charged with a crime if there were violence against the acquitted man.

Injustice on the Eastern Shore

After the Taylor lynching, did anyone really believe his lofty but hollow words?

Noted the *Transcript* the next day, "The Court scarcely believed that there was any body of people who would desire for one moment to offer violence to the [Potts] who had been duly indicted, tried and acquitted."

Meanwhile, the victim's family, including Hill's father, was upset that Potts wasn't found guilty and that two other men, Henry Hynson and John Harrison, were not charged. The latter two testified that they were driving a milk wagon when they passed the doctor on the road, thinking a drunk was driving the dogcart, since the body was oddly slumped.

Samuel Hill and sons were in the courtroom at the time the verdict was read. But the Hills did not agitate for mob justice for Potts, Hynson or Harrison.

As soon as the proceedings ended for the day, the spectators moved out to the courthouse yard to see the prisoners returned to the jail. The crowd was estimated at about five hundred, but Vickers went out to talk to some of them and determined that it was curiosity, not the urge for retribution, that motivated those waiting. Nonetheless, officials prudently waited several hours before moving the prisoners back to the jail, after most of the crowd had broken up.

During the interim, the youngest of the prisoners asked when they would be going home. It was an indication of their naïveté—they didn't understand what had happened.

The *Transcript* reporter asked Brooks if he would rather be husking corn.

"I've been eating so much corn that I want no more corn," Brooks responded.

When asked by a reporter if he had anything to say, Williams lashed out against Bradshaw and Brown, accusing them of lying.

Williams, Brooks and Brown, in leg irons, were placed in the lower cells. "The boys"—Baynard, Comegys, Hurtt, Emory and Benson—were put in an upper cell together.

The older prisoners must have realized what the day meant. The *Transcript* stated the next day that Brown, Williams and Brooks "were depressed." Brooks apparently broke down when fifty cents, left by his father, was handed to him through the bars.

In fact, many people were surprised that the four youngest didn't have their charges downgraded.

That night was tense and unexpectedly quiet, noted the paper.

Darkness fell like a curtain that evening, with only a first-quarter moon to cast dim shadows. There was no sign of violence that night, and "it is to be hoped, as it is to be expected, that the law-abiding citizens of the county

RACE AND THE HILL MURDER TRIAL

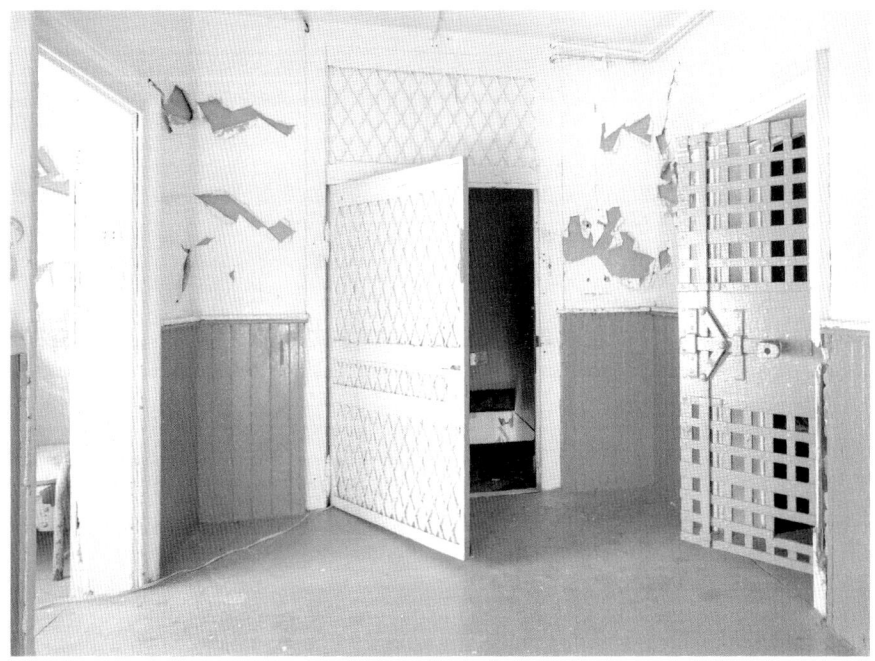

This photo of the Kent County jail after it was abandoned offers a hint of the stark nature of the facility. *Courtesy of Tyler Campbell.*

will bow in humble submission to the majesty of the law, and see to it that no shadow of reproach is cast upon our people and county by mob violence in any way," opined the *Transcript*.

Nevins, the hired detective, was asked to remain until Monday to help keep an eye on the crowds.[157] But for the most part, there was a sense that the climax of the Hill murder sensation had been reached and the rest was just boilerplate.

The second act in a grim theater was over, perhaps, but the script in this real-life drama still held some surprises.

THE MERITS OF HANGING EIGHT

The sentencing came almost as an anticlimax, four days later, on the afternoon of Halloween Day—a propitious omen. Just as a solar eclipse had begun the trial, it ended on All Saints Day. The eight men and boys were brought into the courtroom at three o'clock, and mirroring their cell arrangements, they were separated with the three men as one group and the five teens another. They sat upright in their chairs and listened intently as Judge Wickes passed sentence:

> *A more atrocious and cruel deed has never been committed. With unrelenting ferocity you attacked and killed a man who had never injured you, and whose only offense was that he'd performed a sworn duty. By that cruel act you have deprived the community of a useful citizen; you have blasted the life of the young wife, whose happiness depended on the love of the man you murdered; you have robbe*[d] *her infant child of the father, upon whose support and guidance she would have depended; you have crushed the heart of the aged parents, who, with just pride, had watched over the career of the son in his old age and had seen him enter upon a career of honor and usefulness. As with the patriarch of old, all rise up to comfort him, but he will not be comforted, and well may he exclaim, "I will go down to the grave unto my son mourning."*
>
> *When we consider the motive that led you to commit that fearful crime, and the savage ferocity with which you attacked and assassinated upon the public highway a peaceful citizen, it is not a matter of surprise, that*

> *popular feeling was roused to madness; and that the strong arm of the law might not be able to save you from the hands of an infuriated people, but happily, wiser counsel prevailed, and the people of this county, by practicing that self-restraint which should always govern those who respect the law, forbore to attempt any violence. The charge against you has been submitted to judicial investigations by which you secured the right, which every man should have, of a fair and impartial trial in the court of justice.*
>
> *During the short time you have to live, do not expect human aid, but look to a higher power for forgiveness. You have forfeited your lives by committing the terrible crime of which you have been convicted, and you cannot expect relief from any human power. During the brief remnant of your lives, seek to make your peace with an offended God, who will extend mercy to those who truly repent and ask his forgiveness.*
>
> *The judgment of the court is that you* [it was tediously reiterated for each prisoner]…*be taken to the jail of Kent county from whence you came, and from thence to the place of execution, at such time as shall be duly appointed by the Governor of this State, and there be hanged by the neck until you are dead.*[158]

Potts, Bradshaw, Hynson and Harrison remained extremely nervous after their release from jail the next day. Wickes ordered ten dollars each given to Potts and Bradshaw to get them away from Kent. They bought steamer tickets to Baltimore on the *Emma A. Ford*, leaving on November 2. Potts said he planned to sell his Millington property and move to the city. The *Smyrna Times* said he planned to make his way from Baltimore to Wilmington, Delaware, where he had family. Bradshaw had no firm plans. Both gave fictitious names when purchasing their tickets.[159] Others implicated in the case, including Phillip Mander, left Kent for Queen Anne's County.[160]

Slowly, the true meaning of the verdict and sentence sank in for the prisoners. They were being guarded more carefully than ever. Sheriff Plummer appointed Fred Pote and Jerome Rambo, of Worton, to take the night watch and John H. Greenwood and Thomas Storks for the day shift.

Brown started reading the Bible and praying every night.

There was already talk of petitions to commute some, if not all, of the sentences, but there was also talk of counter petitions. Many in the community were surprised that death sentences were handed out to the five younger prisoners.

There was also controversy about the date set for the execution. Governor Frank Brown signed the death warrants on November 11, setting the date for

December 30. Kent County commissioners, the orphan's court and others bemoaned having eight men hanged just after Christmas. That would mean the celebratory hymns of the season would be interspersed with the macabre beat of the hammers constructing the scaffold. Also, submitted the editors of the *Transcript*, more drinking takes place during the holidays, and that could mean trouble for a hanging spectacle.[161] A request was made for a postponement of a week or two, and the date was changed to January 13.

The change, officially requested by defense counselor James A. Pearce "and other citizens of Kent County, and State's Attorney Slay," required the first set of death warrants to be nullified. The governor had to issue each of the prisoners a reprieve. This was done on November 21. On the same day, new death warrants were issued reflecting the new execution date.[162]

The oddity of the new date, falling on a Friday the Thirteenth, didn't go unnoticed. The correspondent for the *Baltimore Weekly News*, writing later, noted that there were originally thirteen suspects and that on the day of the execution, there were thirteen squads making up the sheriff's security force.[163]

The occasional drama of the trial notwithstanding—the death sentences were a formality for most—the community took aim at the upcoming holidays, but there was another superlative and something that Dr. Hill would have appreciated had his life not been cut short. This was the election of Hill's preferred presidential candidate, Grover Cleveland, on November 8.

Cleveland was the only candidate at that point elected to a second, nonconsecutive term, defeating incumbent Republican president Benjamin Harris. Local Democrats, the Kent voting majority, were ecstatic.

On election night in Chestertown, the streets were crowded until the early hours as the news of the election victory came trickling in from various sources by telegraph.

The local Democrats were headquartered on the second floor of Stam's Hall, which remained crowded. When word was received at about eight o'clock that Cleveland had taken New York City, and when more telegrams arrived with positive election news, "the very roof of the building would almost shake with the shouts," reported the *Kent News*.

Nearby, the *Kent News* building, the former Masonic building across the street, was "thronged."

The Republicans' focal point was the office of Charles T. Westcott on Court Street. They knew about midnight that it was all over, and they closed down their office.

Race and the Hill Murder Trial

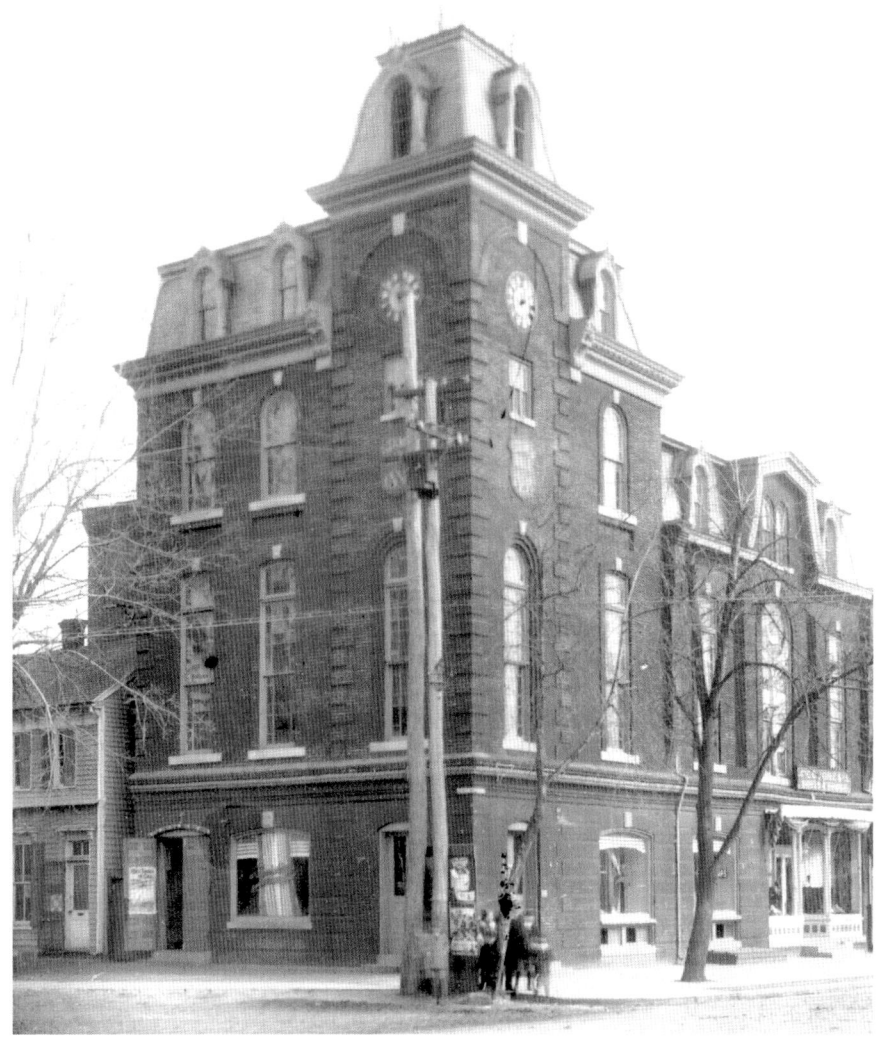

Stam's Hall, built in 1886, is seen about 1900. *Historical Society of Kent County.*

And the African American community?

> *The colored people behaved well. They showed very great interest during the whole day and seemed certain of a Harrison victory. About 8 p.m. a crowd of them cheered lustily, "Hurrah for Harrison! What's the matter with Harrison? He's all right!" A little later the Harrison cheering had ceased altogether, and the colored enthusiasts had disappeared.*[164]

Injustice on the Eastern Shore

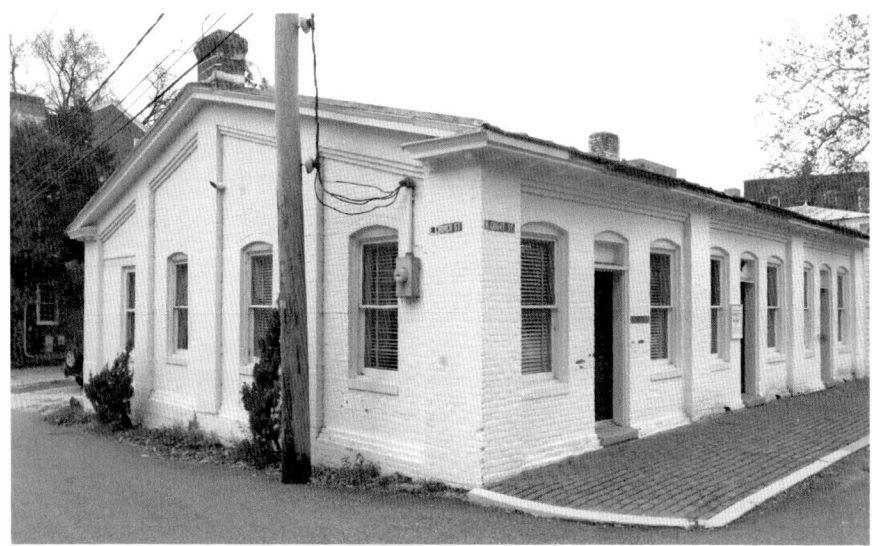

This law office on Court Street in Chestertown was the Republican headquarters for the 1892 election. *Photo by Kevin Hemstock.*

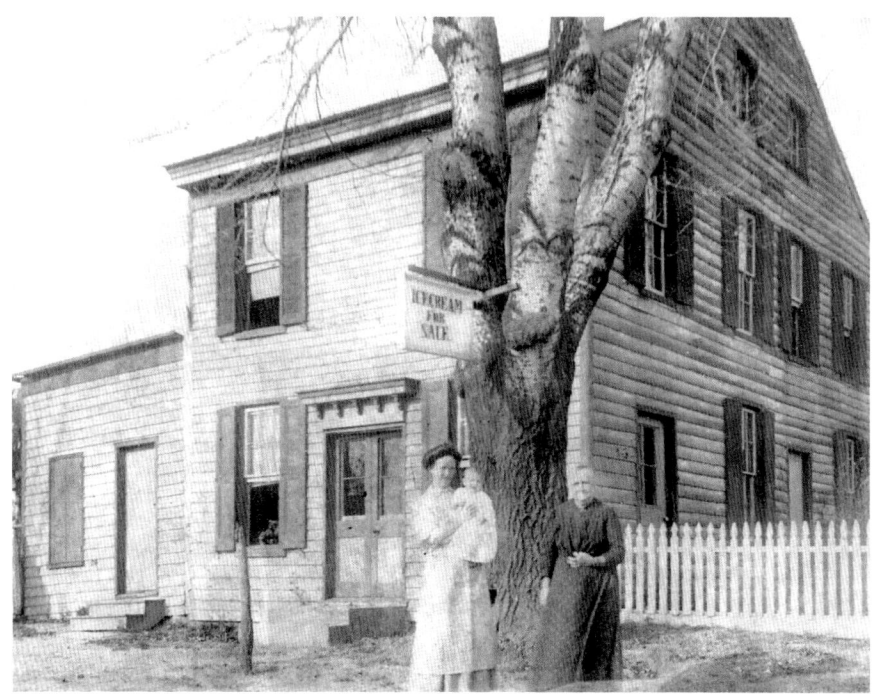

Democrats in Millington celebrated Grover Cleveland's election at the Green Tree Inn, seen here about 1912. *Courtesy of Paul M. Bowman.*

Race and the Hill Murder Trial

In Millington, described as the "Gibraltar of Democracy," Democrats, and probably a few Republicans, celebrated the victory with a torchlight procession and "illumination." For a night, at least, the violent death of one of the town's more ardent Democrats seemed to have been forgotten.

It's doubtful that the prisoners, whiling away the hours in the county jail, cared much at all about who was elected to preside over the nation. For them, life took on a routine that was often dominated by religion. Several preachers, both black and white, visited and prayed. Prominent minister the Reverend Stephen C. Roberts, of the Emmanuel PE Church next door to the jail, delivered Bibles on November 28. All might have benefited from this since all were literate to one degree or another.[165]

On Friday, December 9, the sheriff read the death warrants to his prisoners. It was a melancholy affair, and each prisoner was advised on this occasion to choose a spiritual advisor. Moses Brown, Brooks, Comegys, Emory and Baynard requested the Reverend F.S. Dennis, pastor of the AME church in Chestertown. Williams wanted the Reverend Queeley, pastor of the Janes ME Church. Hurtt and Benson asked for the Reverend J.F. Wallace,[166] pastor of the Golts church, which dated back to before the Civil War, serving the obscure African American community there.

On Tuesday, December 20, the steamer *Emma A. Ford*, with Captain Phineas McConnor at the helm, chugged along on its regular Chester River run, a line of skyward-rising serrated puffs delineating its upriver progress. It pulled up to the wharf near the foot of High Street in Chestertown, dropping off its usual load of mail, freight and humanity with a curtness no doubt magnified by the chilly winter weather. Among those hastily disembarking was Bishop Alexander W. Wayman, a hellfire and brimstone "divine" of

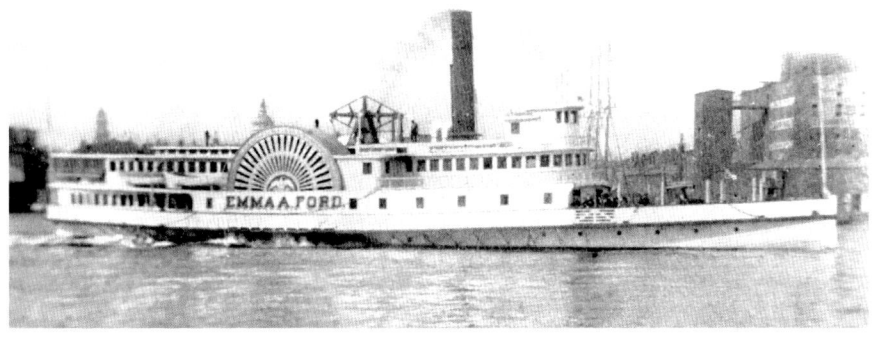

The steamer *Emma A. Ford* plied the waters of the Chester River and brought passenger traffic across the Chesapeake Bay. *Courtesy of Jack Shaum.*

the AME Church, one of the first African American Methodist bishops and a man as highly respected as Frederick Douglass—more so in some circles because it was believed he worked more to alleviate the suffering of the poorest of his race.[167]

Wayman was born in Tuckahoe Neck, Caroline County, in 1821, four years after and across the Tuckahoe River from Douglass. He was the son of a former slave. His father taught him his letters; he was self-educated. Wayman was physically a big man, which he attributed to working as a child on his father's farm.[168] He joined the AME Church in 1843 and became a bishop in 1864. He had served the church in Philadelphia, Washington and Baltimore and, at the time of the trial, made his home in Baltimore, where he would end his days.

After arriving in Kent County, Wayman initially met with the Reverend Dennis. The next day, he visited the prisoners at the Kent County jail. He later told a *Transcript* reporter that his mission was not to ferret out their guilt or innocence.

"I came to pray with them, and to talk about their souls, and not their lives," he said, describing the case as "unusually sad." He said that he was particularly concerned about the younger prisoners, who didn't really understand their predicament.

> *Do the men and boys alike appreciate their situation?...They say they are to die and are preparing for the end, but I scarcely believe that the boys fully realize their fearful position, for three of them particularly are very young. There is no difference between the men and boys so far as appearances go, relative to their appreciation of their fearful fate, for all seem to realize the fearful import of the pending doom that awaits them.[169]*

Wayman said he expected a group of African American Baltimore clergymen to seek a commutation for the younger prisoners but that he wanted a one-on-one visit with Governor Brown to accomplish that aim.

> *I shall visit Gov. Brown in a short time, and simply state that, in my opinion, the boys were too young to appreciate the enormity of their crime, and that it would be a great misfortune to inflict the punishment of death, and will ask for a commutation of the sentence in their cases.*

He did not say that he thought any of the prisoners were innocent or that they had been given an unfair trial.

Race and the Hill Murder Trial

He left the following day, this time traveling by train.

Meanwhile, on the evening of the same day that Wayman was visiting the prisoners, a meeting of the Grand United Order of Galilean Fishermen, Baltimore, was held to determine whether to approach the governor to petition for a commutation.[170] The general feeling at the conference, which "was large and representative," was that the adult prisoners should be hanged, but all "were earnest in their desire that the boys who were now beli[e]ved by many to have been simply bystanders, and interposed no objection because of their fear of the men under threats made against them, should be saved from the gallows."

The group determined to hire Charles W. Johnson, a prominent African American lawyer, to prepare the petition and seek clemency. A committee was also formed to raise funds to cover the cost.

Wayman had a brief audience with the governor on December 27, at which time he dropped off a petition that the governor promised to consider. A similar petition was handed over on December 29 by the Yearly Meeting of the Society of Friends.[171] These weren't the only petitions circulating; another opposed commutation.[172]

Even before Wayman's visit, the thought of having the murderers' sentences reduced was agony to the victim's family. In a December 16, 1892 letter, Arrelee Hill wrote to the governor:

> *There is in circulation a petition soliciting the commutation of the five boys implicated in the murder of Dr. J. Heighe Hill. As a widow of the murdered man, the mother of his orphan child, and one who has suffered most by their act of outlawry, I implore you not to commute the sentence passed upon them.*
>
> *They were tried and found guilty before an impartial Court of three Judges, and assuredly deserve the severest penalty of the law. And their attorney states they are all older than represented. While the forfeit of their lives cannot recall my dead or restore me to a happy home and associations, I realize as the one most interested I would not be enacting my part or doing my duty in behalf of my assassinated helpmate if I did not make this request for justice. Hoping and trusting my insignificant letter may receive your attention and approbation...*[173]

The inmates didn't have a completely empty Christmas. Greenwood, the watchman, brought them some goodies for the holiday. He gave all of them candy, nuts and cake. To Moses Brown, he gave a large piece of mincemeat pie.

Greenwood, an auctioneer, carriage carpenter and onetime constable, was about fifty-five years old. It's uncertain if his charges knew that handling prisoners ran in the family; a member of his family was the jailer during the trial and execution of the three who were convicted of the Cosden family murders.

A day or two after Christmas, a far more important present, for some of the prisoners at least, arrived in Annapolis. It was a petition signed by Bishop Wayman, the Reverend W.M. Alexander, the Reverend Dr. J.H.A. Johnson and other ministers of the AME Church, together with the signatures of one hundred others, both white and black, urging that the sentences of the five youngest inmates—Emory, Hurtt, Comegys, Benson and Baynard—be commuted. The governor turned the petition over to the secretary of state with instructions to file it with the other papers in the case.[174] The governor didn't immediately respond to the petition, and it was not certain whether he would consider it.

It was irrelevant to Sheriff Plummer, who, for the time being, had eight official death warrants. His concern was developing the macabre death device that could effectively carry out the sentences under the guidelines that had been set out for the execution.

On the morning of January 6, a week before the date set for the execution, watchman Pote began the construction of the scaffold against the jail wall, accessible by a short flight of four steps from the door at the end of the jail's west corridor, apparently that which faced Cross Street. Pote would receive $31.25 for his carpentry.[175]

Frederick E. Pote, born in 1852 in Oxford, Maine, came by his carpentry skills naturally. The son of New England blacksmith and cabinetmaker James Munroe Pote, he was a "skilled mechanic" and wheelwright. He lived in Urieville with his wife, Lavinia, and five children.

The scaffold would require a little science because of the statutory constraints. It had to be built to a carefully measured size to accommodate eight condemned people and prevent the anticipated milling crowds from witnessing the horrid spectacle. However, enough room had to be allowed so that the statutory selection of observers, who would be in the corridor, could view the final outcome.

All of it made for a complex carpentry job.

Plummer had already voiced his concern to Judge Wickes that he might not be able to prevent the public from seeing the execution. His concern, he said, was information to the effect that "great masses of people from different counties of the State and from the State of Delaware" had indicated their intent to break the fence around the jail yard. In a January 2 letter, he sought reassurances from the judge that he had the authority to form a large enough "posse" for crowd control.

Not only did Wickes confirm the sheriff's legal authority to conscript any number of men, under the threat of arrest if any refused, but he also made it clear that the sheriff might himself be subject to the law if he failed to secure the peace:

> *It is, therefore, your imperative duty to execute the judgment of the court, in obedience to the warrant of the Governor, in a private manner, as directed by the section of the code which I have quoted. A failure on your part to do so would make you liable to indictment and severe punishment. If you have reason to believe that any disorderly persons will, at that time, attempt to interfere with you in the performance of your duty, or, to be more explicit, to break down the fence or other barrier which you now have to exclude the public from seeing the execution, you have the authority and the power, and it will be your duty to summon before the day of execution the* posse comitatus, *or power of the county; that is, such a number of citizens as are necessary to assist you in preserving the public peace on that day, and in quelling any riot or disorder which may occur before or at the time of the execution. Everyone who is summoned is bound to obey the summons and to assist you in preserving the public peace; and if anyone should refuse to attend or assist, he may be punished by fine and imprisonment.*[176]

Wickes quoted the law, noting that an execution must be undertaken in as

> *private a manner as possible, and to exclude from the view thereof all persons except his deputies, the spiritual advisors of the criminal, the counsel who defended him, his relatives and such other persons, not exceeding twenty, as he may appoint to witness the execution; and the physician of the jail, if there be one, or if there be no such physician, then the sheriff shall procure some other physician of good standing to attend and to furnish him a certificate that the execution was properly performed.*

Plummer published "a card" on January 4, 1893, that ran in the local papers, cautioning people to stay away:

> *The law of this State requires executions to be private. The public cannot view the execution. The law commands me and I shall obey the law to the letter and see that the execution is witnessed only by the persons authorized*

Injustice on the Eastern Shore

by law to witness the same. I therefore counsel all persons not summoned to remain away from the vicinity of the jail on that day.

The mechanism of death was twenty feet wide by eight feet deep and was to have a hip roof. It was later decided to leave off the roof, and a drawing in the January 14, 1893 edition of the *Philadelphia Record* shows what looks like a walled but roofless enclosure on stilts. The wood, including the six- by eight-inch hunk of Georgia pine on which the nooses would be attached, was supplied by Thomas W. Eliason's lumberyard at a cost of twenty-seven dollars.[177]

There would be four four- by four-foot traps, each to accommodate two prisoners. They were located under the broad beam. The traps were divided in half with four hinges—like the doors, laid flat, of a Wild West saloon. But they would swing only one way: down. The traps were to be opened simultaneously by a single lever, which would be pulled by the sheriff.

The law allowed for the execution to be accomplished between the hours of midnight and 2:00 p.m. on the appointed day.[178]

That day was fast approaching.

AN UNEXPECTED VISIT

A week before the execution, the prisoners seemed largely unconcerned. Or perhaps it just seems this way, through history's prism, based on the accounts. Peeking through the barred windows and doors of the 1893 Kent County jail, most would not think that a grisly execution was to take place in a matter of days.

"The sounds of merry laughter that floated out from the corridors of the Chestertown jail last Wednesday morning reminded one more of a jolly party of colored boys than a band of convicted murderers," reported the *Kent News* in its January 7 edition. The paper also said that on that day, Baynard, Comegys and Emory had been allowed the freedom of the corridor. A couple of them played leapfrog while others answered questions posed by reporters.

Hurtt, thought to be the youngest of the prisoners, even asked watchman Storks if he could go visit his mother at Golt's Station for a couple days, promising to return in time for the execution.[179]

The request was denied.

The *Kent News* reporter interviewed some of the prisoners on Friday, January 6, and quoted some of their responses to what appears to be the same questions posed to each.[180]

EMORY: "I am 16 years old last September. My father lives in Millington and works about town. I lived first with Miss Mollie Cacy and have lived with Mr. Gus Hendrickson five years. I was never before with the men now in jail. I am ready to die and do not feel afraid in the least."

Injustice on the Eastern Shore

BAYNARD: "I am 16 years old. Went to school two or three winters. My father works with Mr. Johnny Reese. I lived with Mr. Charles Rolph two months, with Mr. Johnny Reese two years and Mr. S. Johnson one year. Me and Fletcher lived together and I always waited for him when in Millington. I know the time is very short but I am trying to prepare for it. I never belonged to church but attended Sunday school."

HURTT: "I am 16 years old, and have a mother living at Golt's Station. I have worked for Dr. E.G. Clark, [James] Thompson, Lou Hayes, Galena, and at [Joseph] Peacock's. I feel ready to die. I went to school three or four years and can read."

BENSON: "I will be 17 years old next October. I have a father and mother living at Golt's Station, and also seven brothers. I work by the day at different places, the last places being at Mr. [William] Ford's and Mr. John Donahoe's. I know that my time is drawing near but am trusting in the Lord to save me."

When asked about the construction of the scaffold, which he watched from a window, Comegys responded: "It's to hang us on, sir."

The paper reported that Comegys's father had been to see him several times. He said he was seventeen or eighteen years old and had worked for William J. Hurlock, William Price, John Barnes and Clarence Turner. His father worked for William Cully.

Comegys said he wasn't afraid of death.

Brooks remained sullen. He used the interview to reiterate his innocence: "I did not see Dr. Hill on the night he was killed nor did I have anything to do with it."

Although he was thought to be twenty-one, he said, "I will be 18 years, 10 months and 17 days old at 12 o'clock next Friday, the 13th."

He said his parents lived at Golt's Station.

"I have worked for Thomas Donahoe, Henry Gillen and Thomas O'Connor. I feel prepared to die at any time."

Williams also added a denial to his statement: "I am 23 years old and lived with Mr. Charles Rolph. I did not see Dr. Hill on the night of the murder and had nothing to do with the affair. I do not feel uneasy about the hanging as I know I am innocent."

MOSES BROWN: "I am 28 going on 29. I have a wife and one child living and eight dead. I worked by the day at various places, my last home being with Mr. [William] H. Ford. I was not in the crowd when the murder was committed as I left the boys at Ford's gate. I am prepared to go. I know that I have got to die sometime but I don't much like the way I've got to go now. I am trying to teach the boys what the Lord says about death and the home in heaven."

Race and the Hill Murder Trial

While it had been cold enough through the holidays to ice up the Chester River, creating a "blockade" to boat traffic, the first week of January brought warmer temperatures, breaking the ice and encouraging more outdoor activity, particularly the new sport of jail watching that had become fashionable as the time approached for Kent's most populated execution ever.

Meanwhile, the buzz about commutation grew louder and more fevered, as factions inside and outside the county competed for the ear of the governor.

Governor Frank "Farmer" Brown, forty-six, the cigar-chomping Democrat and former Baltimore postmaster from near Sykesville, had been elected the year before for his first and only term, although it was his second try; he had been turned down by the party leaders in 1887. But he won his second bid, approved by the party and the voters. He was sworn in a year to the day before the upcoming execution.

He came by the nickname "farmer" because he ran for office on a pro-agriculture platform that was hugely successful, particularly in Kent County. During the campaign, the *New York Times* described him as "a man of very decided executive ability" and "thoroughly honest and upright, fearless and independent."[181]

On a campaign stop in Chestertown on the wet, rainy Tuesday, October 6, 1891, he was introduced by the chairman of the Democratic Central Committee, Harrison Vickers, who described him as "the people's candidate."[182] He was extremely popular, and the local papers predicted that he would win the statewide race, including the voters of Kent. The prediction was accurate. In Kent, he netted 2,200 compared to 1,817 for his nearest opponent, Republican Colonel William J. Vannort, a Civil War veteran who called Chestertown home.[183]

Vannort lived in the stately Victorian home on the corner of the streets now called Water and Maple. He had a spectacular military career during the war and afterward remained steadily in the Republican political periphery, serving a number of terms as a Chestertown commissioner. But he lacked the charisma, and apparently the marketing skills, of Farmer Brown.

Paul Winchester, in a book of short biographies of the leading personalities of his time published thirty years later, described Brown as energetic and spontaneous:

> *He never seemed to tire. He would go everywhere. He would pay a visit of ceremony and state one day to a county fair and the next day would go through a penal institution in a searching way, often greatly to the discomfort and chagrin of those in charge. He would make the opening speech at a*

great banquet at night, and the next morning, bright and early, he would be scoring some recalcitrant official for neglect of duty. He would attend the Monday german and before noon the following day would be at the House of Correction overlooking improvements going on there, and at night would be in town again dictating letters or making an unexpected visit to the House of Refuge, the Normal School, or some other public institution where his presence was unwelcome because he always found fault, if any fault was there; for nothing escaped. As one disgusted official said, "He hunted dirt, and when he found it he raised a row, swore at us and said if we didn't get a move on ourselves he would fire us all."[184]

He was a hands-on governor, but this time he clearly had a tough decision, magnified by the myriad voices raised, both white and black, which ran the gamut of "hang them all" to "clemency for the youngest." While his greatest concern was being branded as the governor who executed children, it was not at all helpful, from a public relations standpoint, that the ages of Henry Hurtt, Charles S. Emory, Joshua Baynard and Lewis Benson were in doubt and debated. Many in the clemency crowd thought the youngest prisoners were thirteen. It was likely that the youngest, Hurtt, was actually sixteen. The governor also did not want to set the wrong precedent.

The Governor says he feels a hesitancy in granting clemency as the precedent it will establish is that a youth seventeen years old is not criminally responsible. He thinks that unless the prisoners are mentally deficient, they are old enough to judge between right and wrong. If the boys are mentally unsound, he says, the fact should have been brought out in the trial.[185]

The governor also wanted the opinion of one or more of the judges who decided the case. However, that was not immediately forthcoming.

In the January 5, 1893 edition of the *Transcript*, one column stated that the governor had not yet made a decision. Another item in the same paper stated: "Governor Brown has decided not to interfere in any way with the course of the law in the case of the boys under sentence of death for the murder of Dr. Hill."

The confusion of the paper mirrored the governor's indecision.

There was one way to get more information on the topic, and that was to interview the prisoners. Using the hands-on method for which he was

Race and the Hill Murder Trial

notorious, that's exactly what the governor did, acknowledging all the while that his approach was unorthodox.

On the morning of Saturday, January 7, at about ten thirty, Governor Brown rolled into town on a special train, accompanied by his stenographer, J.R. Bowerman, and Colonel Robert L. Holliday, superintendent of the Delaware division of the Pennsylvania Railroad. It was a cold morning, and the train may have been chosen as an alternate mode of travel because the river was icing up. It surely caused quite a stir in town; even in modern days, rare is a visit from a sitting governor to Kent County except at election time.

Brown noted that "though his coming to Chestertown or any other place on such a mission was entirely out of the general order of things, he was unwilling to act until every means of placing himself in full possession of all the merits and the demerits of the case had been exhausted."[186]

He went immediately to the jail and indicated to Plummer his purpose: to interview the prisoners. There is no record that Plummer expected the gubernatorial visit. The surely astonished lawman then set up the interviews in the "jail's parlor." Present with the governor for the interviews were Pearce and Smith, defense counsel; Vickers for the state; William B. Usilton of the *Kent News*; and C. Cox Hopper for the *Transcript*.[187] The attorneys had to be summoned from their homes—another indication that the governor's visit was unanticipated. State's attorney Slay was not at home and could not be reached in time, hence the reason for Vickers's presence.

The prisoners were brought in one at a time. Each was introduced to the governor, who then asked them to tell him a little about themselves and give their sides of the story about the murder.

The first to face the state's chief executive was a nervous Hurtt, the youngest if not the smallest of the doomed octet. He denied any knowledge of the crime. He admitted to being with a group that night on the road near Ford's Hill, but none of them, he said, participated in a murder.

Next up was Benson, who initially denied being involved in the murder but then told the story as it was generally accepted, with one variation: he was the only one to say that Hill was knocked completely out of the cart when Brooks hit him with the stone. When the governor asked why he watched the others attack the doctor, Benson replied, "I don't know."

Sixteen-year-old Emory was described as the one with the "brightest of intellect" among the four youngest. In front of the governor, he was cocky and denied any involvement in a crime, though he admitted to being in Millington on the night of the murder and going with a group past Ford's Hill to Cooper's party.

Injustice on the Eastern Shore

Comegys was quoted as saying, "I can't tell no story, if it would save me to-day. I have told enough stories already." He then denied involvement and stated that his past confession was false.

Baynard, who was the first to confess at the inquest, gave a full account of the attack. He also told the governor that he knew it was wrong to kill but was afraid, on that spring night, to try to stop it. He also verified the motive as being the death of Thomas Campbell at McWhorters's oyster bar four months before the attack on Hill.

The *Transcript* described Moses Brown as a "stupid, good-natured looking negro." When asked by the governor if he was involved in the murder, Brown said, "I can't tell nothing but the truth. I know I have to die, and am not after this world, but am after the world to come." He said he had been "converted" to religion, and "the Lord in Heaven knows I know nothing of the murder of Dr. Hill."

Brooks, the one accused of bashing Hill's head with a rock, was described as "vicious-looking" with a powerful build. He was "sulky and obstinate," declining to answer most questions and proclaiming his innocence.

Williams did the same but added that he was prepared to die.

When the interviews were completed, the governor left without indicating whether or not he favored commutation. According to Hopper, several of the young prisoners, such as Emory, didn't leave a good impression on the governor. It's quite possible that the governor wasn't sure which way he would lean, and it was clear that he felt a great weight of responsibility on his shoulders. He was the last arbiter in the lives of eight individuals, and whatever decision he made would last in the state's memory long beyond his life or theirs.

Meantime, Plummer was instructed to continue with a scaffold for eight and to order eight coffins.[188] That was a sure sign, many thought, that the governor would not interfere.

The next day, Sunday, January 8, was a busy one for the prisoners and perhaps not all unpleasant. It was their last Sabbath, and the mood was relatively light:

> *Jest, laughter and song rung throughout the dismal corridors, and as a small number of visitors stood oppressed and horrified by the fearful solemnity of the occasion, the men and boys were to all appearances celebrating a negro half holiday. After an unbroken night of refreshing sleep, all awoke in excellent spirits and ready for the gay routine which they had introduced into prison life.*[189]

Race and the Hill Murder Trial

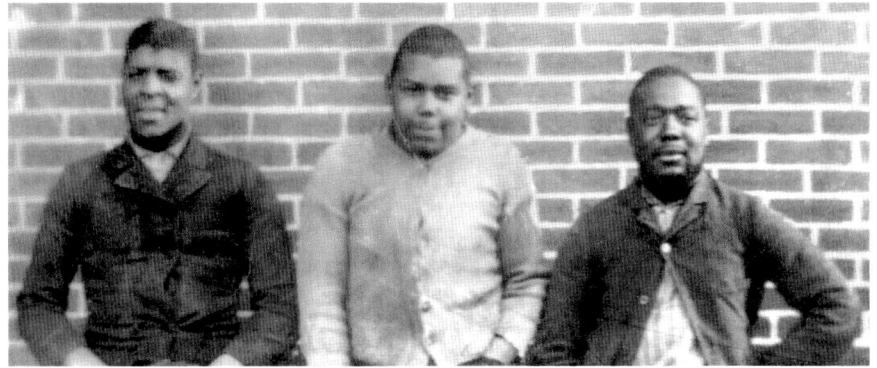

The three eldest of the eight convicted Hill murderers are, from left: Fletcher Williams, Charles Brooks and Moses Brown. This picture was taken just days before their execution. *Historical Society of Kent County.*

There would be a treat on this day: the prisoners would pose for photographer Colonel John M. South.

Confederate veteran South, originally from Shenandoah County and Woodstock, Virginia, likely learned the craft of photography from his sister's husband, Barnett M. Clindinst.

Clindinst, who is listed as an artist in the 1860 census, went on to develop two patents to improve cameras, including a mirror to allow a photographer to see his target right side up through a camera viewer. His son, of the same name, became a prominent Washington, D.C. photographer.

But even in 1893, photography was a complicated business.

Before Kodak debuted the Brownie about 1900, photography was tedious, requiring professional photographers to be chemists as well as artists. It was getting easier; Kodak came out with its first rolled-film camera in 1888. But it was expensive; the early mass-produced camera sold for anywhere from $25 to $100. When it came time to develop the film, owners had to send in the whole camera. South probably used an older camera model more comparable to what he had learned on. It had glass negatives on which the photosensitive emulsion was painted just before use.

South was referred to as "Colonel" South because he fought with the Confederacy. During the war, he signed up with a local artillery unit and ended it with the Forty-eighth Infantry of Virginia. He was wounded near the end of the war. It's not clear if he ever attained the rank of colonel. In fact, there is no evidence he was promoted beyond private,[190] indicating that "colonel" might have been a nickname.

Injustice on the Eastern Shore

His specialty was portraits, and his home in Crumpton included a back porch with double windows all around allowing plenty of natural light, especially suited for portrait photography.

During his fifty-year career, South also recorded numerous scenes and buildings on the Eastern Shore and often sold them to postcard companies. Many of the cards still turn up at ephemera shows and in antique stores.

But on that cold but clear Sunday afternoon in January 1893—the temperature wouldn't make it above thirty degrees—Brooks, Brown and Williams, in leg irons, were led down the steps into the jail yard. The sheriff's bloodhound howled and carried on. Nearby was the partially completed gallows. Standing against the northwest wall of the jail, they waited, shivering in the cold but apparently enjoying the opportunity to be outdoors, even for a few moments. South snapped at least one photograph with his four-by-six box camera.[191] Brown wore an old slouch hat; Brooks was bareheaded in the center and wore an ill-fitting jacket whose sleeves stopped halfway down his forearms; and Williams was wearing a double-breasted coat and an old Civil War–era, kepi-style soldier's cap that Greenwood had given him.[192]

The adult inmates were then herded back inside, as happy to return to the warmth of the jail as they had been to enjoy a brief moment of fresh air. The young prisoners—Emory, Benson, Baynard, Comegys and Hurtt—were then brought out. They were light-hearted, chatting and laughing as if it were part of a game, noted the *Transcript* reporter.

> *Emory grasped both lapels of his coat, Benson pushed his hands well down into the warmth of his pockets, Baynard proudly braced himself back with both hands hanging, Comegys thrust only his fingers in his pockets, while Hurtt assumed an easy attitude with one arm across his breast and one hanging by his side.*[193]

"Just keep quiet for a minute and look at my fingers," South instructed his distracted subjects. He then snapped one or more pictures. It was likely the first pictures they had ever had and would perhaps be the last, at least for the four youngest.

Today, only one picture of the three older prisoners from that session is known to exist. It shows them from the waist up. But a drawing on the front of the January 14, 1893 *Philadelphia Record* shows all eight from head to foot, and it's almost certain South took multiple photos. It is also fairly certain that the drawing in the *Record* was made from two of those photos. A great effort would have had to be made to get the photos to Philadelphia in time for the January 14 edition, and the artist would have had to work quickly from the photographic image. He did a good job based on the extant picture of Williams, Brooks and Brown.

Five days remained to execution day. In that short span, a heavy snow would fall, the sheriff would have a case of the flu and one stealthy surprise would stun the town.

ANOTHER SURPRISE VISIT

The snow, the flu and the surprise all came together on Wednesday, January 11, just two days before the planned execution. But the secret mission to spirit four prisoners out of Kent County actually began two days earlier in Baltimore.

About three o'clock on Monday afternoon, the governor notified Marshal Jacob Frey, Baltimore police chief, that the sentences of Baynard, Benson, Hurtt and Emory had been commuted to life in prison. Frey and Captain Lewis W. Cadwallader, commander of the western city police district, met personally with the governor later in the day to get the paperwork finalized.

Subsequently, Cadwallader and Detectives George W. Seibold, Thomas F. Hogan and Aquilla J. Pumphrey, along with ten policemen, met at Brown's Wharf at the end of South Street about seven o'clock the next evening. They were accompanied by police commissioner John Q.H. Robson and Joel H. Rowlenson, superintendent of the statehouse and the governor's personal representative. Rowlenson, a journalist by profession, was from Queen Anne's County, where his father had been a newspaper editor.

They boarded the police boat *Lannon*, which transported them to the icebreaker *Latrobe*, anchored near Lazaretto Lighthouse.[194]

Up to that point, no one aboard the *Latrobe*, except Cadwallader and Robson, had the slightest inkling of the purpose of the expedition. The vessel then set off across the bay; it was a long and bumpy ride because of the ice.

When the icebreaker made it to the Chestertown wharf about 3:25 a.m. on Wednesday, all was quiet in the little county seat, as should have been expected and no doubt was required by town ordinance. The silence was broken by a knock on the door at the sheriff's house and jail. Pote answered the door and, surprised by the gathering of officials there, summoned Mrs. Plummer.

He didn't call the sheriff because the county's top lawman was suffering from the flu.

La grippe, as the French called influenza, "gripped" Kent almost every year at this time, with a serious spread in 1890. Then, as now, it could be fatal to the frail, young or old. Those who were afflicted were often restricted to bed for a week or more. William Johnson, Millington's justice of the peace, died from pneumonia a year after Hill's murderers met justice, following an attack of la grippe.

There were no antibiotics to treat the contagious malady. A dose of a morphine derivative was often recommended. Quinine was also used.

The sheriff had been laid up for a couple days and probably could not have answered the door in the middle of the day let alone the dead of night.

Mrs. Plummer found on her threshold the white-haired, mustachioed Captain Cadwallader, commander of the Baltimore Police Department's western district. He was accompanied by the substantial party of Baltimore policemen. Mrs. Plummer wasn't completely surprised; Cadwallader had been expected, though perhaps not at that time or in that manner. It had been planned that he would be on hand for the execution and would stay at the sheriff's house. She said she would show him to his room.[195]

"Come, Captain, we have been expecting you and have a bed for you," she said.

"No," said the captain, explaining that his mission was urgent. "I must see the sheriff."

The governor chose the fifty-six-year-old Cadwallader to deliver his final decision on the commutation because he was an acquaintance of Sheriff Plummer. The captain, whose brother Abel was a Medal of Honor winner, had worked his way up through the ranks after joining the police department during its most trying times, the summer of 1861. He was nearing retirement.

He later told the *Morning Herald*: "Sheriff Plummer and I are old friends, and expected me to be present at the execution on Friday. As soon as I got in, the rest of the party filed in and I made our errand known."

His mission was to deliver letters from the governor to the sheriff and to take back with him four prisoners.

The official commutation letter, one for each of the four, stated:

> *Sir, this is to officially notify you that I have this day commuted the sentence of death which was passed upon* [Joshua Baynard,

Injustice on the Eastern Shore

Henry Hurtt, Louis Benson and Charles S. Emory], *who* [were] *convicted at the October Term 1892 of the Circuit Court of Kent County of the murder of Dr. James H. Hill and sentenced to be hung; a warrant for which was issued by me on the 11th day of November, 1892, naming Friday, December 30th, 1892 as the day of execution, but afterwards, to wit: on the 21st day of November, 1892 a reprieve was by me granted suspending the execution of the said* [Joshua Baynard, Henry Hurtt, Louis Benson and Charles S. Emory], *and directing that the same should take place on Friday the 13th day of January, 1893, into imprisonment for life in the Maryland Penitentiary*

The official commutation of the death sentence to imprisonment for life has this day been forwarded to Samuel G. Fisher, Esquire, Clerk of the Circuit Court for Kent County.[196]

There was also another note for Plummer that said:

Annapolis, Md. Jan. 10, 1893.
*Edward J. Plummer, Esq., Sheriff of Kent County.—*sir*: I send by the bearer Capt. Lewis W. Cadwallader, commutation of the sentences of Joshua Baynard, Henry Hurtt, Louis Benson and Charles S. Emory, and I herewith request you to deputize Capt. Cadwallader and all others accompanying him to deliver the prisoners named to the Maryland Penitentiary; thinking it best for you to remain in Chestertown. You, of course, will be surprised by their sudden appearance. But the necessities of the case demand the same. I charge you to be careful that secrecy is preserved, and that these men are delivered instantly aboard the vessel which goes for them, and safely conducted to the Maryland Penitentiary. Caution your deputies that secrecy must be observed, and that nothing must interfere with this order. If you prefer to come with the prisoners yourself, then deputize the men I send as a posse comitatus and bring the prisoners as above directed. I send by the Captain blank papers with the names of the deputies filled in, so you can simply sign.*

Yours respectfully,
Frank Brown,
Governor of Maryland[197]

Race and the Hill Murder Trial

The next day's *Morning Herald* quoted Cadwallader:

> *We then proceeded to the cells of the boys, and quietly awakening them, told them what we intended doing, and they got up and put on their clothing. All seemed pleased, especially Hurtt, who appears to be the most intelligent of the lot, and became so nervous that he got both legs in one leg of his pantaloons.*

"I am so glad, as this will please my mother. She was worrying so about me," Hurtt reportedly told Cadwallader.

The prisoners were ready in about fifteen minutes. They left the jail and walked or trotted the short distance to the waiting steamer, docked at the Chester River Company's wharf at the foot of High Street. The total time between arrival at the wharf and loading of the passengers was twenty-three minutes.

The side-wheel icebreaker *F.C. Latrobe*, owned by the City of Baltimore and named for the city's mayor, had cut through the ice, in some cases as much as fourteen inches thick, to make the trip with Cadwallader's men. The temperature had been above freezing only once the whole week.[198] The iron-hulled steamer was soon heading the other way, with four young convicted murderers who had cheated death at the gallows. Cadwallader probably sighed a vaporous breath of relief into the cold air as the steamer began chugging along the Chester. They

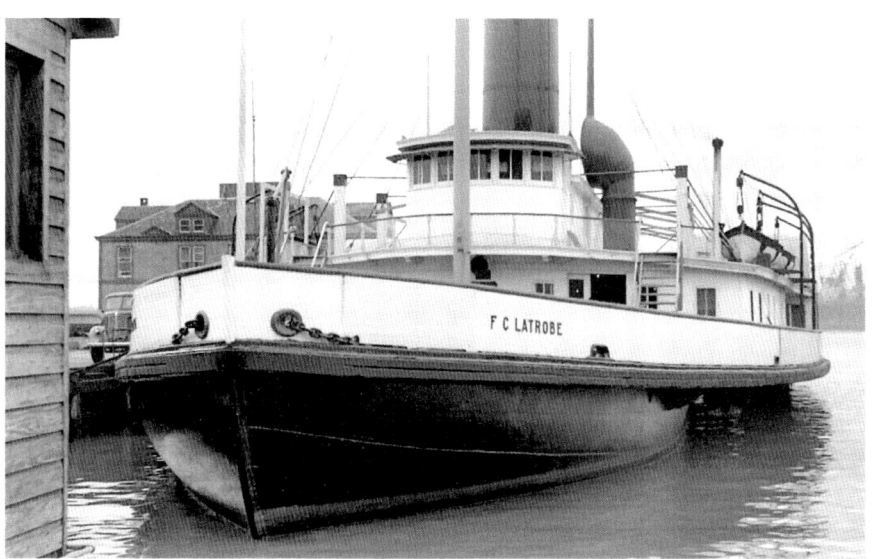

The Baltimore icebreaker *F.C. Latrobe* was named for the Baltimore mayor. *Courtesy of Jack Shaum.*

would be far down the river before the sun rose and the citizenry of the town was made aware of the middle-of-the-night transfer.

The four teens would never again see the other prisoners or set foot in Chestertown or Kent County.

"The trip back was uneventful," Cadwallader told the *Herald*. "The boys sat huddled together in the cabin aft and would have nothing whatever to say, although several attempts were made to get them to talk. The channel which we had made in going up the Chester River had closed, and we experienced more difficulty in coming out than we did ascending."

They arrived at the Chester River Steamboat Company wharf in Baltimore, at Light Street Pier 7, about 1:35 p.m. The Central District patrol wagon was summoned by telephone and arrived with Marshal Frey and a number of additional officers.

A curious crowd had gathered, but there was no trouble, and the four prisoners were transported to the penitentiary.

"They are the happiest prisoners who have come within these gates since I have been warden," John F. Weyler, of the Maryland Penitentiary, told the *Herald*. He said the four "looked like children" and then opined on the governor's commutation. "I think the governor acted wisely in commuting their sentences, for I believe that if they took any part in the murder they were lied into it without knowing what they were about."

The news of the commutation of the four teens "spread like wildfire" in Kent County, which may or may not have helped melt the five inches of snow that fell that day, forming "curly white ribbons, and fantastic figures…wrought upon the beams and braces of the grimly awaiting gallows outside."[199] The scaffold was nearly done; it was raised on Tuesday, and it would be finished the day before the execution.

Neither Vickers, the lead prosecutor, nor Wickes, the judge, offered up any public objection to the governor's commutation of the four teens' sentences. There was "intense feeling" in the upper part of the county, the part that included Millington, created by the governor's decision, but no one seemed inclined to resort to violence, according to the *Transcript*. The opinion of the community was evident and expressed one way or the other. In Millington, the governor was burned in effigy. Samuel Hill, the victim's father, expressed his disappointment in the governor's decision but said he would not support any acts of violence in response.[200]

The governor commented later that a conspiracy was not fully established, "and without this, the boys cannot be said to be equally guilty with the men.

Race and the Hill Murder Trial

"I have acted in the case and feel no regret at the conclusion reached. If I have erred it is on the side of mercy." He added that he hoped no similar case would come before him in his term as governor.[201]

He was quoted in the *Evening Herald* of Shenandoah, Pennsylvania:

> *I had to protect the fair name of Maryland. Such a wholesale execution as this has never been heard of before in the criminal annals of the country. The whole country was aroused over it.*
>
> *The murdered man will be amply avenged, the outraged law of the State will be carried out by the execution of the four whose sentences have not been commuted, and the fair name of Maryland will be preserved from the stain that would have been inflicted on it by the execution of those ignorant boys who were in all probability the unwilling witnesses of a crime that they were powerless to prevent.*[202]

He was quoted in the *Morning Herald* as saying:

> *I made up my mind* [to commute the four] *after having seen them in Chestertown jail. They had been represented to me as strong, robust boys, and at least 17 years old. I determined to see them and judge for myself. I found them to be mere striplings, and, while I am satisfied they were in the crowd, I am convinced that they are not sufficiently intelligent to comprehend that nature of a conspiracy.*
>
> *It is my opinion that they were induced by the men to accompany them without knowing the true object of the conspirators and without any conception of the result. They were only lookers-on. They were convicted on technicalities of the law as parties to a conspiracy. When the case came to me I looked at it in the light of equity. I also procured when in Chestertown much original evidence in the way of confessions which had been taken but which was not submitted at the trial. I read all these papers after my return home, and then decided to have the boys brought to Baltimore without publicity.*[203]

He worried about a confrontation during the mission to remove the four from Chestertown:

> *If I had made the matter public there might have been trouble, and with the responsibility of the safety of such a number of Baltimore policemen under my direction, I felt justified in acting as secretly as possible. Had it been known in Chestertown that the boys were to be taken away, there might have been some*

resistance made by the citizens of Kent County, which would probably have resulted in a conflict in which lives would have been sacrificed.

The African American community in Baltimore celebrated the move.

"The governor of no state could have more wisely settled a serious and perplexing question than Governor Brown settled yesterday by commuting the sentence of the four boys charged with the murder of Dr. Hill. For an executive to have the lives of men to hang upon his decision is a matter of serious importance. Every side of this question was given a full consideration before the governor acted, and the personal visit to the prisoners showed his disposition to do the fair thing," lawyer Harry S. Cummings, a former Baltimore councilman, told the *Herald*.

> *The ends of justice will be fully met when four men's blood will be spilt for this horrible deed. To rescue these four youths from the gallows is to save our commonwealth from what would have been a glaring disgrace, and it has at the same time visited upon the heads of the real murderers a full and just punishment for their crime…This act stamps Governor Brown as a man of a resolute and determined character, and, above all, a man with a heart.*

Cummings correctly predicted that others would be critical of the governor's decision. He was right, and the grieving widow was on top of the list.

She was outraged.

She was quoted in the *Frederick News* and other papers:

> *I have no desire for the death of any one, but as a mother and the widow of a man who was foully murdered, I think* [Governor Brown's] *exercise of his constitutional prerogative in the present case was uncalled for… Three judges of unquestioned ability and integrity sat in trial and found the eight men guilty. They assuredly deserved the severest penalty of the law.*[204]

She wasn't the only one upset by the governor's decision. So was the citizenry. Louis Justiss summed it up: "You can hardly realize the pitch of excitement to which the people are worked. If the secret [of the commutation] had leaked out the police would not have had so easy a job to get these men."[205]

Local officials commented benignly, if at all. Marian deK. Smith, as comptroller and essentially the governor's co-worker, said that the state's chief executive acted "honestly and according to the dictates of his judgment."

Race and the Hill Murder Trial

Vickers, a Democratic Party supporter of Brown's, said he always believed in upholding the law.

The sheriff would say only, "I was surprised."

Plummer said there would be no change in the construction of the scaffold.

The governor's action simply added more sensation to what surely would be the most infamous execution in the county and of interest to the whole nation.

THE GALLOWS BECKON

It wasn't the first hanging in Kent County, and it wouldn't be the last. In fact, it was just slightly less than a year since the last one, but that one had involved only one miscreant. It caused a huge stir in Chestertown and set the pace for what was to come.

It started on the night of Saturday, August 22, 1891, when Thomas Thompson, a Chestertown native and son of Richard and Mary Thompson, approached itinerant laborer William "Bully" Adams at the corner of Calvert and Kent Streets and stabbed him in the heart with a forty-cent, five-inch penknife. Adams dropped dead almost immediately, a cigar still clutched in his right hand.

It was the result of a dispute over a game of craps and a contest over the affections of twenty-one-year-old Kate Mitchell. After the fray, Thompson disappeared into the night, fleeing through the Barnett brickyard, today about where Garnett Elementary School is located. He was caught by Constable Miller about a week later near Galena and charged with murder. He was held in the county jail. In November, he was found guilty and sentenced to hang.

It was thought by some to be the perfect hanging. It went without a hitch.

Plummer bought the three-quarters-inch rope at J.K. Aldridge's shop. T.J. Joiner built the fourteen-foot-tall scaffold on the Cross Street side of the jail, with its five-foot drop from the platform. The six-foot-tall, 180-pound Thompson watched and listened as the death machine was constructed. And just after dawn on a cool January 29, 1892, he was led out onto the platform,

Race and the Hill Murder Trial

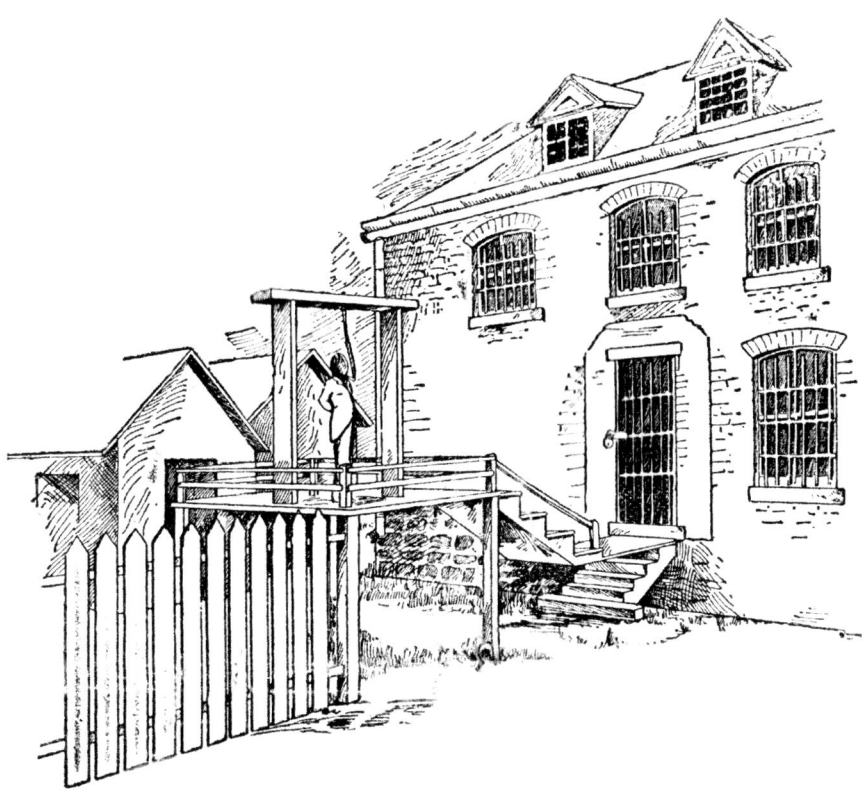

A graphic depicts the hanging of Tommy Thompson at the Kent County courthouse. *From the* Kent News, *January 30, 1892.*

and he said his last words before a hood was placed over his head. The noose was then placed around his neck, and Plummer, already in position, pulled the lever of the double-door trap.

> *There was a distinct swish as the doors to the trap sprung apart and the man shot down. The drop nearly five feet, and his death must have been instantaneous. There were a few convulsive motions, then all was quiet and the body hung still. The body was examined by Drs. Hines, Whaland, Kelley, Cooper and Wethered, and all pronounced death to have been almost instantaneous, resulting of the severance of the bones* [of] *the neck.*[206]

It was at Thompson's execution that Plummer, his brother Frank, Dugan, Storks and Greenwood cut their teeth on the science of hanging. The paper gave high marks for the end result:

Injustice on the Eastern Shore

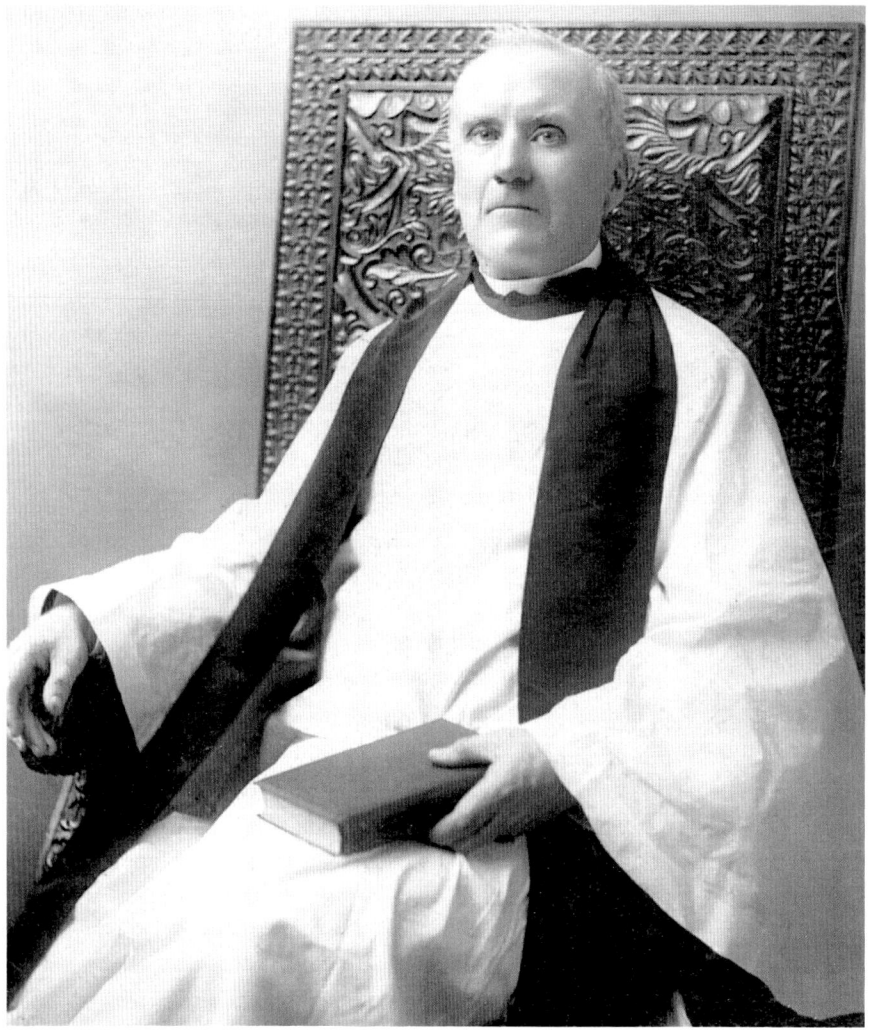

The Reverend Stephen C. Roberts. *Historical Society of Kent County.*

> *Sheriff Plummer and his watchmen, Messrs. Dugan and Starks [sic] are to be congratulated upon the wisdom shown in the management and successful culmination of this sad affair. It could not have been carried out more perfectly.*[207]

The Reverend S.C. Roberts and the Reverend F.S. Dennis were spiritual advisors for the confessed murderer then, too.

The training didn't do the lawmen much good. Maybe it was because multiplying it by four created four times the complexity. Perhaps it was a physics experiment that would create different and unpredictable results each time. But much would go awry in the execution of the four sentenced to die in the death of Dr. James Heighe Hill. And it simply was beyond the sheriff's control.

By Thursday, January 12, 1893, the hotels in the county seat were full—with the curious, those employed in keeping order, those who came from afar to witness the ordeal and the throngs of local and visiting press (there were twenty or more outside correspondents, including representatives from papers in Baltimore, Philadelphia and New York).[208]

The media "invasion," unprecedented in the county's history, was demonstrated by one superlative: an assistant was hired for telegraph operator William S. Culp, at the Adams Express office on High Street, to handle the crush of communication.[209]

On the last full day of their lives—the day before those lives would end—three condemned men and one teen woke early and had a good breakfast. They then went about the business that one would expect of condemned people: they read their Bibles. Brooks and Brown wrote or finished letters.

Brooks wrote to his two sisters and his mother. He also wrote a letter for Williams to his mother, which brings into question whether Williams was literate. However, the *Kent News* indicated that Williams had sent a letter to Charles Emory, one of the four removed to the penitentiary. In it, Williams allegedly wrote: "You have gone and left us but I have a better chance than you because you have lied and I haven't."[210]

The day before, Brown had written a letter to his wife and started another to his mother. The *Daily Herald* reporter read and recorded the latter, at least as much as he saw:

> *My Dear Mother: I will write you my last letter. It leaves me well. I hope will find you well. I would love to see you once before I am to be strangled away from this life, but if I don't, will meet you in glory, for I feel as though when I am done. Going to write something else before I die.*[211]

Both men wrote out statements for visiting reporters.

In fact, the *Philadelphia Record* reported that three of the adult prisoners had learned to read and write while residents of the county jail:

> *The four colored murderers of Dr. J. Heighe Hill…were of an exceedingly low order of intellect, yet three of them learned to read and write during the few months of their incarceration, and almost by their unaided*

efforts….Moses Brown, the weakest-minded one of the quartette, was the most accomplished penman…He appeared to take more interest in his chirography than he did in his salvation.[212]

None of the letters or statements has come to light in modern times.

Preachers visited throughout the day. They included African American ministers the Reverends Queeley and Abraham A. Murray of Edesville; the Reverend Dennis; and the Reverend Lemuel Wilmore. There was also a white minister, the Reverend Roberts, rector of the Emmanuel PE Church.

About six o'clock, another man of the cloth visited and spent an ample amount of time locked in the cells with each prisoner. He was Father Henry R. Sargent of the Society of the Holy Cross, who came from Westminster. Sargent's Protestant Episcopal organization was dedicated to improving the plight of the black man, particularly in the South. Sargent said his special function was to visit African American jail prisoners. He wouldn't say what the prisoners told him, owing to a creed of confidentiality.

About the same time, State's Attorney Slay stopped in to bid the prisoners goodbye. Harrison Vickers did likewise, telling them that while he had done everything he could to secure their convictions, it wasn't personal, and he was only doing his job.

The prisoners, when not talking to visitors, spent their last night writing more letters and reading the Bible. Oddly, all of them penned notes to Watchman Greenwood—apparently they all had an affinity for the man. There were numerous members of the press on duty, too. The account in the *Transcript* Extra the next day told about some of their doings and what they said.

The prisoners stayed up late, with most of their time involved in spiritual activities, praying with the preachers and singing religious songs. The activity, said the *Baltimore Weekly News* reporter, "was of a highly excitable character and not at all calculated to produce sleep."

The Reverends Queeley and Dennis left at midnight, admonishing the four prisoners "to confess their guilt, even at the last moment, if they had committed the crime."

There would be no confessions forthcoming. But that didn't prevent the reporters, waiting out the night in the corridor nearest the cells, from trying to coax one or more of the condemned four into admitting guilt.

Each reporter had some idea of his own as to how to get a confession from the murderers. Sympathy, strategy, mild abuse and a variety of other means were employed to accomplish the desired end. But all were equally useless.[213]

Race and the Hill Murder Trial

Some of the reporters even wrote out confessions and exhorted the convicts to sign them, but it was no use. The prisoners refused to sign anything admitting their guilt. They did, however, give out autographs to any and all who requested them.

When the preachers had left, Comegys fell asleep. Brown lit up a cigar and said he felt sure he was going to be in heaven about the same time the next night. Williams bundled up his things, including his coat, and asked Watchman Storks to make sure they were sent to his family.[214]

Most, except for the guards, had left the area of the cells.

At one point, an oil lamp in Williams's cell ran out of fuel. "What's the matter with my lamp?" Williams asked out loud.

"Don't you see what's the matter?" one of the guards said. "The oil in that lamp is like the lantern of your life—it has nearly burned out."

"That's so, boss," Williams was said to have replied. "But the lantern of my life is going to be relit, and the lamp ain't."[215]

As the night wore on, only Brooks remained awake, and he began pacing back and forth in his cell. After about a half hour of this, he fell on his knees at his bunk.

> *Beginning in a low tone he prayed to God for forgiveness. Louder and louder grew the negro's voice, more intense became his temporary religious fervor, and finally he wor[k]ed himself to a high pitch of excitement.*
>
> *His vocabulary was wonderful. Few of those who heard the praying murderer's prayer had any idea that Brooks possessed such a command of the language. He used many words of whose meaning it is scarcely possible he could know. On he went for more than 15 minutes until, at the expiration of that time, he sank down upon the stool at his cell door and looked the picture of misery.*[216]

Just as he finished, about one o'clock, the prisoners received a surprise visit from Samuel Hill and his adult son, Walter, the latter a well-traveled commission merchant.[217] It was also a surprise to the jailers and caused quite a stir in the middle of a night that was filled with nervous tension. The Hills arrived with a group of about twenty men, and those in the jail at first thought a group of lynchers was approaching. Immediately, the guards got their weapons at the ready. Someone rang the bell that was on the door. A reporter, at first, opened the door and told the men waiting outside that he was not the doorman.

"Hold up there," said Watchman W.W. Stephens. "No one can enter here."

At that point, the elder Hill, wearing a wide-brimmed hat, stepped to the front of the group and said he wanted to give the prisoners one more chance to confess.

"I haven't the slightest doubt of their guilt," Hill said. "But I thought I would come over tonight and see if these men would, now that they are about to die, stop their lying and confess the murder."[218]

He and his son were allowed to enter the jail, but the others had to remain outside.

Samuel Hill went first to Brooks.

He said, "Brooks, you have only a few hours to live, and I don't want you to die with a lie on your lips, but tell me all you know of the killing of my son."[219]

Brooks replied, "I know nothing about it, I did not see the doctor that night. If I knew anything, I would have told long ago."

"Tell the truth, Brooks," Hill said. "You will soon meet the doctor at the judgment bar of God, and if you tell the truth, he will be glad to see you, but if you lie, he will turn his back upon you."

Brooks repeated his denial. "I'm sorry, Mr. Hill, I can't tell you who killed the doctor, but I don't know."

Then Hill went to a dozing Williams, who seemed perturbed that his slumber had been interrupted.

"Williams," he said, "do you know me?"

"Yes, Mr. Hill, I know you," came the response.

"Tell me all you know about the murder," requested the sad father.

"I know nothing about it," Williams replied. "I had nothing against the doctor or anybody else. I have known you ever since I was a little shaver, and have known the doctor for five years, and indeed, I had nothing against him and do not know anything about it. I met the doctor on the street that night about twenty yards from his house and stepped to one side to let him pass, and when he looked up and saw me, he said, 'Hello Fletch.'"

He continued, "I know I have to go to die, and it would do me no good to lie about it…I told the boys if they knew anything against me, tell it, and I would be glad of it, and would not hurt them. I liked the doctor, and do not know anything about it. I wish I could tell you something, and as God's in heaven I would do it."

Moses Brown was the next to be awakened. He recognized Hill, and he, too, denied any involvement in the doctor's murder. He told the story that he said he had heard from Potts, that a white man named Bill Darhl, who lived on a farm between Millington and Massey, was involved in the murder.[220]

Race and the Hill Murder Trial

According to the *Philadelphia Record*, Harrison Vickers had checked out this story and found no substance to it.

The youngster, Comegys, also denied involvement. The boy looked up at his two visitors for a moment but then claimed ignorance and innocence.

Hill and company left without the hoped-for nugget of truth.

A little later, there was some more excitement. About a dozen reporters, writing copy, were aroused when one of them, L. Stevens, looked out the window and saw shadows. Again, they thought it was lynchers. At just that point, there was a knock on the door. The reporters all hid in closets and alcoves. But it turned out to be a watchman who wanted to come in and get warm.[221] After that, an anxious quiet retook the night.

FOURSOME FINALE

Throughout the night, as many as seventy newly sworn deputies were on duty, along with the sheriff, his brother Frank, Greenwood, Pote, Storks, Rambo, William Stephens, John Prettyman and Robert Carter.

At some point during the night or in the early morning, Brooks asked for Thomas Donahoe, son of an Irish immigrant, with whom he had once lived. Donahoe must have been in Chestertown. He gave Donahoe some items to give to his parents. During their conversation, Brooks started crying.[222]

The condemned men slept fitfully, but none awoke before 7:00 a.m. It was as if they didn't want to start their last day. Who alive can possibly imagine what it would be like to wake up on the day you know will be your last? But the day dawned cold and bright, and activity soon could be heard outside as people started arriving for the upcoming spectacle. Sleigh bells, for those using that mode of transportation, could be heard echoing from the increasingly busy town streets.

Newspaper correspondents from throughout the region, and even the editors of the local newspapers, were on hand at first light, and when the prisoners were roused, there was an impromptu press conference at which the doomed were again asked to repent. The stories were the same.

"I am innocent, and God must be my judge," said Brown.[223]

Three of the condemned men wore worried, frightened looks on their faces. Only Moses Brown maintained his clown-like smile, for which he had now become famous.

About 8:00 a.m., the prisoners were fed their last meal, prepared by Mrs. Plummer; the breakfast menu included ham, beef, light bread, biscuits and honey. Brooks and Brown had hearty appetites. Williams and Comegys ate only small portions, complaining of eating too many cakes the night before.[224]

Afterward, the Reverends Murray, Dennis and Queeley led the men in prayer. Brooks prayed aloud:

> *Oh Lord Jesus, look at my condition. I pray Thee. Thou art a God of mercy; Thou art a fountain of light for my soul; Thou hast warned me; Thou hast pleaded my guilty cause. Oh, heavenly master, I thank Thee for Thy kindness. This may be the last time I bow down to Thee.*
>
> *Master Jesus, come this way, I pray Thee, and anoint me with the anointment of Thy love. Oh, Lord, I ask Thee to make a pure heart, if it is Thy blessed—in Thy righteous will. Reach down Thy lily-white hand, and snatch me from a burning hell. Keep me in the love of Thee every moment of my life, and me not go astray. Take care of me while I lay down to my sleep, oh Lord, that I may wake up in Thy righteous Kingdom. Oh, Lord, turn my mourning into joy, and my hell into a heaven. Oh Lord, have mercy upon those who have no mercy upon themselves. Look upon the servant, who ventures to call upon Thee.*

The moment of truth was upon the condemned men.

Even as Brooks was praying, Sheriff Plummer was busy in his bedroom preparing the five-eighths-inch cotton rope nooses that would be used to end the four lives.[225]

The prisoners boxed up their belongings, and each directed that the articles go to his parents. Brown even packed up his shoes to give to his brother. He would end his day, and his life, in his stockinged feet. Comegys sent his coat home; he would go to his end coatless on a cold day.

Meanwhile, patrols were going on outside around the jail grounds. People began to gather early, initially on the other side of Cross Street and what is now Memorial Plaza (at the time, it was considered a green median in the middle of that part of High Street). There were crowds in front of the Rockwell House, directly across from the jail. Curtains had been placed on the corridor windows to prevent the curious from peeking. An eight-foot fence surrounded the fifty-square-foot jail yard.[226]

It was crowded in the jail now. At about ten o'clock, Brooks asked a reporter what time it was and when the execution would take place. When told, he responded he wasn't concerned and simply said he was ready to go at any time.

At 11:00 a.m., Samuel Hill and his sons Walter and Harry[227] quizzed the prisoners one last time. The response was no different than before.

At about 11:25 a.m., the sheriff and Queen Anne's County constable C. Sydney Jump "noosed" and attached the ropes to the crossbeam and tested the trap releases. Deputy Pote had bathed the nooses with rosin soap so the knots would slip properly.

The sheriff then gathered his deputies, Dugan, Stork, Pote, Prettyman, Stephens, T.D. Starks, Carter and Rambo, to give them last-minute instructions. They proceeded downstairs to the jail, where the doomed awaited their inevitable fates.

A few minutes later, preparations began for the prisoners. Deputies Dugan and Stork secured their hands and arms; the accounts differ on whether steel handcuffs were used or rope. Nor is it clear when the leg restraints were removed and when they were replaced by looser leg chains before it came time to walk down the corridor to the door and then to the gallows box.

Plummer intentionally waited until after noon, which was when the crowds were expecting the execution to take place. That didn't make much of a difference. About one thousand people were waiting outside in the ankle-deep snow, and their muttering was a steady drone outside the fence. The *posse comitatus* had retreated to inside the jail yard, congregating around the scaffold.

The cells were unlocked about 12:15 p.m.

Brooks and Williams, whose cells were entered first, had little to say. They seemed nervous but showed little outward emotion. While Williams was being secured, the others began singing.

While his arms and hands were being bound, Brown said he was ready to die.

The deputies had trouble removing his leg irons, also part of the process. When he joined the other prisoners, Brown began to break down, claiming they were about to hang an innocent man.

Last rites were read by the Reverends Sargent, Queeley and Dennis.

Sargent read the "Four Lessons" of "hope," "love," "faith" and "contrition." He prayed with each of the four.

Murray, described as an "old-time clergyman" with a "hallelujah voice as deep as a coal mine," sang and prayed. Comegys said several times, "Save me, Jesus, save me." The preachers and condemned men then sang "Nearer Thy God to Thee." Dennis then closed with a funeral service.[228]

Race and the Hill Murder Trial

The last ceremonies dragged on too long for the sheriff. He had to walk down the corridor several times to see what the holdup was. In the meantime, the crowd outside was getting loud and boisterous. There were shouts of "bring them out" and other such cries. Finally, Plummer walked up to Williams and said, "Follow me." He told the guards to bring up the other three.

Comegys was a concern for the deputies since he had shown signs of panic in the early morning hours. He began to sob hysterically when the cells were opened.

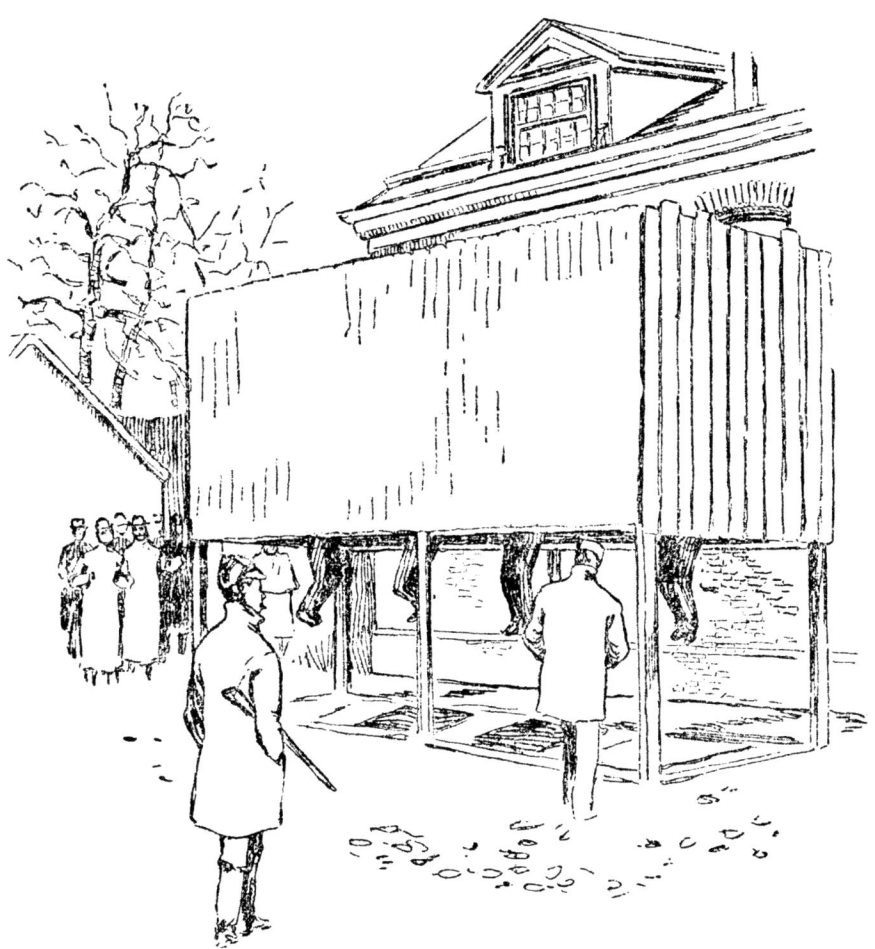

This drawing depicts the executions of four of the eight charged with the death of Dr. Hill. *From the* Philadelphia Record, *January 14, 1893.*

Injustice on the Eastern Shore

A stretcher had been prepared but wasn't needed; the teen was "serene" when it came time to walk down the corridor to the door that led to the scaffold. Had he known how ugly his end would be, he might have tried to bolt just then.

They walked down a flight of steps from the back of the building, turned around a corner and climbed the wooden steps of the scaffold.

Williams, who was in the lead, caught a glimpse of the crowd. The watchers were lit by the sun, just showing up above the roofline of the jail and courthouse, steep pitches from that angle. It was cold, and his first quick breath outside would have been exhaled as a vaporous cloud. He was followed by Brooks and then Comegys. Brown brought up the rear. He was probably the most endearing of the ill-fated prisoners, and many in the crowd could be heard to say, "Poor Moses!"

He hesitated for a moment, then he dropped his head and shuffled up the steps, the chains on his feet rattling in time with those of his cohorts, who followed in a line.

On the way, Brooks asked Williams, "How do you feel?"

"All right," was the response.

Brown began to reveal an obvious nervousness and said, "Gentlemen, I am going for nothing. God knows I am."

Someone told him to keep his nerve.

"I am, I have enough left," he responded.

On hand were the deputies, Storks, Pote, Frank Plummer and Stephens, along with physicians, reporters and others. The sheriff then led the march up to the platform, followed by Deputy Dugan, Williams, Brooks, Comegys, Brown, the preachers and the watchmen.

Williams chewed on a plug of tobacco as he shuffled along.[229]

The prisoners were led onto the scaffold. Brown was over the trap nearest the steps, followed by Brooks, Comegys and Williams.[230]

As they stood on the gallows, with only moments to live, Comegys began to tremble, and the chattering of his teeth was audible. However, while one newspaper attributed this to fear, it may also have had a lot to do with the weather. The temperature was in the upper teens, and he was without a coat.

Otherwise, the condemned four stood quietly ready. The sheriff did not ask them if they had any last comments.

Their legs were then bound at the ankles. Dugan and Rambo drew a black hood over the head of each prisoner, and the nooses were placed around their necks.[231] All the while, the preachers remained with the condemned.

Race and the Hill Murder Trial

For the most part, the watchers could see none of it because the fence around the jail yard and the walls around the scaffold kept the dismal spectacle hidden from casual observation. The fences, initially at least, kept spectators at a distance. However, they could hear the creaking of the freshly assembled death machine, the testing of the levers and traps and the footsteps and muffled voices of those orchestrating the event. They also "heard" the hush before the final moment.

Dugan stepped back, and Sheriff Plummer gave one last inspection of his charges and what would soon be their instrument of death. It was about at this time that the fence was breached, and some of the spectators began creeping, unimpeded, into the jail yard.

The last words from the condemned men came from Brown just before the traps were sprung: "God knows I am innocent."[232]

The sheriff, at precisely 12:28 p.m.,[233] pulled the lever. Then, *thunk, thunk, thunk, thunk*. As the *Transcript* stated, "Williams, Brooks, Brown and Comegys were ushered into eternity."

Unfortunately, it wasn't that simple, quick or neat. While Dr. Frank Hines and the sheriff made the official times of death 12:28 p.m., that was the time the lever was pulled. Even that time differed among those watching and varied from 12:30 to 12:35 p.m. Regardless, death was either agonizingly short or terrifyingly long for the four convicted murderers.

Williams, the alleged ringleader, died almost immediately. He was the lucky one.

Brooks was less fortunate. The rope slipped to one side, and though he remained motionless for a while, after about a minute he began to writhe and drew up his legs and arms spasmodically for six or more minutes. The action forced his hood up enough that his neck and associated bruising caused by the noose could be seen.

Brown drew his legs up several times and, after about a minute, ceased struggling.

The youngest of the four, Comegys, writhed for a lengthy period in obvious, horrifying convulsive agony.

> *The boy, Comegys, was fearful to behold! It was evident that he was strangling to death! His cries of "oh, Lord! OH! OH!" were audible, and his bodily contortions made strong men shudder. His pinioned arms were lifted almost to his head while his legs were both drawn up and straightened out again in his horrible agony.*[234]

There are three ways to die in a hanging. One is by a broken neck, facilitated by the rate of descent, weight of the body, length of the drop and the placement and angle of the knot. Williams, possibly the tallest and heaviest of the four, clearly died in this manner. Brooks also had a broken neck.[235]

Another way is to be strangled, and sometimes the throes of death can go on interminably, as was demonstrated by Comegys.

Many things can go wrong, and often did, in this manner of execution. In the Kent County of 1893, there were still people living who remembered the triple hanging of the Cosden murderers in 1851 on a hill north of Chestertown. One of the condemned men in that case, forty-five-year-old waterman Nicholas Murphy, fell through the trap, and when the rope stretched taut, the knot slipped, and he fell to the ground stunned and bleeding, staring up at the quivering legs of his two co-conspirators. They made Murphy wait about an hour while the rope and trap were redone so that he could be re-hanged. After falling through the trap a second time, his life continued for another eleven minutes as he died slowly of strangulation. It was an ugly business.

In rare cases, the execution victim can be decapitated. For example, on April 2, 1880, in Washington, D.C., James Madison Wyatt Stone, convicted of murdering his wife with a razor, was decapitated by the rope at his hanging.[236] In more recent times, it happened in the execution of Barzan Hassan, the half brother of Iraqi dictator Saddam Hussein. When he was hanged in January 2007 in Baghdad, the drop was too far, the rope too short and the man too heavy. His head just "snapped off."[237]

Comegys's agonizing death at the end of the noose was attributed to his light weight and the way the noose gathered around his neck after the drop. It happened, quite possibly, because the weight-drop calculation was in error; the teen had lost weight during his incarceration.

The physical contortions of the dying youth continued for a full five minutes. At one point, he drew his knees up to his chin. At another, his heels reached toward the back of his head. His left shoe fell off.[238] Even when the writhing stopped, death was not declared for another twelve minutes—seventeen minutes after the drop.

Those who witnessed the scene were horrified.

Hines was assisted by Drs. Charles W. Whaland, J. Horton Kelley and John L. Wethered. Kelley said Williams's neck had been broken. Whaland, feeling for a pulse, pronounced Brooks dead in ten minutes, his neck also broken. Whaland said Brown was dead fifteen minutes after the drop, while Hines said Comegys died from strangulation and dislocation of the neck.[239]

Race and the Hill Murder Trial

Hines, the official jail physician, signed a "certificate of hanging" for each one of those executed. The certificates were duly filed with circuit court clerk Fisher.[240]

And many people, far more than the sheriff had intended, witnessed the final gruesome spectacle.

Just before the execution, hundreds had gathered around the jail yard fence. Before noon, some in the milling crowd began to pull some of the boards away. The local papers downplayed what outsiders described as a "mob" of the curious, who attempted to get a view of the execution. Not so the visiting reporters, who didn't have to worry about repercussions:

> *The streets around the jail were crowded early in the forenoon by a mob of men howling for admittance within the enclosure. By 11:30 o'clock the citizens were swarming on top of the high board fence and trees in the vicinity. A disgraceful riot ensued…A rush was made to defend the fences, which had meanwhile been partially demolished.*[241]

There was some scuffling reported, and some in the "posse" of deputies were said to be involved in assisting the rioters. By the time the traps were sprung, there were open holes in the fence and a number of gawkers in the jail yard.[242] While the scaffold remained enclosed and only the legs of the hanged men could be viewed from outside the platform, many of the bolder ones peeked up under the enclosure.

"For God's sake, men, as you expect to die yourselves, let these men die in peace!" shouted Reverend Sargent.[243]

The bloodlust of the crowd prompted Plummer to say, "Some of these men about here are no better than brutes. How they long to have the blood of these unfortunate creatures."

According to one news account, some of the "mob" in the yard continued to taunt the prisoners in the sixty seconds before the lever was pulled, then touched their twitching bodies after the drop. Some of the brazen gawkers peering underneath the scaffold enclosure were nearly struck by the bodies as they fell through the traps.

> *Then, as the bodies dangled in the air, barely striking some of the mob, some of the more hardened poked their fingers in the quivering bodies of Williams and Brooks, and exclaimed, "That's the one who drove the knife in Dr. Hill," or "that's the one who heaved the rock."*[244]

It's also possible the execution could be witnessed from the upper floor of the Armstrong Hotel or the Rockwell House across Cross Street and other nearby buildings; however, there is no mention of spectators peering through second-floor windows into the jail yard.

There was a "rumble" between the town bailiffs and the *posse comitatus*. About fifteen town bailiffs were under the command of Thomas Jefferson Joiner. They ordered members of the posse to get off the Cross Street sidewalk so that the latter had to patrol in deep snow. When the sheriff was made aware of the situation, he ordered T.E.W. Crew, captain of the posse, which in the morning had numbered nearly two hundred men, to arrest Joiner.

"Arrest him," said Plummer. "I'll have no interference with the guards."[245]

Joiner was locked up in the jail, the key being turned by Mrs. Plummer, since the sheriff was busy.

> *With a determination which might have saved the fence later, Captain Crew marched right up to the [b]ailiff, and gracefully drawing and presenting his sword caught the bailiff by the collar, and after a vigorous fight, in which the [b]ailiff's forces were ignominiously routed, took Joiner over to the jail and locked him in a cell.*[246]

Joiner was soon allowed to go free and witnessed the hanging.

One person who didn't see the final act was Samuel Hill; he left before the hanging was completed. It's uncertain whether other family members remained.

The corpses were permitted to hang for about twenty minutes, during which time spectators ghoulishly examined the bodies. The only thing that dispersed the crowd was the announcement that the area would have to be cleared of spectators so that a photographer could take photos of the still hanging bodies.

> *A space was cleared and the kodak [sic] man leveled his camera and proceeded to take several snap shots, the results of which, he stated, would in due course of time be placed before the public.*[247]

Afterward, the bodies were taken down and examined. When the hoods were removed, it was seen that Brown's eyes remained opened, while the eyes of the others were closed.[248]

The *Baltimore Weekly Herald* described all their faces in death:

> *The face of Comegys when the body was laid in the coffin was terribly drawn, indicating that the boy murderer had suffered great agony. Moses Brown had the same smile in death that had been his characteristic in life. Brooks' face wore a very natural expression, but Williams, who apparently died the easiest looked as though death had not been as easy with him as he thought it would be.*[249]

The bodies were placed in the coffins that had been waiting directly beneath the scaffold. They were then placed in the care of undertaker John N. Dodd. There is no indication that any of the prisoners' relatives attended the execution. No one claimed the bodies. Dodd transported the coffins to the almshouse cemetery, outside Chestertown, and they were buried within an hour in unmarked graves without ceremony there, though certainly not without difficulty. The high temperature that day was twenty degrees, and it had been below freezing most of the week. The grave digger, whoever it was, was paid eight dollars for his services. It was an additional thirty-four dollars for the undertaker and the coffins.[250]

AND THEN THERE WERE NONE

The lives remaining for the four teens who evaded the noose—Charles Emory, Henry Hurtt, Joshua Baynard and Lewis Benson—were only by a slight degree an improvement over the fates of the other four. The Maryland Penitentiary in Baltimore was run by a hard-fisted disciplinarian in a facility that was counted as one of the oldest prisons in the nation.

And John F. Weyler, its warden, started and ended his reign in controversy.

The penitentiary, located on four acres near Jones Falls, housed its first prisoner in 1811.[251] Those entering through the Madison Street front gates in 1893 found an eclectic collection of four brick buildings constructed between the time of the first prisoner and January 11, 1893, the day that the four Hill murder teens were trundled into the facility.

After being transported across the bay on the state's icebreaker, Benson, Baynard, Emory and Hurtt were dutifully received into that system, in that order, prisoner numbers 13020, 13021, 13022 and 13023. Each had his name recorded, along with age, height, eye and hair color, former residence and occupation (all were listed as laborers). The crime and sentences were also noted.[252] There was also a place on the admission form to indicate their anticipated discharge dates; since their sentences were for their natural lives, that would be when they died.

It wouldn't take long.

The prison was made up of a three-story administration building with three structures housing the dormitories.

It was crowded. There were 816 inmates counted in 1899. The dungeon-like dorm cells were about forty-two inches wide by nine feet

Race and the Hill Murder Trial

John F. Weyler. *From* History of the Baltimore Police Department, *1907.*

long and seven feet high. Solid cell doors had only small slits, and many of the rooms had no windows. There were no toilets in the cells—that would be an improvement added in the 1899 expansion and upgrade. The four remaining Hill murderers had only what were generally termed "filth buckets." Inmates were segregated by race and gender. Female offenders were housed at the penitentiary until about 1927. Nor was age much of a factor in the criminal population. Youths as young as eleven shared the facility with adults. They all shared their cells with lice, bedbugs, rats and cockroaches.[253]

Weyler, a former saloon owner and Democratic president of the Baltimore City Council, had no previous penal experience when appointed as warden in 1888. He stepped into the position at a time when morale was low among prison personnel, the facility was aged and in decay and the productivity of its inmates in generating income for the facility was disappointing to state officials.[254]

One of the warden's first moves after starting the job was to create a new set of rules, improving operations. He signed a contract with the Baltimore Boot and Shoe Company to have prisoners produce footwear.[255]

Emory, Hurtt, Baynard and Benson were soon put to work in the shoe shop, assigned there on the recommendation of the prison physician, Dr. Theodore Cooke Jr., primarily because they couldn't be used for hard labor.[256]

By June, all four of the prisoners were reported to be in bad health. Oddly, Emory was paralyzed below the hip.[257] Hurtt had developed a case of pneumonia, possibly as a symptom of tuberculosis.

Hurtt died at about five o'clock in the morning on Friday, June 30, attended by Dr. Cooke and prison chaplain the Reverend Edward D. Boone, of Loyola College,[258] who administered last rites. Said the *Transcript*: "He received the attention of the prison physician and everything possible was done by the prison officials to make his condition comfortable."

Boone declined to talk about what Hurtt said in confession, but Weyler, who seems to have enjoyed getting his name in the news, told reporters that he had discussions with the teens, and all claimed innocence. Boone buried Hurtt's body at St. Vincent's Cemetery on Rose Street, near Johns Hopkins University.

Emory was the next to go. After his condition continued to deteriorate, he died on Tuesday, August 8. He was also attended by Cooke and Boone. Boone took his confession, which did not include revelations about the Hill murder. Emory was also buried at St. Vincent's.[259]

The other two lasted a little longer.

A *Baltimore Herald* reporter interviewed Benson and Baynard in July 1895. The portion quoted in the July 18, 1895 edition of the *Transcript* demonstrated classic white-on-black stereotyping in the media, particularly with the use of vernacular:

> *The boys, who are now rather stouter than when placed in the institution, are otherwise changed since their confinement in the penitentiary, which commenced on January 3, 1893* [sic]. *It was explained to the boys that they need not talk unless they so desired. Bainard is now 18 years of age, and Benson 17. Bainard, when questioned, remained sullen and silent. Benson, the more intelligent of the two, in response to a question as to what he would do if he got out, said he would like to "run around a little," as there was not much room in the yard for that. He also said he would "like ter git something good ter eat." The warden said it was hard when they first came to the institution to make them understand that they had to work, but they had at last learned it and were doing their tasks faithfully, in the shoe department, which is the lightest work in the penitentiary.*

Benson was next to die, in what the *Kent News* described as "the strange fatality" among the prisoners in Baltimore. He drew his last breath on Friday, November 20, 1896.[260] His death came after he suffered in the infirmary for months with what was described as "cerebro-spinal meningitis." He also had tuberculosis. He apparently was delirious in the last days of his life.

Benson's body was turned over to Boone and was buried on the day of his death at Laurel Cemetery on Belair Street in Baltimore.[261]

The *Morning Herald* sought comments from Weyler, who seemed ever ready to opine. In this case, he said he felt his four charges, who were so quickly dying off in his care, were actually innocent:

Race and the Hill Murder Trial

> *Governor Brown never did a more humane act than that which saved the lives of those four boys…It was, I think, the wisest of his administration. I have had many interviews with Benson and the others, and I feel convinced that they were entirely innocent of Dr. Hill['s] murder. Of course, I have no other grounds upon which to base an opinion than my talks with them.*

He did not think they were part of a conspiracy, he said in comments that also made his racial prejudice clear:

> *You know the way of country negroes of a Saturday night to go to the nearest town and drink. I think that these boys, if they did leave Millington with the real murderers, turned off before Dr. Hill encountered the crowd. I cannot help but believe that they had no hand in the crime. But public sentiment down in Kent was strong, and so they were convicted.*

And he added, no doubt to the different direction of the interview questions:

> *I have nothing to say against the conduct of the three dead convicts while they were in my charge, nor have I of Baynard's behavior. They seemed utterly shocked at their conviction and heavy punishment, which resulted, I am inclined to think, in breaking down their health.*[262]

The remaining prisoner, Baynard, was recognized in the *Baltimore News* in August 1897 as one of six prisoners serving out life sentences at the penitentiary.[263]

He died on Sunday, September 10, 1899, about a week after being operated on by Cooke and Dr. Joseph Ward for appendicitis.[264] At the time of his death, he had built up an account of about $200—a substantial sum—for overtime work at the prison, probably in the shoe shop.

The *Transcript* hailed his death as the "End of a Bad Gang."[265]

It's uncertain where his body was buried. However, the paper reported that his mother, who lived on Green Street in Baltimore (her name was not given), had been informed of his death.

It may seem odd that all four prisoners died within seven years of their incarceration at the Maryland Penitentiary, and there were suggestions in the tone of some of the news reports that it was a conspiracy. However, there is absolutely no evidence that their deaths were anything other than natural—if you count the condition of the penitentiary as being "natural."

INJUSTICE ON THE EASTERN SHORE

Given the state of squalor existing in many state prisons, and especially the Maryland facility, it's not surprising that infectious diseases such as tuberculosis were the chief cause of death among the inmates.

Another of Kent's murderers died young after receiving a long sentence. Sarah Bradshaw was convicted of second-degree murder in the 1887 poisoning of her grandmother. The girl, whose age was listed variously as twelve to fifteen years old, lived with the elderly Deborah Bradshaw in their home at Riley's Neck, just east of Millington. It is not surprising that scientist Tonry was called in to consult on that case, and it was determined that rat poison, mixed in the grandmother's tea, was the cause of her demise. Sentenced to fourteen years, the teen was in the penitentiary when the four Hill murderers arrived. She died on November 5, 1893, from unknown causes.

Maryland's wasn't the only facility where a non-death sentence was considered a quick way to the grave because of unhealthy conditions. The state penitentiary in Delaware also had a bad reputation. When Hattie Reese was convicted of the shotgun murder of her husband in Dover, she feigned a loud cough when the judge sentenced her to life in prison. The cough "showed to those about her that she was probably receiving a death sentence between the order of the court and the ravages of tuberculosis, Nature's penalty for the peace that kills."[266]

Cooke complained about conditions in the Maryland Penitentiary and ultimately lost his job because of it. In April 1910, at a meeting of a medical faculty organization, he claimed Weyler's only interest was in turning a profit in the prison shops, "regardless of the health or the lives of the prisoners"; that a prisoner with "abdominal tuberculosis" was whipped and eventually died from the beating; that the food "is the worst that he ever saw"; and that work was carried out on the Sabbath.[267]

He claimed Weyler saved money by replacing meat purchases with a low-grade product that was mostly bone and tendon, that the flour and vegetables were below minimum standards of quality and that prisoners who couldn't meet production quotas were routinely punished with solitary confinement.[268]

Cooke started at the prison about 1891, freshly graduated from the University of Maryland and Johns Hopkins University. He recommended medical exams for the inmates, even before they were adjudicated. He also campaigned for greater authority by the prison physician, who, he said, should be more involved in monitoring the food supply and evaluating the prisoner before and after corporeal punishment and should even have input in the design of the facility. He said diseased inmates should have separate facilities:

> *The criminal* [sic] *insane and tubercular hospitals should be absolutely under the medical profession. Every state should build these hospitals. It is not right that the criminals suffering with insanity and tubercular trouble should be sent to the ordinary reformatory, because there they do not get the proper treatment and they endanger the lives of the other prisoners. Neither is it right that these criminals should be sent to hospital where the poor free man is sent. The most favorable spot in the state should be selected for these hospitals, the tubercular in the highest section of the state, as far as possible from civilization, and the insane in some rural section.*[269]

It's clear that at the time Cooke made his comments to the American Prison Association, undiseased inmates cohabited with the ill and were consequently exposed to infectious diseases such as tuberculosis. That may explain the quick demise of Emory, Hurtt and Benson.

Cooke's complaints about Weyler's management fell on deaf ears in 1910. In May, Weyler was reappointed as warden, and all of the prison staff, except Cooke, was retained. The board of the Maryland Penitentiary dismissed Cooke's charges against the warden.[270]

Two years later, Weyler retired as the longest-serving warden in the state's history. He was credited with making the prison shops profitable, stewarding the expansion and upgrade of the penitentiary and banning the lash as a form of punishment. He was made "warden emeritus" and given a yearly salary in his retirement. However, the following year, an investigation confirmed Cooke's allegations that the prison was filthy, bugs occupied every corner, the food was unfit for human consumption, rats thrived, prisoners were mistreated and the medical facilities were unequal to the task of treating the inmate population.[271]

By 1929, the facility had been rated by the National Society of Penal Information as being "in a poorer condition than any other in the east."

> *The report called morale of penitentiary prisoners plainly low and ascribed this to poor working and living conditions. Among details of the report on the penitentiary were named a cell-house, dark and poorly ventilated, which should be abandoned; the main bathhouse, called unsanitary and dangerous because proper supervision of the men is impossible; and condition of most of the shops, constituting "as grave a fire hazard as any noted in the country."*[272]

With such conditions prevalent, it's not surprising that Emory, Hurtt and Benson died of "natural causes." In this manner, three of the four whose sentences were commuted to life were effectively "executed" by a filthy, unhealthy prison environment in less time than the average death row inmate in the present day would take to face his punishment. The fourth, Baynard, died from complications of a surgery that can go awry even today but back then would have had a much higher risk because of the lack of sanitation at the facility, primitive medical equipment and less advanced surgical techniques.

WAS THERE A MISCARRIAGE OF JUSTICE?

If Dr. Hill's murder had happened in the present day, the fates of the eight suspects convicted would have been vastly different, according to Robert H. Strong Jr., who recently ended his fourth term as Kent County's state's attorney.

Strong examined news articles and some of the material related to the case. He questioned the way the defense attorneys handled the case. Although times and courtrooms are different now than in the era of the Hill murder trial, he notes, many of the legal guidelines and attorney practices are the same.

Strong commented extensively from the standpoints of both procedure and the evaluation of the evidence.

Under the heading of procedure, he first considered the question of the accused men's ages:

> *Maryland law has come a long way since 1892. However, the five juveniles, all ages 16 or 17 would be charged and stand trial as adults—(Criminal Procedure 4-202 [c]), murder in the first degree being a crime which carries a maximum penalty of death. If any of them had been 15 or younger, at the time of the offense, they could have requested a removal to juvenile court jurisdiction.*

Those charged were represented by only two attorneys, James Alfred Pearce and Marion deKalb Smith. Strong notes that this would be an ethical lapse in today's legal arena:

> *For two attorneys to represent eight charged defendants in modern times would be an egregious violation of due process and of the ethical obligation attorneys must recognize. The newspaper article [Chestertown Transcript, October 6, 1892] explaining the victim's father's and the general public sentiment of relief that the two court-appointed lawyers would be handling the defense speaks volumes. The rumor that the defendants would hire a city attorney were quelled, but all opportunities for a fair trial by modern standards were over at that appointment.*

And Strong notes that a change of venue should have been sought, regardless of the general lofty reputation of the defense attorneys:

> *We have no indication that the defense attorneys even attempted a change of venue. Since the northern county was in a near lynch mob mentality, no attempt to remove this trial to another part of Maryland was malpractice—then or now. With a local physician as a victim, with the victim being white, with the defendants being black and of no appreciable social standing, who would not want to have their case removed?*

It was common legal practice—even early in the nineteenth century—in controversial cases, in the face of strong public sentiment, to request a change of venue.

In 1831, Thomas I. Bond, a white man, was charged with murdering Daniel Plater in Talbot County. Plater, a free black man who worked for Bond, was trying to leave the area. Bond caught up to him on the Miles River ferry, and a heated argument ensued. Plater received a fatal stab wound when the fight became physical. Bond's defense attorney, Ezekiel F. Chambers of Kent County, a War of 1812 veteran, noted politician and future judge, sought and received a change of venue for his client. Bond was tried in Queen Anne's County. The change didn't keep Bond out of prison but may have saved him from a first-degree murder conviction. On November 14, 1831, a jury found him guilty of second-degree murder, and he was sentenced to twelve years in the penitentiary.[273]

In the case of the Cosden murder trial, one suspect, William Shelton, was tried in Kent. In fact, Pearce's father was one of his defense attorneys, the other being E.A. Moore. But murder suspects Abraham Taylor and Nicholas Murphy sought and received a change of venue to Elkton.

It was likely that the public approved the selection of Pearce and Smith because the perception was that they would make sure, since they were local favorites, that the outcome would be convictions. In fact, it would have been political suicide for these two had the trial resulted in acquittals.

Strong continues:

> *In that same vein, what competent attorney would permit all of the defendants to be tried in one court trial? With the risk of accomplice liability hanging over the heads of those present who may not have taken an active part, any competent professional would have demanded bifurcation. The risk that some of the accused may have gone along with no idea of what was about to happen should have been reason enough for separate trial.*

To use the Cosden case again as an example, all three of the white suspects received separate trials, and all had jury trials.

Strong also looked at the failure of the defense to request a jury trial:

> *It appears that the court-appointed attorneys waived the defendants' right to a trial by jury, a right handed down by English Common Law and which was certainly available to the accused. This was the lynchpin for any of the juveniles who may have been unwitting participants. Even though their presence at the scene, if proven beyond a reasonable doubt, would have placed them in serious jeopardy, the prosecutor, State's Attorney Slay, would have had to prove that each of the juveniles, who may not have physically attacked Dr. Hill, actually aided, abetted or encouraged the actual attack upon the victim. Their presence alone does not equate to guilt—ipso facto. By modern standards, the waiver of jury trial and having a consolidated court trial left little doubt of where the tribunal was headed.*

Strong also wondered why there wasn't an appeal:

> *Within three and a half months of verdict, four of the defendants were hanged. Even though the governor personally took statements from the juvenile offenders and commuted their sentences to life in prison (which turned out to be less than eight years), I see no evidence that an appeal was requested. As of this writing, it takes about twenty years from verdict to execution, with the state paying exorbitant resources to provide a death row inmate with every conceivable appellate review. For these hangings to occur in such an expedited manner is another negative mark against the legal system of 1892.*

Strong also questioned letting Arrelee Hill forego an appearance in court in favor of a written statement: "The defense had no opportunity to cross examine [her about] his sobriety or lack thereof on the night of the attack, his appearance, the nature of the injuries or the times he was away from home and his routine and travel habits."

Kent County sheriff John F. Price IV has served in that elected office since 1994. He notes that the Campbell case should have been handled better, eliminating the motive for the attack on Hill:

> *From what I have read, the white men who participated in the attack should have been held responsible for Campbell's death and certainly contributed to his death. In today's world, we certainly would have arrested someone or several people who obviously contributed to Campbell's death.*
>
> *Once Dr. Hill rendered his decision on the autopsy report of Campbell as "heart disease," this just added additional unrest in the African American community. Unfortunately, we still see levels of distrust in our criminal justice system throughout our country. In 1891, I can only imagine how unfair the law was applied by an all-white leadership within the county. Times have changed, and I believe that there is consistent and fair law enforcement for all in our county. Communication and a constant display of fairness while maintaining law and order are extremely important. It appears to me that this was certainly not the case back in those days.*

EXECUTIONS REMOVED TO PENITENTIARY

African American Joseph Wright was the last man legally executed, by hanging or otherwise, in Kent County.

On the night of Thursday, November 4, 1897, Wright, who had an unsavory reputation, got into an argument with William Newcomb, a popular African American who had loaned Wright money. However, in a drunken rage during a quarrel at a country store at Big Woods, Kent County, Wright pulled a pistol and shot his unarmed victim in the heart.

He was initially tried in Kent County, but when it was clear it would deadlock the jury, the trial was moved to Talbot, where he was found guilty of first-degree murder.[274]

Wright's court-appointed attorneys, Richard Hynson and Harrison Vickers, sought an appeal based on a question about a self-incriminatory statement Wright made to a bystander within an hour of the shooting. The case was heard by the Maryland Court of Appeals. It decided on December 21, 1898, to uphold the circuit court jury's verdict of guilty.[275]

Since there was only one sentence that could be handed out for a first-degree murder conviction, Judge James Alfred Pearce sentenced the Cecil County native to death. It was the first time that Pearce, defense attorney in the Hill case, ever handed down a death sentence in Kent County.

Wright's sentence caused a public outcry against the death penalty by many of Kent's socially well-placed white women, but to no avail.

The drop fell on March 24 at 9:23 a.m. Wright died "without a struggle," and like the four executed in the Hill case, he was buried in an unmarked grave at the almshouse graveyard.

Injustice on the Eastern Shore

In 1908, the Maryland legislature changed the law to allow a judge the option of sentencing a person with death or life in prison for first-degree murder. The law amended Section 335 of the state codes to read:

> *Every person convicted of murder in the first degree, his or her aiders, abettors and counselors shall suffer death, or undergo a confinement in the penitentiary of the State for the period of their natural life, in the discretion of the court before which such person may be tried.*[276]

That saved one man from the gallows five years later.

It was a sensational case in Kent County that resulted from the murder of James Coleman on December 23, 1913. National Guard troops were sent to Chestertown to prevent a lynching. The two charged in the case, Norman Mable and James Paraway, were tried outside the county. Mable was sentenced to eighteen years in the penitentiary after a jury found him guilty of second-degree murder. Paraway received a life sentence after being found guilty of first-degree murder in a non-jury trial.

If it had been just a few years earlier, Paraway would have faced the death penalty.

The Coleman murder had parallels to Hill's murder. It was another case of a lone white man in a single-horse carriage being stopped by African American assailants. One grabbed the horse; the other ran up from behind and around the side and bludgeoned Coleman. Coleman's lifeless body was then positioned in the carriage by wedging his head into the ironwork of the folding top.

The perpetrators might well have taken their murder crib notes from the account of the Hill murder.

The motive in this case, however, was robbery. The thieves' haul was thirty dollars.

In the legislative session of 1922, state senator David Gregg McIntosh Jr. introduced a bill to have all executions in the state take place in a special, permanent "death chamber" at the house of corrections.

It was similar to other bills proposed earlier over concerns that hangings at the county seats had become barbarous spectacles. The *Sun* supported the bill in an editorial in its March 10, 1922 edition:

> *It is difficult to understand how, in supposedly decent communities, thousands of men and women could be found who seemed to delight in witnessing such spectacles and who flocked to them as to a circus…*

Race and the Hill Murder Trial

Whenever an execution occurs, in the counties there is almost invariably such an exhibition of human degradation and savagery as almost makes us wonder who is the greater brute—the fiend on the gallows or the hardened man in the crowd who revels in the ghastly drama.

It's uncertain whether the Hill murder was recalled for the purpose of this debate, though it would have been appropriate. The *Sun* referenced hangings in Towson and Easton.

The Easton case was that of Isaiah Fountain, an African American man found guilty of raping a fourteen-year-old white girl in 1919. The process of his trial, conviction and execution was marked by sensation and controversy because he escaped twice and tried to commit suicide in his cell twice. At one point, the Maryland National Guard was called in to protect the prisoner from lynching.

His execution at the Talbot Jail in Easton in July 1920 went without a hitch. It was done inside the jail with a gallows constructed within the building to limit access to spectators. Nonetheless, the case became a point of reference in the debate about public execution.

McIntosh's bill was changed as it went through the committee process and was ultimately approved by both the House of Delegates and the senate.

The final bill called for executions to take place at the Maryland Penitentiary in a special room or building:

The Warden of the Maryland Penitentiary is hereby authorized and directed to provide and maintain a permanent death chamber within the confines of said Penitentiary, and which said death chamber shall have all the necessary appliances for the proper execution of felons by hanging by the neck until dead.[277]

Even after both houses of the legislature approved it, the bill remained controversial. The state Board of Prison Control filed a protest asking Governor Albert C. Ritchie not to sign it into law. The complaint was that it would be bad for prison morale at the penitentiary to have a death chamber on the premises.[278]

The bill became law on April 11, with the change effective for those convicted after January 1, 1923.

Professional skeptic and acerbic satirist H.L. Mencken, of the *Baltimore Sun*, who supported hanging as a form of capital punishment, favored the change: "A new State law has got rid of the obscene crowds that used to flock to hangings, and of the bungling that once made them revolting. The gallows at the Penitentiary is admirably designed."[279]

But the method ending the lives of the state's most ill-mannered criminals, no matter how private, fell out of favor.

The last hanging in the state was on June 10, 1955, when William C. Thomas was executed for rape and murder. After that, the state switched to death by asphyxiation with the use of gas until 1961. The most recent method of execution in Maryland was by lethal injection.[280]

Maryland was not superlative, compared to other states, regarding the number of executions held within its jurisdiction. Between the time of the original settlements in the seventeenth century and 2002, 312 executions were recorded.[281] States including Alabama, Texas and New York, to name a few, had double or more. However, the period from 1866 to 1899 was the most active in the state, with 74 people—almost one-fourth of the total—executed during those years.

Kent County has had a relatively small number of executions in its history. There were thirteen recorded between 1729 and 1770. There were at least nine in the nineteenth century and none in the twentieth century.

What does stand out is the number of multiple executions in the county's early history. There have been two triple executions. One of them, in 1746, was also the most horrendous, when one of three convicted murderers, a convict servant named Esther Anderson, was burned at the stake. It's uncertain why she was treated differently than her two male co-conspirators, who were hanged. The other triple execution was for the Cosden murders. There were two double hangings, too, and of course the quadruple hanging for Hill's murder.

The Hill murder didn't set the state record for simultaneous executions. Seven slaves were hanged and quartered in Calvert County in 1742.

As the twenty-first century approached, the death penalty in the state continued to be an issue of passionate debate. A death penalty moratorium was considered; it was begun in 1996—largely on racial grounds, for good reason. Since the executions were switched to the penitentiary in 1923, 77 percent of those executed have been African American.[282]

The issue crystallized in 2009, when Governor Martin O'Malley, a former prosecutor, began a long-touted campaign to repeal the death penalty. On March 15, 2013, the General Assembly voted to abolish the death penalty altogether.

It wasn't unanimous. The House of Delegates voted eighty-two to fifty-six for the ban, while the state senate followed with a twenty-seven-to-twenty vote.

Race and the Hill Murder Trial

The voting paralleled party lines, with the majority Democrats gaining the upper hand. Attempts to reach a less partisan compromise failed as numerous Republican amendments were unsuccessful for lack of Democratic support.

With that legislative approval, Maryland became the eighteenth state to abolish the death penalty.

O'Malley, who was rumored to have an interest in a 2016 run for the presidency, was elated:

> *Today the Maryland General Assembly voted to repeal the death penalty in Maryland. And in so doing, we just released Maryland from the ranks of other places in the world—including Iraq, Iran, North Korea, and others—that still do commit public executions.*

He added a philosophical note:

> *Because in our state, we understand that there is no spare American. Every single life is needed, and every single life is important. So let's continue to do more of the things that work, and thereby really do right by those who have gone before us…those who have lost their lives to violent deaths…that we remember their lives, and that we honor them—not by taking life, but by saving life.*[283]

Republican state delegate Jay Jacobs, from Kent County, voted against the repeal. He said it eliminates a tool in punishing the worst criminal offenders. "It takes away a bargaining chip" in dealing with murder suspects. It also leaves in question how you punish someone who commits a crime in prison, such as murdering a prison guard or another inmate, after already being given the maximum sentence for an earlier capital offense. "They're already in there for life. What have they got to lose?"

Jacobs said there's no doubt that O'Malley's efforts to repeal the death penalty were political. "He was punching the ticket," he said, pandering to his liberal state and national constituency.

Republican state senator Richard F. Colburn also voted against the repeal. He cited one case in which a man raped and murdered a child. The suspect wouldn't admit his role in the murder until he was given the option to plead guilty with a guarantee of a life sentence in order to avoid the death penalty.[284]

THE VICTIMS

The indelible mark left by violent crime fades with time but never completely disappears. It may vary by scale—Hitler's massacre of six million Jews dominates the global conscience, while national pundits still speculate on alleged conspiracies behind the two Kennedy assassinations and that of Martin Luther King Jr. On a local scale, it would be difficult to find a Kent County native who hasn't heard of the Hill murder, even after more than 120 years. Some locals still have original copies of news clippings, handed down from their ancestors. Those who don't have originals have copies of the 160th-anniversary edition of the *Kent County News*, published in 1953, which included copies of several of the original Hill murder articles from the *Kent News*.[285]

Such crimes directly affect the victims' friends, associates and relatives for generations. For example, there is still a newsletter published on the topic of the 1851 Cosden murders.

In January 2011, a descendant of Henry Cook asked why there was a copy of a drawing of Dr. Hill taken from a contemporary newspaper in a family scrapbook in his possession. The answer, of course, was that Cook was a member of the Hill murder grand jury and a witness at the trial.

What happened to the doctor's immediate family?

From the little available in the public record, Arrelee Hill was inconsolable, certainly for years and perhaps for the rest of her life. She remained in a "nervous condition" throughout the investigation and trial of her husband's murderers.

Race and the Hill Murder Trial

She and baby Ethel moved in with her parents near Baltimore. She was reported to be too "ill" to testify. The *Transcript* reported that she became ill on the first anniversary of the assault, while on a visit to the Hill family in Kent County, where she spent the summer.

While money was probably not a concern for her, she did receive a $3,000 life insurance payment after her husband's death.[286]

Arrelee never remarried. With her daughter, she lived out her life in Baltimore with her parents until their deaths. Her mother died on January 6, 1916. Her father died in January 1922 at his home on East Twenty-second Street.

Arrelee died on the afternoon of July 20, 1932, forty years after her husband's death. The notice in the *Baltimore Sun* stated that she was the "beloved wife of the late Dr. James Heighe Hill." Funeral services were held at the Govans ME Church, and her remains were interred in Oak Lawn Cemetery.[287]

Ethel Heighe Hill went by her middle name. She was a bright child and as a toddler would "chatter away like a magpie."

She graduated from the Maryland Normal School and in 1911 became an elementary school teacher in Colgate, Baltimore County.[288] She continued as a teacher through the rest of her life. She never married.[289] She earned a bachelor of science degree from Johns Hopkins University and a master of arts degree from Columbia University. Maryland state school records indicate that for a number of years she assisted in the development of education policies and was among the faculty, teaching elementary education, at the State Teachers College at Towson. She retired sometime after 1950. She died at the Manor House in Seaford, Delaware, on July 9, 1976.

She moved to Delaware in retirement to live with or near her cousin Florence Hill Mitchell, Dr. Hill's niece, who lived in Millsboro.

Mitchell's daughter, Barbara Wharton, said in 2011 that she recalled her cousin and remembered the retired teacher had items that once belonged to the doctor, including the medical case now on display at the Historical Society of Kent County.

Wharton also recalled seeing an original photograph of the dogcart.

However, she never talked about her father, Wharton said.

Ethel Heighe Hill's grave is located in Oaklawn Cemetery in Baltimore. On September 6, the year she died, her estate apparently donated to the museum in Chestertown the medical case that her father had carried on the night of his fatal encounter.

Hester Hill, the doctor's mother, didn't live to see the demise of Benson and Baynard. She died on April 5, 1895, probably from the flu, at her

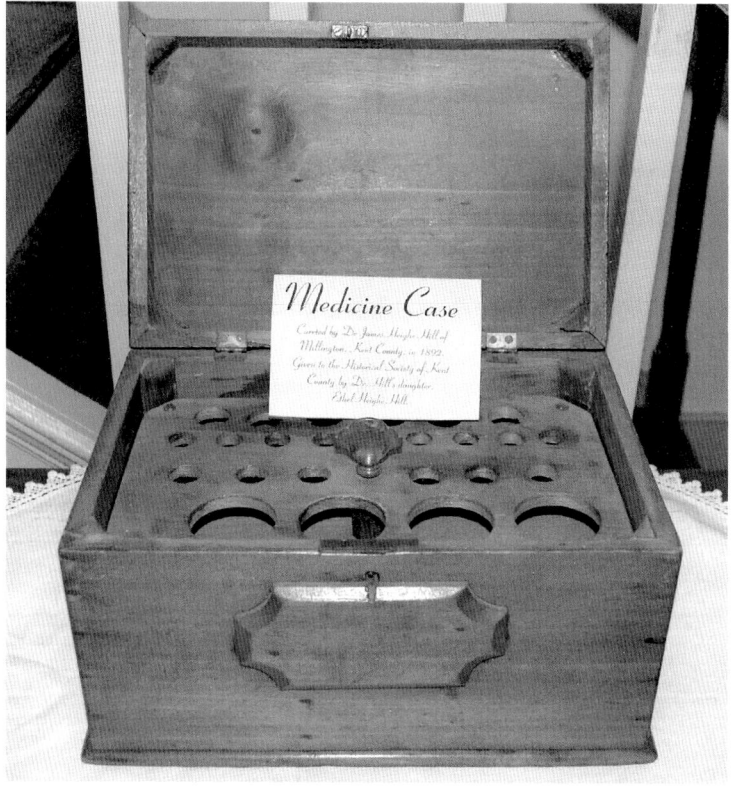

Dr. Heighe Hill's medical case, which he carried with him on that fateful night in April 1892, is on display at the Historical Society of Kent County in Chestertown. *Photo by Kevin Hemstock.*

home in Locust Grove. Her husband, Samuel, went to his grave in July 1900 with the knowledge that all those involved in the death of his son, except for John Potts, had had an audience with their maker.

Even in his obituary, Hill was remembered for doting on his little granddaughter and vice versa. She was with him during his fatal illness.[290] In his will, he left her one-fourth of the money raised from his estate: $1,110.69.[291]

James Heighe Hill, the doctor's namesake nephew, son of his brother Charles, eventually bought Colin Stam's Victorian Gothic home on Washington Avenue in Chestertown. It's now a bed-and-breakfast called Hill's Inn.

John Ahern, who lived next door to Hill at the time of the murder, had a son, born in 1894, whom he named John. John's middle name was Heighe.

RIPPLES TO THE PRESENT

Thomas Dodd was elected sheriff in November 1893. Plummer didn't run. The Plummers moved out of the jail on November 20 to Rock Point Farm.

After the execution, the former sheriff received several offers from people wanting to buy the scaffold on which Brown, Brooks, Williams and Comegys came to their end. In one case, a group of speculators offered $2,000 for it in order to put it on display at the World's Fair.[292] There was also an offer from someone interested in displaying it at the Tolchester Beach Amusement Park. However, Plummer kept the scaffold erected in the jail yard until his term ended. He then had it disassembled and moved to his farm, where he used the wood to build a smokehouse. The *Kent News* picked up a *Wilmington Morning News* story, adding a racist twist:

> *Ex Sheriff E.J. Plummer, of Chestertown, has on his farm near this town a smoke-house which is safe to bet will not be robbed by any of the light-fingered people who sometimes find it cheaper to take meat from a smoke-house than to buy it. It is also doubtful if any of the colored laborers about the place would* [go] *to the smoke house even if they were employed to do so.*
>
> *Mr. Plummer is the man who hanged the four murderers of Dr. J.H. Hill over a year ago. After the men had been hanged a number of persons wanted to purchase the scaffold. One man wanted to take it to the World's Fair to exhibit. Another man wanted to take it to Tolchester Beach for the same purpose, but the sheriff did not think that it would be right to allow*

the scaffold to be exhibited and so it was allowed to remain in the jail yard until his term as sheriff of Kent County expired. When Mr. Plummer's term as sheriff expired he removed to his farm in the county. With him he took the big scaffold on which the four men were hanged, and built a smokehouse. It is still doing duty in that capacity.[293]

It's not clear on which farm the smokehouse was located. Plummer rented Rock Point farm, on Plum Point, owned by Theodore Diehl. The former sheriff may have purchased the farm in 1894, which is what a newspaper article indicates. However, there is no deed in his name, or that of his wife, for that property on file in the Kent County courthouse. The house there burned in a fire on May 15, 1895. No one was injured, but the structure was a total loss.[294] According to news reports, the fire started over the parlor, where there had not been fire in the fireplace since winter. It was never clear how the fire started.

Another fire later that year burned a stand of trees on the property. In neither case is a smokehouse mentioned.

In 1896, Clayton Dulin, who was living on William Ford's farm, near the site of the attack on the doctor, found the knife thought to be the one wielded by Moses Brown and used to cut Hill's throat. Dulin found it behind his house while crossing the stream several hundred yards below the bridge.[295]

Watson Spear, Hill's employee, went to work for Dr. Nathaniel Comegys. In 1893, Spear's brother John was charged with murdering farm laborer John Brophy. He was acquitted of manslaughter charges the following year. Soon after, the brothers moved to Colorado.

The dogcart in which Dr. Hill was riding at the time of the attack was sold by Hill's father to J. Frank Ernest in October 1892. It was placed in a Baltimore museum less than a year after the trial.[296] It's uncertain what happened to it. Hill's wooden medical case remains on display at the Historical Society of Kent County, located in the Geddes-Piper House, Church Alley, Chestertown.

Edward Comegys, Frisby Comegys's brother, was charged with the attempted rape of a white woman in Blanco, Queen Anne's County, in 1904.[297] Another brother, Harry Comegys, was charged with the December 1921 murder of William Epps at the victim's house in Golts.[298]

JAIL FALLS TO THE WRECKING BALL

The grand brick testimony to the local penal system, designed by J. Crawford Neilson, constructed by H.M. Stuart and completed in 1885, was disparaged throughout much of its twentieth-century existence. County lockups were regularly inspected from the late nineteenth century on. Initially, the inspections were undertaken by the Prisoner's Aid Society. That role was taken over by the state's Department of Welfare early in the twentieth century.

Although it was once referred to as a "mansion," the facility seldom passed muster by the inspectors. In 1929, the jail was determined to be "deplorable, wretched and entirely unsatisfactory," as were the jails in five other counties, in a review by the Welfare Department's director Stuart S. Janney. A lawyer, Janney was a good friend of Governor Albert C. Ritchie, with whom he had once partnered. Kent County sheriff Thomas J. Hadaway at the time blamed the legislature for failing to pass a $30,000 bond bill to upgrade the facility.[299]

Just three years later, Janney declared the jail to be much improved:

> For the first time since these inspections have been made, this jail showed a number of improvements, among which was the installation of a set of new cots designed by the sheriff and made by the prisoners under his supervision. The frames made are of pipe and the canvas kept in a taught [sic] position by wire fasteners. Another improvement was the cutting of window and repairing of bathroom on the second floor.[300]

Janney lauded Sheriff John Vickers for segregating the female prisoners. However, he noted that the room set aside for the ladies on the third floor was, at the time of the inspection, occupied by "a number of federal prisoners," no doubt incarcerated for moonshining. Additional improvements included a new floor for the end cell on the second floor, "which has been a source of unfavorable comment."

In 1935, there was a new state director of welfare, Charles J. Butler, and he slammed the local slammer but added in his report: "With some additional attention, this jail, which generally has been listed among the worst, can become reasonably satisfactory."[301]

And so it went. In 1947, the county's own grand jury, which also inspected the jail regularly, recommended numerous improvements and repairs to both the jail and the sheriff's living quarters. However, this body unanimously opposed a proposed regional jail for Kent, Queen Anne's and Caroline Counties.[302] The issue of a regional jail continues to crop up periodically in modern times.

When the courthouse was expanded in 1967, with the modern Greco design side entry (now the front) extending within feet of the back of the jail, it was assumed that something would be done with the jail, with replacement on or off the site.

A proposal for a bi-county jail was dropped in 1978. But by then, there was no doubt that the old facility needed to be replaced; it was too small and obsolete, and it clashed with the new courthouse. One plan was to build a new structure on the parking lot to the rear of the courthouse. That was opposed by Chestertown's town officials, and residents of Queen Street there objected. The Maryland Historic Trust opposed razing the old facility.[303]

In January 1986, the Kent County commissioners approved a new facility on Flatland Road, signing a $3.3 million contract with J. Roland Dashiell & Sons, Inc. One month later, the commissioners agreed that if a private concern didn't take on the cost of moving the old jail building to a different site, it would have to be demolished.

The old jail ceased operation in October 1987, when the operation was moved to the new site.

There were several plans floated to save the old structure. The most serious, championed by the late Walter Harris of the Kent County Historical Trust, was a proposal by Bradford and Tyler Johnson. Their concept involved moving the building about one hundred feet northeast onto the county parking lot with a plan to then lease the space for offices.

Harris, representing the Historical Society of Kent County; Preservation, Inc.; the Kent County Historical Trust; and Preservation Maryland, pleaded

Race and the Hill Murder Trial

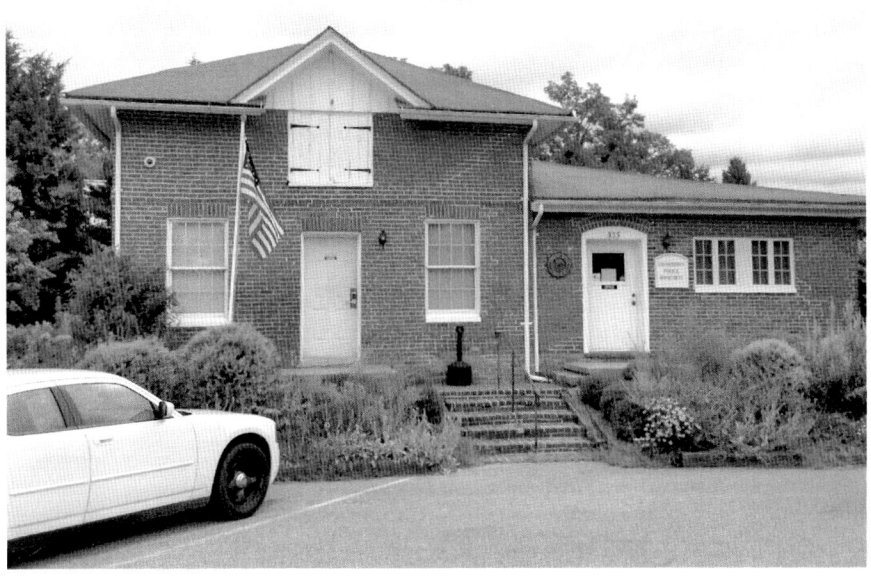

The Chestertown Police Department is currently housed in a building on Cross Street that was originally the stable of the old Kent County jail. *Photo by Kevin Hemstock.*

with the commissioners in December 1987 to save the building. A new plan, moving the building 130 feet, would mollify some opponents of preserving the building, he said.

"We should preserve every square inch of our heritage…not only for the people who live here, but for the visitors who come here to see the county, and Chestertown's preserved, historical buildings," he said.[304]

The county advised him to continue his efforts but also approved going forward with an application for a demolition permit from Chestertown.

In May 1988, the demolition permit was approved and a demolition contract awarded. The Historical Society of Kent County and the Kent County Historical Trust again pleaded with the commissioners to hold off until preservation plans were formulated. But on Friday, June 3, 1988, the wrecking ball went into action, and the building was quickly reduced to rubble.

Most people have forgotten the old jailhouse. The side of the courthouse where it was located is now a verdant open space, shaded by a dozen or more spreading oaks and maples planted when the jail was demolished. It's an attractive vista, particularly in spring, well suited for the venerable seat of local justice.

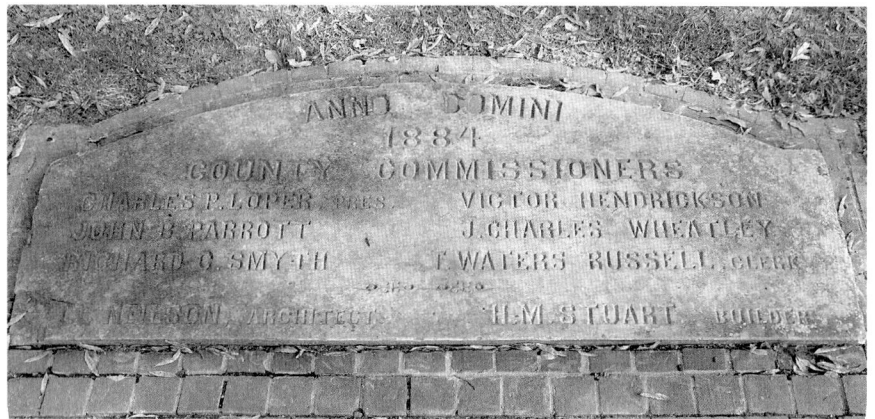

This monument once adorned the front of the old Kent County jail. It's now located on the courthouse lawn. *Photo by Kevin Hemstock.*

Two vestiges of the old jail remain. The stable, once located behind the jail, was moved to Cross Street and is now the Chestertown police station. Plans are now in the works to move the police station, and when that happens, the fate of the old "stable" is uncertain.

The original 1885 concrete dedication marker, once displayed above the jail's central first-floor front window, is now inset in the ground on the northeast side of the courthouse property, little noticed under shady trees next to the brick path on that side. It is within a couple dozen feet of where three men and one boy were hanged on January 13, 1893.

NOTES

COLLECTING A DEBT

1. *Chestertown Transcript*, June 23, 1892.
2. Ibid.
3. *New York Times*, April 27, 1892, 1; *Kent News*, January 2, 1892, 3; June 25, 1892, 3. The June 23, 1892 *Transcript* says Joe Potts was alone at this confrontation. That seems unlikely.
4. *Transcript*, December 31, 1891, 3. The *Transcript* is not clear on the number of blacks; the *Kent News* stated that there were three people, including John Potts and Campbell. The June 25, 1892 *Kent News*, in describing the conspiracy theory in Hill's death, says there was a "gang of negroes." None of the papers indicates how many whites were involved. The June 25, 1892 account differed from the other accounts on numerous particulars.
5. County incorporation records, Book JKH Book 1, p. 237.
6. *Kent News*, December 27, 1879.
7. Ibid., June 25, 1892.
8. Ibid.
9. *Transcript*, August 18, 1892, statement of expenses for the county levy. The county paid Hill's estate.
10. *New York Times*, April 26, 1892.
11. *Transcript*, June 23, 1892.

MILLINGTON IN THE 1890S

12. Taylor, "Down the Eastern Shore."
13. *Transcript*, January 15, 1891.
14. *New York Times*, May 27, 1884.

The African American Community

15. A handout titled "History of John Wesley United Methodist Church," 1976, shows that the feeling continued into modern times.
16. 1900 census statistics. The percentage of blacks in Kent in 1890 was 38.96. It grew to 39.45 percent a decade later.
17. 1900 census statistics, by physical counts on the individual pages.
18. *Kent News*, August 25, 1888.
19. Ibid., July 26, 1875.
20. Ibid., September 22, 1866.
21. Ibid., May 21, 1870.
22. Ibid.
23. Supplement to the laws of Maryland, 1868, Article 14.
24. *Evening Telegraph*, April 4, 1870.
25. *St. Clairsville Chronicle*, May 19, 1870.
26. The *Columbian and Bloomsburg Democrat*, of Bloomsburg, Pennsylvania, on June 17, 1870, carried the piece by the *New York Herald*. It's uncertain how the size of the voter parcel was changed; however, the May 4, 1870 deed (JKH 315-317) on file in the Kent County courthouse states the total size as thirty-four feet, nine inches, just a little bit more than one inch per person.

Hill Sets Up House in Millington

27. *Sun*, January 13, 1893.
28. Kent County Land Records, JKH10-662.
29. Maryland Historical Trust: School, K-566; store, K567; church, K-568.
30. Derby and White, *National Cyclopedia of American Biography*, vol. 9.
31. *Transcript*, December 15, 1887.
32. *Kent News*, January 14, 1893.
33. *Sun*, October 18, 1892.
34. *Transcript*, October 3, 1889; *Kent News*, October 5, 1889.
35. According to Dr. Hill's administrative accounts in the Register of Wills Office, "James E. Edwards" was owed $22.60 "for house rent." James A. Edwards, carriage maker, owned property on the south side of Cypress Street, in the vicinity of what is now 403 Cypress. The *Lake, Griffing & Stevenson Atlas of Kent and Queen Anne Counties* does not show a double house on that side of the street. A double is on the other side, but there is no indication that Edwards, using whatever middle initial, owned property on the north side of the street. Kent County Land Records, SB7-628; JTD 10-448; JTD 13-182; APR7-216.
36. Kent County Register of Wills, inventory of the "goods and chattels personal estate of James H. Hill."
37. Bill from Shoemaker & Busch, wholesale druggists of Philadelphia, December 2, 1891.
38. Kent County Land Records, JKH10-651. The transfer was made on New Year's Eve 1872 but was not recorded until April 24, 1874.
39. Records of the Asbury ME Church.

Notes to Pages 39–50

A House Call

40. *Kent News*, October 29, 1892, transcript of written testimony of Arrelee Hill.
41. Ibid., April 30, 1892.
42. Ibid., May 26, 1883.
43. Ibid., July 13, 1889; J.P. docket of William Johnson, pp. 173–74. While the July 6 incident was attributed to "drunken negroes," it was actually an unidentified, and apparently unpunished, white man "from Queen Anne's County" who was described as the "leader."
44. *Transcript*, April 14, 1892.
45. There were two men by the name of James Shaw in the county's first district on the 1900 census. James and Annie are listed directly under the household of Clarence Hurlock. This conflicts with *Tales of Kent County*.
46. *Kent News*, April 30, 1892.
47. *Transcript*, May 5, 1892, for sorrel; June 23, 1892, for mare.
48. Diary of Dr. William Maxwell Jr., p. 213.

Ford's Hill and Destiny

49. Measured by automobile odometer; both local newspapers said the distance was one mile. They also added one mile to the distance between Millington and Massey.
50. Goodykoontz Perpetual Moon Chart, 1898.
51. *Kent News*, April 30, 1892.
52. *Transcript*, May 12, 1892. At an "indignation" meeting held by area blacks in Chestertown, a resolution was passed bemoaning the use of liquor as "a means to the end of the committal of this dreadful murder which we deplore."
53. *Transcript*, May 5, 1892, testimony of Joshua Baynard.
54. Ibid., June 23, 1892.
55. *Sun*, November 1, 1892, said Hill offered money.
56. *Transcript*, May 5, 1892; *Kent News*, April 30, 1892, testimony of Joshua Baynard.
57. Baynard initially said the stone was thrown, but most said it was not. The *Sun* of November 1, 1892, quoted Judge Wickes as stating that Benson and Brown "hacked" Hill after Brooks hit him with the rock and Williams stabbed him.
58. *Kent News*, April 30, 1892; *Transcript*, May 5, 1892, Joshua Baynard's testimony at the inquest.
59. *Transcript*, June 23, 1892.
60. *Kent News*, April 30, 1892.
61. Ibid.
62. *Transcript*, October 26, 1892, "Daily."
63. *Kent News*, October 29, 1892.
64. Ibid. She did not appear in court but gave a written response to questions.
65. *Transcript*, October 26, 1892, "Daily."
66. *Smyrna Times*, April 27, 1892.

67. *Sun*, October 26, 1892.
68. *Transcript*, October 26, 1892, "Daily," trial testimony.

It Was No Accident

69. *Transcript*, October 26, 1892, "Daily," trial testimony.
70. Ibid.
71. *Washington Times*, March 4, 1906, interview with Wilbur Bates.
72. *Olean Democrat*, April 28, 1892.
73. *New York Times*, April 26, 1892.
74. *Transcript*, May 5, 1892.
75. His name was Mander, but in many of the articles and paperwork concerning the killing, he is called Manda.
76. The hotel in Millington would eventually come under the management of John Bailey and thereafter become known as the Bailey Hotel. It burned down in 1904. Rebuilt, it remains to the present day as a locus for apartments and shops and is still sometimes referred to as the Bailey Hotel.
77. *Transcript*, May 5, 1892.
78. *Sun*, April 29, 1892. The article did not say that Nevins was there but that "Detective Wm. Pippin" was there. That had to be an error since Nevins was the only "detective" in the case. Bates, of the *Philadelphia Press*, was never mentioned in the *Sun* articles. That's either because he was the competition or he *was* the correspondent for the *Sun*. However, it seems likely that he also accompanied the group taking Baynard to Chestertown.
79. From the May 2, 1892 minutes of the board of trustees of Asbury ME Church, courtesy of the Reverend Larry Jameson.
80. *Kent News*, April 30, 1892.
81. Kent County Register of Wills, administrative accounts.
82. BY-LAWS of ToghWogh Tribe, No. 169, IORM, 1913.

Lynching Prevented

83. James Crawford Neilson (1816–1900), often associated with John Rudolph Niernsee, was a prominent architect from Howard County. He was educated in Europe. He was involved in the design of hundreds of buildings in Maryland, Virginia and South Carolina. The jail wasn't his only partnership with Stuart. They also worked together in 1885 on the design and construction of the home of William N.E. Wickes, on Water Street near the Chester River Bridge. It was the site of the Buxton murder in 1935. He also designed two of the Washington College houses, once located on Washington Avenue, including the president's residence. The "Spanish House," one of his designs built by the Duyer Brothers in 1890, was demolished to make room for a temporary dining hall, while Hodson Hall was expanded in 2007. The temporary dining hall was removed in 2009, and a lawn is there now.

84. *Transcript*, April 9, 1885.
85. Ibid., August 1, 1908. Stutsman, a Methodist minister originally from Indiana, where he resided at the time of the Hill case, was general secretary of the Prisoners' Aid Society. It is uncertain whether he was familiar with the Hill murder case, sixteen years earlier, but his report also noted, "It would be impossible to conduct an execution anywhere about this institution and keep out the crowds."
86. *Kent News*, October 22, 1887.
87. *Transcript*, May 5, 1892.
88. *Kent News*, May 7, 1892. "We are reliably informed also that a secret meeting of colored men was held near Millington for the purpose of attacking any lynching party that might be formed, and there certainly would have been trouble."
89. Tales of Kent County, 16; see also the *Kent News*, January 3, 1903. A new depot was built at the west end of Cross Street in 1903.
90. *Smyrna Times*, May 4, 1892.
91. *Transcript*, June 23, 1892. The account was given several times. The December 3, 1896 *Transcript* copied a story from the *Washington Times* when Bates was a promotional manager for the stage production of *The Great Train Robbery*. The *Times* either rehashed the same interview, or Bates gave it again almost verbatim in the March 4, 1906 *Times*, in a story about psychic powers.
92. *National Police Gazette*, October 29, 1892.
93. *Transcript*, May 12, 1892.

African American Deliberations

94. *Kent News*, supplement, May 7, 1892.

Unpreventable Lynching

95. *Transcript*, May 19, 1892.
96. *Kent News*, May 21, 1892.
97. At least one book printed in the last decade erroneously associated the lynching with the Hill murder.
98. *Transcript*, June 2, 1892.
99. Ibid., May 14, 1891.
100. *Annapolis Evening Capital*, November 29, 1884, Maryland Archives transcription.
101. Kent County Circuit Court records, report of the grand jury, October 31, 1892, Cornelius J. Scott, foreman.

The Long Summer

102. *Kent News*, May 14, 1892.
103. *Transcript*, August 11, 1892, list of county expenses for the circuit court. *Kent News*, August 5, 1893, list of "costs attendant upon the arrest, conviction and execution of the Hill murderers."

104. *Transcript*, June 23, 1892.
105. Ibid.
106. Ibid., January 31, 1889.
107. *Kent News*, June 22, 1895.
108. Interview with Benjamin Jones; *Kent News*, December 11, 1926.
109. *Transcript*, August 4, 1892.

Columbus Day

110. *Kent News*, December 11, 1920, Pearce's obituary. The biographical information was augmented by numerous other newspaper abstracts—i.e., references to his elections to the town commission, school board appointments, etc.
111. 1850 and 1860 slave censuses.
112. 1850 slave census.
113. *Kent News*, December 6, 1890. Smith prosecuted the controversial "Club Case," while Pearce was the defender.
114. *Transcript*, October 26, 1892, "Daily."
115. Hanson, *Old Kent*.
116. *Kent News*, June 10, 1911.
117. Legislative Session of 1894, Chapter 552, approved April 6, 1894.
118. *Kent News*, October 27, 1928.
119. Moore, *Murder on Maryland's Eastern Shore*.
120. Reports of the Cases Argued and Determined in the Courts of Appeals of Maryland, Vol. LXIV, 1886.
121. *Kent News*, May 3, 1890.
122. Hanson, *Old Kent*.
123. *Kent News*, May 22, 1915, obituary.
124. Ibid.
125. Surles, *Commissioned Slave Statistics*. Wickes held nine slaves in 1864.
126. Report of the Seventh Annual Meeting of the Maryland Bar Association, 1912.
127. Earle and Skirven, *Maryland's Colonial Eastern Shore*.
128. *New York Times*, September 19, 1901.
129. *Kent News*, June 13, 1863. Wickes and Robinson were co-counsel for defense in the murder trial of William Perkins, who was found innocent of the murder of Matthew Wood.

The Trial

130. *Kent News*, October 22, 1892.
131. Ibid.
132. Report of the Grand Jury, October 1892 term, filed October 31, 1892.
133. *Transcript*, October 26, 1892, "Daily."
134. *Sun*, October 26, 1892.
135. Ibid., January 13, 1893.

Notes to Pages 106–123

136. *Kent News*, December 10, 1881.
137. Ibid., April 30, 1892.
138. Surles, *Commissioned Slave Statistics*.
139. *Sun*, October 26, 1892.
140. *Transcript*, June 23, 1892.
141. Heights for all the suspects are from the Maryland Archives, Prisoner Record, Maryland Penitentiary.
142. *Transcript*, June 23, 1892.
143. Kent County Circuit Court file, October term, 1892, *State v. Fletcher Williams et al.*
144. *Kent County News*, August 5, 1893.
145. *Sun*, October 18, 1892.
146. *New York Times*, June 16, 1898. Tonry was not fired for incompetence but because of the woman he married: Anna E. Surratt, whose mother, Mary, had been hanged for complicity in Lincoln's assassination.
147. Viennese doctor Karl Landsteiner discovered the four major human blood types in 1901.
148. *Transcript*, October 26, 1892, "Daily."
149. *Smyrna Times*, November 2, 1892.
150. *Transcript*, October 27, 1892.
151. *Sun*, October 27, 1892.
152. *Transcript*, October 27, 1892.
153. Ibid., October 28, 1892, "Daily."
154. *Kent News*, October 29, 1892.
155. *Transcript*, October 28, 1892, "Daily." The paper did not have the comments in quote marks but treated the words as a direct quote.
156. *Baltimore Weekly Herald*, January 20, 1893.
157. *Sun*, October 28, 1892.

The Merits of Hanging Eight

158. *Kent News*, special Monday night edition, October 31, 1892. (The same report was reprinted in the November 5, 1892 regular edition.)
159. *Transcript*, November 10, 1892.
160. Ibid., November 3, 1892. Neither Potts nor Bradshaw shows up in later available censuses or other local records after the trial. It is uncertain what became of them.
161. Ibid., November 17, 1892.
162. Maryland State Archives, Proceedings of the Executive Department, November 21, 1892.
163. *Baltimore Weekly News*, January 20, 1893.
164. *Kent News*, November 12, 1892.
165. Ibid., December 3, 1892: "The men and boys pray, sing and read the Bible regularly"; *Transcript*, December 22, 1892: Wayman noted that "all of them can read and have Bibles."
166. *Kent News*, December 10, 1892.

167. *New York Times*, December 8, 1895.
168. Wayman, *Cyclopedia of African Methodism*.
169. *Transcript*, December 22, 1892.
170. *Kent News*, December 24, 1892.
171. Ibid., December 31, 1892.
172. *Transcript*, December 29, 1892.
173. Ibid., January 19, 1893.
174. *Kent News*, December 31, 1892.
175. *Transcript*, August 17, 1893, list of county expenses.
176. Ibid., January 12, 1893.
177. Ibid. The scaffold specifications can be found in the December 29, 1892; January 5, 1893; and January 12, 1893 editions of the *Transcript*, the December 29, 1892 *Sun* and the January 7, 1893 edition of the *Kent News*. The January 5 *Transcript* said the beam was six by six.
178. *Kent News*, December 3, 1892.

An Unexpected Visit

179. *Kent News*, January 7, 1893.
180. Ibid.
181. *New York Times*, July 31, 1891.
182. *Transcript*, October 15, 1891.
183. Ibid., November 5, 1891.
184. Winchester, *Men of Maryland Since the Civil War*, vol. I. This was the same Winchester who reported the Hill murder for the *Baltimore Evening News*. By the time he wrote his book of biographical sketches, he was in his seventies.
185. *Transcript*, January 5, 1893.
186. Ibid., January 12, 1893.
187. The accounts of Governor Brown's visit are taken from the January 12, 1893 *Transcript* and January 14, 1893 *Kent News*. The latter did not mention the presence of the editors, stating only that "reporters" were present. The papers differed on the time of the governor's arrival; the *Kent News* said noon.
188. *Transcript*, January 12, 1893.
189. Ibid.
190. National Park Service, Civil War Soldier's and Sailor's System; other web sources. South was a private in Berryman Zirkle Price's Danville Artillery, which became part of the Eighth Star Artillery, New Market Battery. Records indicate that he was a private when he mustered out of the Forty-eighth Virginia Infantry.
191. There is no mention of the size or type of camera used. However, the extant South glass negatives all seem to be of the same size.
192. *Transcript*, January 12, 1893. The account of the photo session is detailed, indicating there was a reporter or editor who witnessed the scene. Additionally, clothing details and postures compare with a drawing of the prisoners on the front page of the January 14, 1893 *Philadelphia Record*.
193. Ibid.

Notes to Pages 138–153

Another Surprise Visit

194. Much of the account of the "expedition" to Chestertown by the officials from Baltimore is taken from the *Daily Herald* (Baltimore, MD), January 12, 1893.
195. The *Transcript* said Mrs. Plummer answered a "ring." The January 14, 1893 edition of the *Kent News* said that "Watchman Pote" answered "a rap" at the door. The *Daily Herald*, which quotes Cadwallader at length, mentioned both a ring and a knock.
196. Maryland State Archives, Proceedings of the Executive Department, January 10, 1893.
197. *Transcript*, January 12, 1893.
198. Ibid., February 2, 1893, Weather Notes.
199. *Transcript* Extra, January 13, 1893.
200. Ibid.
201. Ibid.
202. *Evening Herald*, January 12, 1893.
203. *Morning Herald*, January 12, 1893.
204. *Frederick News*, January 14, 1893.
205. *Evening Herald*, January 12, 1893.

The Gallows Beckon

206. *Kent News*, January 30, 1892.
207. Ibid., January 30, 1892.
208. *Baltimore Weekly Herald*, January 20, 1893: "a score or more of newspaper correspondents."
209. *Transcript*, January 12, 1893.
210. *Kent News*, January 14, 1893.
211. *Baltimore Daily Herald*, January 12, 1893.
212. *Record*, January 17, 1893.
213. *Baltimore Weekly Herald*, January 20, 1893.
214. *Kent News*, January 14, 1893. He would go to the gallows, on a cold winter day, without a coat.
215. *Baltimore Weekly Herald*, January 20, 1893.
216. Ibid.
217. The *Philadelphia Times* says the Hills visited at 3:00 a.m.
218. *Baltimore Weekly Herald*, January 20, 1893.
219. *Transcript* Extra, January 13, 1893.
220. Sam Hill's visit is pieced together from accounts in the *Philadelphia Record*, January 14, 1893; *Hamilton (OH) Daily Republican*, January 14, 1893; *Baltimore Weekly Herald*, January 20, 1893; and several other papers.
221. *Kent News*, January 14, 1893. The *Philadelphia Record* reported that there had been a lynching attempt.

Notes to Pages 154–162

Foursome Finale

222. *Sun*, January 14, 1893.
223. *Transcript* Extra, January 13, 1893.
224. *Kent News*, January 14, 1893.
225. *Transcript* Extra, January 13, 1893.
226. *Transcript*, January 12, 1893.
227. *Kent News*, January 14, 1893. The *Transcript* said only one son accompanied the father.
228. *Philadelphia Record*, January 14, 1893.
229. Ibid.
230. *Sun*, January 14, 1893.
231. The *Philadelphia Times* says that Dugan slipped the nooses on the prisoners and Rambo hooded them. The *Kent News* says that Dugan hooded them.
232. The *Philadelphia Record*, January 14, 1893. The *Baltimore Weekly Herald* said only three words were spoken on the platform.
233. Kent County Court Minutes, SGF 1, folios 25, 26, 27 and 28. (The book is located in the courthouse attic.) The *Transcript* said both 12:32 p.m.—"the town clock marked twenty-eight minutes of one o'clock"—and 12:25 p.m.; the *Kent News* said 12:25 p.m. The *Sun* said 12:30 p.m.
234. *Kent News*, January 14, 1893. The January 19 *Transcript* quoted Plummer, who denied that Comegys had spoken after the trap dropped. Since the teen was strangling, it seems unlikely he would have been able to form discernable words. All the accounts agree on his physical contortions.
235. There is no indication that the doctors performed an autopsy on the hanged men's corpses but were merely on hand to confirm their demise, as required by law. The January 14, 1893 edition of the *Middletown Daily Times* and January 17 *Frederick News* also reported that Williams and Brown had broken necks.
236. *New York Times*, April 3, 1880.
237. CNN.com, January 16, 2007.
238. *Sun*, January 14, 1893.
239. *Kent News*, January 14, 1893.
240. Certificates of Hanging, Liber 1, Folio 28, etc., of the Proceedings of the Circuit Court for Kent County.
241. *Frederick News*, January 17, 1893.
242. Accounts vary. Several papers say up to three hundred. The *Transcript* notes that many of the visiting news reporters sensationalized the story, and there were only minor incidents.
243. *Philadelphia Record*, January 14, 1893. The *Transcript* of January 19 said the *Record* and *Philadelphia Press* "compromised their profession, and rendered themselves notorious for the glaring inaccuracy and sensational nature of their misstatements." However, the *Record* contained many accurate statements and included a large amount of material that was not reported by the locals.
244. *Philadelphia Record*, January 14, 1893.
245. *Baltimore Weekly Herald*, January 20, 1893.
246. *Philadelphia Record*, January 14, 1893.

Notes to Pages 162–172

247. *Baltimore Weekly Herald*, January 20, 1893. No such photos have come to light. This is the only account, of dozens, that mentions photographs of the dead prisoners.
248. *Sun*, January 14, 1893.
249. *Baltimore Weekly Herald*, January 20, 1893.
250. *Kent News*, August 5, 1893.

And Then There Were None

251. Shugg, *Monument to Good Intentions*.
252. Maryland Archives, Prisoner Record, Maryland Penitentiary.
253. Shugg, *Monument to Good Intentions*. A House of Correction and House of Reformation for Colored Children was operated by the state for petty offenders.
254. Shugg, *Monument to Good Intentions*.
255. Ibid.
256. *Transcript*, January 19, 1893.
257. Ibid., June 29, 1893.
258. Ibid., July 6, 1893.
259. Ibid., August 17, 1893.
260. *Kent News*, November 28, 1896. The *Kent News* actually lifted the words "strange fatality" from a headline in the *Baltimore Morning Herald* that ran six days previously.
261. *Transcript*, November 26, 1896.
262. *Baltimore Morning Herald*, November 21, 1896.
263. *Transcript*, August 19, 1897, quoting the *Baltimore News*.
264. This is according to prison records; both the *Transcript* and *Kent News* say he died on Monday, September 11, 1899.
265. *Transcript*, September 14, 1899.
266. *Kent News*, March 4, 1911. Reese's mother was from Chestertown, and it's likely Hattie was also from Kent.
267. *Washington Post*, April 29, 1910.
268. *American Magazine* 73 (November 1911–April 1912): "An Ounce of Correction, A Pound of Corruption."
269. Proceedings of the Annual Congress of the American Prison Association, Richmond, VA, November 14–19, 1908.
270. *Daily Mail of Hagerstown*, May 5, 1910.
271. Shugg, *Monument to Good Intentions*. The investigation also found Weyler had expropriated large quantities of prison supplies for his personal use.
272. *Salisbury Times*, December 23, 1929.

Was There a Miscarriage of Justice?

273. *Centreville Times & Advertiser*, November 19, 1831.

Notes to Pages 175–187

Executions Removed to Penitentiary

274. The account of the Wright murder case is taken primarily from the *Transcript* of March 23 and March 30, 1899, and the *Kent News* of March 25, 1899.
275. Reports of cases argued and determined in the Court of Appeal, pp. 706–08.
276. Maryland State Archives, Session Laws 1908, Chapter 115, p. 84.
277. Laws of Maryland, Chapter 465.
278. *Sun*, April 6, 1922.
279. Mencken, *Mencken Chrestomathy*.
280. Maryland Department of Public Safety & Correctional Services.
281. Executions in the United States, 1608–2002, Espy File, W. Matt Espy, 2004 edition.
282. State Department of Public Safety & Correctional Services statistics.
283. Governor Martin O'Malley's blog, www.governor.maryland.gove/blog/?p=8495.
284. Separate interviews with Jacobs and Colburn, June 24, 2013, at the Maryland Municipal Convention in Ocean City, MD.

The Victims

285. The *Kent News* and the *Transcript* merged in 1946 to become the *Kent County News*.
286. *Kent News*, May 7, 1892.
287. *Baltimore Sun*, July 21, 1932.
288. Department of Public Education, annual reports for the forty-fifth year ending July 31, 1911, and fiftieth year, ending July 31, 1916.
289. Federal censuses for 1910, 1920 and 1930.
290. *Kent News*, July 28, 1900.
291. Kent County Register of Wills, Administrative Accounts, JTD1-508.

Ripples to the Present

292. *Transcript*, January 26, 1893.
293. *Kent News*, June 2, 1894.
294. Ibid., May 18, 1895.
295. *Transcript*, September 17, 1896.
296. *Denton Journal*, December 17, 1892.
297. *Kent News*, July 23, 1904.
298. Ibid., December 31, 1921.

Jail Falls to the Wrecking Ball

299. *Kent News*, November 16, 1929.
300. Ibid., December 17, 1932.
301. Ibid., August 31, 1935.
302. *Enterprise*, April 23, 1947.
303. *Kent County News*, October 17, 1979.
304. Ibid., December 16, 1987.

BIBLIOGRAPHY

Archival Sources and Collections

Asbury United Methodist Church, Millington
Historical Society of Kent County
International Order of Redmen
John Wesley United Methodist Church
Kent County (Maryland) Office of the Clerk of Circuit Court
Kent County (Maryland) Register of Wills
Library of Congress
Maryland Bar Association
Maryland Historical Trust
Maryland State Archives
National Park Service
Tombstoning in Kent County
U.S. Census Bureau

Books, Periodicals, Essays and Journals

Derby, George, and James Terry White. *National Cyclopaedia of American Biography*. New York: J.T. White, 1899.

Espy, W. Matt. *Executions in the United States, 1608–2002*. N.p.: The Espy File, 2004.

Goodykoontz, Jasper. *Goodykoontz's General Reference Guide*. Atlanta, 1911.

Hanson, George A. *Old Kent: The Eastern Shore of Maryland*. Baltimore, MD: Genealogical Publishing Co., 1876.

McCabe, Clinton. *History of the Baltimore Police Department, 1774–1907*. Baltimore, MD: Fleet-McGinley, 1911.

Bibliography

Mencken, H.L. *A Mencken Chrestomathy.* New York: Knopf, 1949, 1982.

Moore, Joseph E. *Murder on Maryland's Eastern Shore.* Charleston, SC: The History Press, 2006.

Shugg, Wallace. *Monument to Good Intentions: The Story of the Maryland Penitentiary, 1804–1995.* Baltimore: Maryland Historical Society, 2000.

Surles, Trish. *Commissioned Slave Statistics, Kent County Md., 1864.* Gambrills, MD, 2002.

Tales of Kent County. Kent County News, 2006.

Taylor, Bayard. "Down the Eastern Shore." *Harper's New Monthly Magazine* (1871).

Wayman, Alexander. *Cyclopaedia of African Methodism.* Baltimore, MD, 1882.

Winchester, Paul. *Men of Maryland Since the Civil War.* Baltimore: Maryland County Press Syndicate, 1923.

Media

Annapolis Evening Capital
Baltimore Herald
Baltimore Sun
Centreville Times and Advertiser
Chestertown Transcript
CNN.com
Columbian and Bloomsburg (PA) Democrat
Denton Journal
The Enterprise
Evening Telegraph
Frederick News
Kent County News
Kent News
Middletown Daily Times
National Police Gazette
New York Times
Philadelphia Record
Philadelphia Times
Salisbury (MD) Times
Smyrna (DE) Times
St. Clairesville Chronicle
Washington Post
Washington Times

INDEX

A

Accooe, Reverend John H. 75
Adams, William "Bully" 99, 146
Ahern, John 34, 50, 62, 182
Aldridge, Samuel W. 106
Armstrong Hotel 78, 162
Arrelee 191
Asbury ME Church 25, 36, 190, 192

B

Baltimore Boot and Shoe Company 165
Baltimore & Delaware Bay Railroad
    Co. 70
Bates, Wilbur 54, 192
Baynard, Frank 84
Baynard, Joshua 45, 55, 85, 108, 139,
    164, 191
Benson, Lewis 45, 108, 132, 164
Bond, Benjamin Franklin 33
Bond, Sarah J. 33
Boone, Reverend Edward D. 165
Bottomley, Frank 40
Bowers, James 90
Bradshaw, Deborah
  Sarah Bradshaw 111, 168
Bradshaw, Perry 45, 54, 56, 107, 112

Britton, Thomas M. 53, 61
Brooks, Charles 44
Brown, Governor Frank 119
Brown, Moses 45, 71, 76, 78, 83, 107,
    114, 123, 125, 130, 134, 150,
    152, 154, 163, 184

C

Cadwallader, Captain Lewis W. 138
Camp, Augusta 107
Campbell, Thomas 12, 29, 134
Cantwell's Bridge 30
Carter, Robert 154
Chestertown 15, 17, 19, 23, 26, 27, 28,
    54, 55, 56, 57, 63, 64, 66, 68,
    70, 71, 73, 74, 76, 82, 84, 85,
    87, 89, 90, 91, 92, 97, 98, 100,
    101, 102, 104, 105, 107, 120,
    123, 129, 131, 133, 138, 140,
    142, 143, 146, 154, 160, 163,
    172, 176, 181, 182, 183, 184,
    186, 187, 188, 191, 192, 193,
    197, 199, 202
Chestertown jail 65
Chesterville 26, 32, 36, 62, 106
Clark, Carroll 112

Index

Clark, Dr. Enoch G. 46
Cleveland Club 40, 41, 53, 113
Cleveland, Grover 40, 41, 120
Columbus Day 87, 88, 101, 105
Comegys, Charles E. 52
Comegys, Frisby 45, 55, 56, 75, 107, 114, 184
Comegys, Samuel 75
Cooke, Dr. Theodore, Jr. 165
Cook, Henry S. 55
Cooper, Stephen 44, 83
Cornelius J. Scott 193
Cosden case 99, 173
  William Cosden 99
Cosden family murders. *See* Cosden case
Cosden murderers. *See* Cosden case
Crumpton 106, 136

D

Darrell, William 111
Dennis, Reverend F.S. 123, 148
Dodd, Undertaker John N. 163
dogcart 44, 50, 54, 102, 109, 116, 181, 184
Donahoe, Thomas 107, 130, 154
Dugan, William O. 55, 57

E

Emma A. Ford 96, 123
Emmanuel PE Church 123, 150
Emory, Charles 54, 56, 75, 105, 149, 164
Emory, Samuel 75, 107
Evans, Dr. Britton D. 33

F

Fifteenth Amendment 26, 74
Fisher, Samuel G. 109, 140
Ford's Hill 43, 44, 53, 113, 133
Ford, William H. 55, 107
Fountain, Isaiah 177
Frey, Marshal Jacob 138

G

Galena 32, 51, 59, 102, 108, 130, 146
Garnet, Henry Highland 26, 74
Godey's 61
Golts 19, 38, 106, 107, 108, 112, 129, 184
Golt's Station. *See* Golts
Gracie, steam launch 76, 77
Grand United Order of Galilean Fishermen 125
Green, Asbury 80
Greenwood, John 84
Greenwood, John H. 119

H

Hadaway, Sheriff Thomas J. 185
Harrison, John 84, 116
Harris, Walter 186
Heighe, Dr. James 32
Hendrickson, Gus 46
Hill, Arrelee 39, 49, 50, 51, 83, 109, 125, 174, 180
Hill, Ethel Heighe 37, 181
Hill, Heighe 9, 13, 33, 56, 87, 97, 125, 149, 181
Hill, Samuel 30, 109, 116, 142, 151, 152, 156, 162
Historical Society of Kent County 184
Hopper, C. Cox 133
Huey, Adam F. 48
Hurlock, Clarence 41, 191
Hurtt, Henry 54, 83, 108, 114, 132, 140, 164
Hynson, Henry 84, 116
Hynson, Richard 90, 92, 96, 175

I

Improved Order of Red Men 35, 62

J

Jacobs, Dr. J.K.H. 51
Janes Church 73, 75
Janes ME Church. *See* Janes Church

INDEX

Janney, Stuart S. 185
Jim Crow laws 23, 94
Johnson, Charles W. 125
Johnson, Colonel Richard C. 46
Johnson, William 191
Johnson, William M. 19, 52, 139
John Wesley ME Church. *See* John Wesley United Methodist Church
John Wesley United Methodist Church 22, 190, 201
Joiner, Thomas Jefferson 162
Jones, Edward 11
Judge Lynch 63, 78, 82, 115
Jump, Constable C. Sydney 56

K

Kelley, Amos B. 57
Kelley, Dr. J. Horton 51
Kennedyville 30, 32, 51, 70, 76, 90
Kent and Queen Anne's Railroad 33
Kent County 7, 9, 11, 13, 15, 21, 26, 30, 36, 71, 75, 80, 85, 90, 92, 93, 95, 96, 97, 98, 99, 100, 101, 102, 111, 113, 120, 124, 129, 131, 133, 138, 140, 142, 144, 146, 160, 171, 172, 174, 175, 176, 178, 179, 180, 181, 184, 186, 187, 190, 191, 192, 193, 195, 198, 200, 201, 202
Knock, Jesse 90
Ku Klux Klan 85, 86

L

Lamden, Joseph 53
Latimer, Dr. John W. 51
Latrobe 138, 141
Lauretum 92
Legg, Willie 111
Locust Grove 30, 32, 33, 37, 59, 62, 83, 85, 182
Long Meadow Branch 43, 44, 71, 72
Loper, Charles P. 55, 111

M

Mallalieu, Sam 56
Mander, Phillip 55, 56, 85, 119
Maryland National Guard 177
Maryland Penitentiary 140, 142, 164, 167, 168, 169, 177
Massey 17, 33, 39, 41, 42, 43, 46, 47, 51, 52, 56, 70, 102, 108, 152, 191
Maxwell, Dr. William, Jr. 51, 191
ME Church South 35, 36
Mencken, H.L. 177
Millington 9, 11, 12, 15, 17, 19, 21, 22, 23, 25, 30, 32, 33, 34, 35, 36, 37, 39, 41, 42, 43, 49, 51, 52, 53, 54, 55, 56, 57, 58, 59, 61, 66, 73, 75, 83, 84, 85, 86, 87, 90, 96, 105, 106, 107, 108, 109, 110, 111, 113, 119, 123, 129, 130, 133, 139, 142, 152, 167, 168, 191, 192, 193, 201
Morgan Creek 80
Murray, Reverend Abraham A. 150

N

Neilson, J. Crawford 66, 185
Nevins, James (Pinkerton detective) 57

O

Oaklawn Cemetery, Baltimore 181
Odessa 30, 32

P

Pearce, James Alfred 88, 171, 175
Perkins Hall 74, 95
Perkins, William 73, 194
Pinkerton National Detective Agency 58
Pippin, Dr. William M. 83
Pippin, Robert K. 55, 92
Plummer, Deputy Frank 78, 158
Plummer, Sheriff Edward J. 64, 69, 140
Plum Point 114, 184
Porter, William J. 49

INDEX

Pote, Fred 119
Potts, John 12, 84, 105, 109, 111, 115, 182, 189
Potts, Joseph 12
Prettyman, Eliza J. 64
Prettyman, John 154
Price, Sheriff John F., IV 174
Price, William H. 53

Q

Queeley, Reverend Benjamin A. 73
Queen Anne's County 11, 21, 22, 56, 76, 77, 80, 84, 99, 108, 109, 119, 138, 156, 172, 184, 190, 191

R

Rambo, Jerome 119
Reese, John 41, 111
Ritchie, Governor Albert C. 177, 185
Roberts, Reverend Stephen C. 123
Robinson, John M. 80
Rockwell House 78, 155, 162
Roe, Walter 46, 51, 84
Rolph, Charles 105, 110, 130
Rowlenson, Joel H. 138
Ruddell, Thomas C. 88

S

Sandfield 12, 22, 23, 34, 112
Sand Town 22
Sargent, Father Henry R. 150
  Society of the Holy Cross 150
Sassafras 11, 12, 13, 24, 33, 36, 38, 42, 56, 62, 112
Sassafras, village of 23
Scott, Cornelius J. 102
Seward, Sheriff Frank 57
Shaw, James 41, 191
Showaker, Carl 30
Showaker, Hester 30
Shrewsbury Church 59, 61
Silcox, Nellie 76
slavery 21, 36, 90, 97
Slay, William M. 92

Smith, Marion deKalb 88, 171
Smith, Thomas J.F. 53
South, John 105
Spear, James 46, 111
Spear, Watson 39, 111, 184
Starks, T.D. 156
Stephens, W.W. 151
Still Pond 25, 51
Storks, Thomas 119
Strong, Robert H., Jr. 171
Stuart, Horace M. 36, 66
Stump, Frederick 80
Stutsman, Reverend Jesse O. 66
St. Vincent's Cemetery, Baltimore 166
Sudlersville 21, 36
Sumner, Charles 94

T

Taylor, Bayard 15
Taylor, James 76, 78, 104
Thomas, William C. 178
Thompson, Thomas 99, 146
Todd, Dr. Alonzo R. 13
Tolchester 86, 183
Tolson, Mary A. 80
Tonry, Professor William P. 110

U

Urieville 126
Usilton, Frederick G. 55
Usilton, William B. 14, 66, 133

V

Vannort, Colonel William J. 131
Vickers, Harrison 56, 131, 153, 175
Vickers, Senator George 91
Vickers, Sheriff John 186

W

Wallace, Reverend J.F. 123
Washington College 90, 97, 99, 192
Wayman, Bishop Alexander W. 123
Westcott, Charles T. 100, 120

Wethered, Dr. John L. 160
Weyler, Warden John F. 142, 164
Whaland, Dr. Charles W. 160
White Caps. *See* White Caps and cross-bones
White Caps and cross-bones 85
White, Reverend E.E. 59
Wickes, Joseph A. 80, 92, 96
Williams, Fletcher 44, 53, 56, 105, 111, 114, 195
Winchester, Paul W. 50
Wright, Joseph 175

ABOUT THE AUTHOR

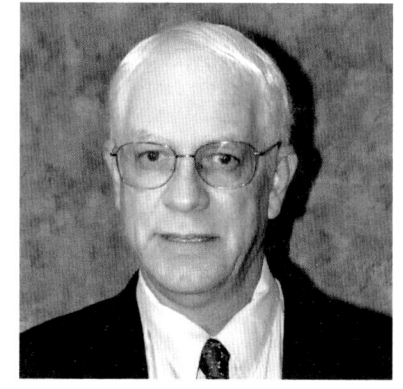

G. Kevin Hemstock, a native of Delaware, resides in Millington, Maryland, with his wife. While attending college in Wyoming, his first history project was researching the nineteenth-century Overland Trail stagecoach stations of southwestern Wyoming. He has also lived in Florida and Idaho.

As a journalist, he has worked as a reporter, photographer and editor for various newspapers, publishing hundreds of articles on the topic of history. From 2009 to 2014, Hemstock worked with the Kent County Office of Tourism to plan activities associated with the War of 1812 bicentennial. As part of that project, he authored numerous articles about the War of 1812.

He left the *Kent County News* in 2012 to operate Old News, a genealogical and historical research service and ephemera shop in Millington, where he continues writing about local history.